# Love a la Carte

## DR. SHIRLEY JORDAN BAILEY

This book is a work of non-fiction. Unless otherwise noted, the author and the publisher make no explicit guarantees as to the accuracy of the information contained in this book and in some cases, names of people and places have been altered to protect their privacy.

LifeRich Publishing is a registered trademark of The Reader's Digest Association, Inc.

LifeRich Publishing books may be ordered through booksellers or by contacting:

LifeRich Publishing
1663 Liberty Drive
Bloomington, IN 47403
www.liferichpublishing.com
844-686-9607

Because of the dynamic nature of the Internet, any web addresses or links contained in this book may have changed since publication and may no longer be valid. The views expressed in this work are solely those of the author and do not necessarily reflect the views of the publisher, and the publisher hereby disclaims any responsibility for them.

Any people depicted in stock imagery provided by Getty Images are models, and such images are being used for illustrative purposes only.
Certain stock imagery © Getty Images.

ISBN: 978-1-4897-2800-5 (sc)
ISBN: 978-1-4897-2802-9 (hc)
ISBN: 978-1-4897-2801-2 (e)

Library of Congress Control Number: 2020917218

Print information available on the last page.

LifeRich Publishing rev. date: 11/18/2020

# DEDICATION

In memory of my loving parents, Adeline Nadine Wilson Jordan and Limuary Alja Jordan Sr., with heartfelt appreciation love and admiration.

You provided a loving Christian home and a unified spirit of educational encouragement and support for me. You were living examples of an authentic and good family life. You raised us with unconditional love. You are missed every day and loved forever. I learned from you because you both spent your extraordinary lives helping all people. Everything I am or hope to be, I owe to you my parents.

# CONTENTS

# ACKNOWLEDGMENTS

I wish to express my profound gratitude to my granddaughter Sofia N. Walton. Sofia, your loving support, enthusiasm, skill sets, and creativity assisted me immeasurably in organizing and editing this memoir. My dream of publishing this memoir surely would not have been realized without your technical expertise and keen interest in helping me, as well as your sacrifice and dedication to accomplish what we have.

I also appreciate all my family and friends who encouraged me to write about our family for so long.

Special appreciation to dedicated Teachers everywhere. A special thank you to all the ones who touched my life. The unforgettable ones I must mention. Fifth grade Mrs. Simms at Monroe Colored High School in Monroe Louisiana. Tenth Grade Mrs. Nash Algebra teacher Manual Arts High School, Los Angeles, California. Fisk University, Nashville Tennessee, Biology Professor Mrs. Ray, and Chemisty Professor Dr. Samuel Massey. Lastly, Howard University College of Medicine, Dr. Walter Booker and Dr. Tureman of the Department of Pharmacology. Howard University College of Dentistry, Dr. Percy Fitzgerald, Dr. Harold Flemmings, Dr. Frank Barbee, Dr. Joe Henry and my personal recruiter and mentor the Dean, Dr. Russell Dixon.

Profound appreciation to my four children. Paula, Pamela, Patricia and Danny. My life has been so enriched by the privilege of being your Mother. I have received a hundred fold more blessings of joy and happiness than I deserve. Each of you have pioneered, blazed new paths and built extraordinary lives. You have hit walls where many would have quit but you didn't. In the darkest of times you knew God was your compass and your family had your back, you found your way again. I have been blessed by your loving devotion to me and to your father Dr. Henry Dan Bailey, during his lifetime and his long illness. In the words of my chemistry teacher Dr. Massey each of you was truly not just a vessel to be filled but a torch to be lighted. You caught the vision and continue to light torches of love and enlightenment to all you meet in your lives of service and dedication. God has smiled upon our lives. I am blessed to call you friends as well as my children.

*When you put down the good things you ought to have done and leave out the bad things you did, well, that's memoirs.*

*—Will Rogers*

# FOREWORD

As a wife and mother of four children, I knew and believed in full family support which meant involvement in clubs such as the medical wives' Charles Drew auxiliary; Jack and Jill of America, Inc.; the Links, Inc.; and Pilgrim school and The Buckley School as well as church activities that involved the children. For fun, playing bridge and trying to play the elusive piano, We had season tickets to the Los Angeles Lakers and the Los Angeles Raiders, Dan and I loved all sports and went on Friday nights. We gave tickets to Doctors as referral perks or friends if we could not attend. Those are great memories at the Forum in Inglewood. We loved watching old movies, listening to good music, and spending time with old friends. A typical weekend for the family was when husband, Dan, cooking or smoking meat for a barbeque in the backyard and the music was playing Aretha Franklin singing anything, Al Green Love and Happiness, and Ray Charles singing ballads and all those love songs Ruby, Georgia, and Hallaluia I just love her so, now ain't that love. We were making happy times indeed.

The children swam, filled their tummies with good food, entertained the neighborhood children which were beautiful times. We lived on Enoro Dr. "Pill Hill" as I later heard it described in View Park, California. It is an area where Black Doctors, Black Lawyers, Black Entertainers lived. Ray Charles, Tina Turner, Nancy Wilson, Black Atheletes and Black Business people lived as close neighbors, We had fireworks parties, and wonderful networking of Black culture in home after home in this area. This was the late1960's when we moved in and life there is cultural history. It was like the songs we heard in the Civil Rights struggles. "We shall overcome". Well all the surrounding families had overcome. These families were the ones who walked through the doors of opportunity as they opened. My Dad used to say as the humorist that he was It is better to say "We is rich" than "We are poor", Times were good, you could buy a whole watermelon, eat expensive shrimp, buy better cuts of meat that you did and not have to braise or bake forever but cut with a fork. As they said "meat as tender as a mothers love". Ha Ha Ha. Those memories are sweet. Dan was a great cook and hunter of deer at Crater lake in Oregon and he would hunt in Utah. Venison was packaged and shippped home. He was a master at cooking Lobster as well.

This did not mean all problems were solved. However this was a joyous time for many Black families. Every home with swimming pools and shake roofs, flocked wall covering's to grass cloth and children attending private schools. Yes, we had worked hard and continued to work hard, but we were seeing some rewards. The Jefferson's Television show featuring Sherman Hemsley sang a song in the opening scene whereby the lyrics scream "we finally got a piece of the pie". That is how we felt. For my parents living around the corner on Monteith Dr. with a swimming pool as well, My Dad said to me when I was planning a vacation to the Bahamas with all seriousness, "Just go into your backyard girl," That's a vacation right there! We had come a long way from the U-haul trailer with the washing machine in the back in 1952 motoring to California from Louisiana to now "living on the hill". We know God lifted us!

I am grateful to the many hands who were on my support team that made everything work. My office staff of dental assistants, hygienists, and associate dentists and my home-support of live in housekeepers and child support (Maria, Allie Smith,Lydia). It was also such a blessing to live around the block from my parents, Adeline and Limuary Jordan. As extended family, grandparents added so much wisdom and value to the lives of our children. One can do nothing alone. We were blessed.

Without the support of good friends, the journey would not have been as meaningful or as much fun. Without a strong spiritual base, the journey would have been impossible. This memoir explores that journey's many paths, musings and challenges and invites you to explore how and why one Black woman walked it in those times and beyond.

To God be all the glory!

# That's All

—Alan Brandt and Bob Hayme

I can only give you love that lasts forever
And a promise to be near each time you call
And the only heart I own
For you and you alone
That's all, that's all
I can only give you country walks in springtime
And a hand to hold when leaves begin to fall
And a love whose burning light
Will warm the winter night
That's all, that's all
There are those, I am sure, that have told you
They would give you the world for a toy
All I have are these arms to enfold you
And a love time can never destroy
If you're wondering what I'm asking in return, dear
You'll be glad to know that my demands are small
Say it's me that you'll adore
For now and ever more
That's all, that's all
If you're wondering what I'm asking in return, dear
You'll be glad to know that my demands are small
Say it's me that you'll adore
For now and ever more
That's all … that's all

# When You Wish Upon a Star

—Leigh Harline and Ned Washington

When you wish upon a star,
Makes no difference who you are,
Anything your heart desires will come to you.
If your heart is in your dreams,
No request is too extreme,
When you wish upon a star as dreamers do.
Fate is kind, she brings to those who love, the
sweet fulfillment of their secret longing.
Like a bolt out of the blue,
Fate steps in and sees you thru,
When you wish upon a star, your dream comes true.

# Theme Song of My Life

**Dreaming**

I was born in Monroe, Louisiana, on September 25, 1937, at four thirty in the morning. At only six pounds, I arrived in the deeply segregated South to a young mother from Des Moines, Iowa, and a young father from Monroe, Louisiana. I was delivered by Dr. Shapiro, a young, uncertain Jewish doctor who was just out of medical school, at the segregated Catholic Saint Francis Hospital. I was my parents' firstborn.

My parents just out of college and had little money and very few options for where blacks could work with dignity and freedom of racial oppression. Those jobs mainly were to teach school, become a professional doctor or lawyer, or go into business. My mother was a pragmatist, and my father was a visionary.

We moved to Detroit, Michigan, when I was two years old. They labored hard, helped many others, and were very successful. Dad worked at the Ford Motor Company, while Mother tended to the household. As they bought gas stations and other small businesses, our ascent into the middle class began. By the time I was thirteen years old, this journey upward took us to even better opportunities in Los Angeles, California. We were now a part of black society, a blessed family of the industrial revolution who made it up and out. This migration of our family was noted with my parents names in the book *The Warmth of Other Suns* by Isabel Wilkerson.

I knew for sure that education was the key to my best life. I took advantage of every opportunity and knew what I wanted. I was not deterred by closed doors or rejection. Subsequently, I enjoyed a very successful and highly honored pioneering professional career as a black woman dentist. Being elected a commissioner of the American Dental Association by my peers was among many other firsts as a black woman dentist, including serving as the first black woman dentist on a state board and serving as president of the California Board of Dental Examiners.

I married the man I fell in love with, Dr. Henry Dan Bailey, a surgeon. I became the mother of our four children and grandmother of eight. Our children are all successful professionals who give much back to the world. We enjoy a loving family, and the legacy goes forth. It's who we are; it's who I am—a dreamer and an achiever.

Why this song? Because I believe in miracles! I am a dreamer like Dad and a pragmatic capitalist like Mother. At my core, I think the poorest people in the world are not those who don't have wealth but those who do not have dreams.

As a parent and grandparent, I have tried to be a dream-builder and to expose our children to as much of the world as possible through Camp Shirleywhirl travel and talks. What is CampShirleywhirl?, It is all eight Grandchildren coming together with me and we travel and spend weeks together bonding as a family. The cousins come to know and love one another and family bonds strengthed. We have been to many places. Las Vegas, The Grand Canyon, The Carribean Islands on the Royal Caribean Cruise ship Azure, Barcelona, Paris, Rome, Capri Sorrento, Singapore, Bangkok,Viet Nam, Hong Kong just to name some highlights.

*Nothing ventured, nothing gained.*

*—Geoffrey Chaucer*

# CHAPTER 2

## By My Side, Always

*Mom and Dad*

*Big Mama at Home*
*611 Layton Avenue*
*Monroe, Louisiana*

*Louisiana—Shirley and Big Mama*

*Big Mama, paternal grandmother*

*The Jordans, my first family*

This book is about the very special people who have been at every juncture of my life and are the threads of the fabric of my life—my companions, friends, and family, who, through the years, have impacted my journey and have been on the trail with me. I have been blessed with the gift of friendship from some great women and great men, and these relationships are very special. In the words of Gladys Knight's songbook of life

If they should ever write my life story

For whatever reason there might be
You'll be there between each line of pain and glory

Well, they are special, and my memoir will include those memories. My father often said that "friendship is essential to the soul." The Bible says, "A friend sticketh closer than a brother" (Proverbs 18:24). You probably have heard the sayings, "Birds of a feather flock together," and "A man is known by the company he keeps." Jacqueline Bouvier Kennedy said of marriage that the first is for love, the second for money, and the third for companionship.

I think, for the most part, this book will be positive and an adventurous read, but I promise to be honest as my memory serves me and to share the good the bad and the worst as I remember the events.

This book is for my children, grandchildren, and great-grandchildren, so they can know more about me and the life I have lived, what I feel has been important and unimportant, the best moments and worst, and any thoughts of do-overs, whatever they might be.

My life began in the deeply segregated South in 1937, in Monroe, Louisiana, a city today that still looks like it did in the thirties. Saint Francis Hospital, where I was born, is still there. DeSiard Street is still the main street. But it seems to be a forgotten city, as if the world went forward and forgot this city. Houses fall down or burn down, and the rain still beats the paint off the houses. Isabel Wilkerson's *The Warmth of Other Suns* depicts the great migration to the factories of the northeast and west, draining the intelligent leaders and families of the day. My family is one such family mentioned in that book, one who left the South in search of the promise of America. My life is about getting prepared for the opportunities in life and taking them when they came.

My parents, Adeline N. Wilson and Limuary A. Jordan, met at Arkansas Agricultural Mechanical and Normal College in Pine Bluff, Arkansas. They married after their freshman year, deferred their education, and began a family. I am the oldest of three children. Adeline is from Des Moines, Iowa, and went South at the urging of her minister to attend a black college. Limuary, who wanted to expand his experience and leave Louisiana, stayed close and went to Arkansas.

After some years and much sacrifice, Limuary and Adeline continued their education while working and rearing children. Their value of education and the merits of knowledge being the key to a good life was the ever-present mantra in our family. The only professions really open for blacks in those days were doctor, lawyer, teacher, or business person; there was little employment outside of those areas except in the service area. Maids and chauffeurs were common jobs, as were cooks, nurses, house cleaners, waiters, dishwashers, or farmers. Education was the path out of servile labor.

I am eager to tell you about my two grandmothers, Alzenia Jordan and Rosa E. Wilson, who were very independent women for their time. I will tell you about my grandfathers as well, but their history pales in comparison to these determined, strong, and powerful women.

Rosa E. MacDonald Wilson was a black-skinned, heavy-set woman. I never saw her in high heels, as her stout legs were more suited to a black oxford shoe with stockings. I also never saw her in pants, it was not the custom of the day for women to wear pants. Rosa should have been a philanthropist, as she thought and acted like of woman of considerably more means than she had. She was a giving woman who lived for her church work. The mother of five children, she espoused the pursuit of excellence for her children, and they responded. Anna and Mac went to the University of Iowa but suffered tragedy. Mac was to become a doctor, but he drowned mysteriously. Anna, also an excellent student, succumbed to a ruptured appendix and died of peritonitis, due to neglect by the attending doctor. Kermit became a musician and played the drums with various bands, and Fannie excelled at the violin and became a housewife. Adeline was the next-to-youngest and left home to try to build her life, attending Arkansas State University at the urging of the family minister, who knew of this school. After Adeline left for college, she never returned back home to live.

Joseph Wilson was a small-framed, black-skinned man who worked hard in the coal mines of Alabama. He and Rosa moved to Iowa as a young couple and raised their family there. Rosa, however, was never cut out to be a housewife, cooking or doing the mundane routine of family life. She was up and out in public, doing various jobs and loving it. Joe a hard worker, wanted to come home to a hot meal and rest and comfort, but Rosa was more excited by meetings and the activities of the community.

Rosa came from a huge family with twelve sisters and brothers, and she enjoyed them. She was culturally and intellectually adept for someone of her limited education. She sent me packages when I was in college from Yonkers department store, gift-wrapped exquisitely; there would be one handkerchief or a small cake with hearts on Valentine's Day.

While Rosa and Joe were kindred spirits, a husband was not the thing that made the sun rise for Rosa. Joe was pragmatic and thought mainly of work and home. In addition, Joe was plagued by poor health, rheumatoid arthritis. Rosa and Joe lived into their late eighties and were happy people, although in later years, they divorced.

My memories of Grandmother Rosa are sweet. She had a large home at 844 West Fifteenth Street, Des moines Iowa with a big porch. She had roomers who paid to live there. It was a grand house, with a basement and an attic filled with trunks and all kinds of treasures. We enjoyed our summer visits there. My fondest memories of her are her million dollar smile, even in the rest home the last time I visited her. Sitting in a wheel chair you would have thought she owned Yonkers Department store, the finest Des Moines Iowa offered of the day as she had a spirit of loving and giving the smallest of things in the grandest of ways. What a woman! Grandmother Rosa. Tears are rolling as I lay these words on paper because my heart is so full. What a blessing to me.

Alzenia Collins Jordan Kidd Flowers Holiday Hood was a colorful woman. Though a Christian, she cursed as commonly as she spoke. I think she used curse words for emphasis and impact, as she surely got everyone's attention. Her mother died when she was fourteen years old, and as the oldest, she raised her brothers and sisters: Rob, Elbert, John, Alenia, and David. This was a lot of responsibility, but she made biscuits, sausage, and grits for them and made them all exemplary citizens and successful people. She rose early in the morning to sweep the yard of chinaberries that had fallen from the trees and to gather the pecans from the tree. She also would see who was up and walking at that time of morning. She loved the scents of the morning air after the frequent rains. Hibiscus and blooms, fig trees and persimmons she loved mornings.

When she went back in the house to make breakfast and wake everyone, she would say, "Get up now." When no one moved, five minutes later, she would say, "Get up now. Breakfast will be ready in ten minutes." No sounds. Finally, she would come through the house, calling out, "You bastards will never amount to anything. Get your asses up, brush your teeth, feed those chickens, and get into this kitchen!" Action!

She lived on a paved street, where she had rental houses. Mr. Vick, Jewish, was her neighbor on the right. He had a neat little store, with pickles in brine in a large barrel and pigs' feet on the counter. We used to buy the pickles, put a Tootsie Pop stick up the middle, and suck on the sweet and sour—all for a nickel.

Alzenia's rental houses on the left extended to the corner, where the Black Cat Saloon was located. Men sat there all day on chairs with cane backs and watched people go by. Some smoked; most had missing teeth and were uneducated and unemployed. Occasionally, you'd see a young woman go into the bar, but women never sat around. Across the street from the saloon was George, an Italian, who made the best pan sausage. People spoke of others by ethnic identity in those days, as there were differences. My grandmother got along with all of them, and they called her Ms. Alzenia or Ms. Jordan. White folks called her Alzenia. She called them White folks, but they lived peaceably there together.

Alzenia was a light-skinned black women and rather striking in appearance. She was tall and stout, and she wore big hats and high heels. She later acccumulated money and influence and never rode at the back of the bus. If she took a bus and a white driver told her to go to the back, she would say, "Let's go, children." And we would get off the bus and walk the rest of the way.

She knew Judge Harper, the most influential person in town. She had nursed his children, and there was nothing he could refuse Alzenia. She helped a lot of people who got into trouble.

Alzenia was married seven times. She shot and killed one husband. She took him to the hospital and was not charged. She tortured the others by tying them to the four-poster bed and sticking them with a fork if they spent any of their paychecks before coming home. She cooked ten or twelve cakes, biscuits, chicken, and other food and drink and always had company. She always had a swing on the screened-in porch. When our work was finished for the day, we would sit in the swing and talk into the night.

She had many occupations—nursing, owner of a tearoom, beautician, businesswoman—and she owned blocks of houses. She kept money all over, even in the fireplace. She sewed hundred-dollar bills into quilts. She buried money. She bought silver dollars and kept coins in barrels and pots. She put money in her bosom and forget who gave it to her. She did not trust banks and enjoyed money hunts because people buried their money in la louisiane coffee cans. Metal deterctors could find them. When people died often noone knew where their money was buried. People would hunt for it.

Bigmama was very superstitious and was a fortune teller; she went by the name Madam Zenia. She used to say there were only a few things people were concerned about: romance, jobs, finances, and health. She must have helped a lot of people, as they would come night and day for advice. She always had a nice house, by black or white standards. She had indoor plumbing, a parlor, beautiful furniture, and chickens. Her house was on a paved street with trees. She had lots of money, but her description of herself was "a poor widow woman." She always attracted men who had something, and they were always younger than she was.

She lived to be ninety-four years old. She was an unforgettable character and had quite a life and sense of humor.

Daddy was essentially Alzenia's only child. He had a brother, Leamon, but he died of an infection. Medical care was at a premium back then. Either the doctor was too far away, or he cost too much, or he did not know what to do. Antibiotics were not available; people could die from almost anything, as help rarely got to them in time. Daddy got a lot of his humor from his mother, who dearly loved him.

Mother, a Northern woman who had never eaten grits or Southern food, was a newcomer to all of this. She felt somewhat bewildered, but as a young woman and mother, she had to learn quickly. One thing she and Daddy both knew was that they had to finish their education and build a better life for themselves and their children.

I am in my eighth decade of life and Louisiana is still one of the poorest states and least progressive in the United States. Corruption and political dynasties like the Huey P. Long families played a role. So, I am thankful my parents migrated away. I am sure my life would have been very different had they not sought opportunities and sacrificed for them. When my Dad was leaving Louisiana the principal of Carroll High and most influential Black man called "Mr. Henry Carroll" in town came over to my grandmothers house and said to my father "Limuary a rolling stone gathers no moss" Dad turned to him and said "Henry I am not wanting moss just a better life for my family." but thank you.

Bigmama was in the middle of all of this as she did not want her only son to leave Louisiana and all she had built. There was acrimony between them for some years, I think Dad gained some energy from it as he was determined not to fail. He loved his mother, but he loved Adeline my mother as well and he was strong enough to cleave to his wife. We are all the better for it. Bigmama adoped a young boy Calvin and raised him. Down there people gave children away. She just said to the girl give me this boy I will raise him and that is what happened. That was her response to Dad leaving. Years later all was forgiven and Dad always took us back in motorhomes and the like to visit. I would call Bigmama a survivor! I am not sure if she ever found love or happiness, or even knew what it was but it was not for lack of trying. Bigmama was

13

a comely woman as they said in the day. My Dad's father was a white man. A physician in Columbia Louisiana and Coroner with two white sons, My dad was not a recognized son. However my mother told me the story of how they took me to meet him when I was born. Later years through the television program Roots, Henry Louis Gates was engaged to trace our roots. The two sons came to visit my sister Carolyn Booker and my nephew her son, U. S. Senator from New Jersey Cory A. Booker. The family name is Brown and the heritage roots extend to England. Bigmama gave birth to my Dad at age 14 and my dad had a brother two years older Leamon. You might think of her life as a tragedy and in many ways the hand she was dealt in life does seem awfully tough. But she whatever it was she chewed it up and spit it out, or as Paula says she ate the fish and spit out the bones. Her advice to me was "Push, Pull, Shove, If you give out daughter don't give up, It takes wit grit and bullshit to make it, An empty wagon makes the most noise. Keep quiet. She had one a minute.

Bigmama was such a humorous woman. When I was in her presence she was always in the past telling stories or in the future dreaming of riding the Missouri Pacific train to Corpus Christi, Texas but never quite with you in the moment. An Unforgettable woman.

I was two years old when my parents moved to Detroit, Michigan. Over the following years, I developed an adaptability as I grew and saw a lot of changes and a lot of people. We lived through food rationing, race riots, roomers with people migrating from the south and my parents helping them. They opened their home and helped them find jobs. Mom and Dad had wonderful friends for life.

As children we spent summers in Louisiana after moving to Detroit. When school was out we started summer vacation and drove to Bigmama's house. Mom and Dad were completing their education, establishing themselves, So my life in Louisiana is vivid. I went to school there a couple of years and kept friendships from all those years of many of my Louisiana classmates. Almeta, Minnie V, Isaac, Mary, Gloria, Abe Pierce and Jimmy Heywood and many more and actually attended a fifty year high school reunion. That was a blast, Our whole family went as we were reviewing some of Bigmama's properties as well for a sale.

One, two, buckle my shoe

Three, four, close the door

Five, six, pick up sticks

Seven, eight, you'll be late

Nine, ten, big fat hen.

(This is how I learned to count to ten.)

# CHAPTER 3

## The Early Years

*Baby Shirley Anne*

My life as a young girl was one of wide-eyed learning, seeing, and adaptability. My parents made it seem like a grand adventure. One thing was clear: my parents were looking for and were determined to find a good life, one better than their hardworking, racially oppressed parents had experienced.

My mother, the fourth child of Rosie and Joseph Wilson, lived in Des Moines, Iowa. She was a smart student and was talented, singing in a group called the Wee Sisters. They had performances with Jimmie Lunceford and the big bands that came through the city. Mother got a scholarship to Arkansas State, a long way from home and a different

17

culture. Her older brother and sister went to Drake University and both had died. The minister thought a change would be good. Mother's parents were hardworking members of Corinthian Baptist Church. Rose and Joe were from large families, from Alabama originally.

Mom met my dad, Limuary Jordan, at college. Dad was the only surviving son of two children born to Alzenia Jordan. Dad's mother and my colorful grandmother was a stalwart member of Zion Traveler Baptist Church in Monroe, Louisiana. I was born in Monroe at the Catholic Saint Francis Hospital. Mom and Dad moved to Detroit, Michigan, after a year as the opportunity was booming for Negros along the northeastern corridor in the automobile industry and the manufacturing companies of the big cities. Farming and animal husbandry, which had been my dad's major, was no longer the dream. Mother was majoring in home economics in college, and she too saw other ideas were possible.

They attended Wayne State in Michigan and later taught school. My dad joined the auto union, the AFL-CIO, of Ford Motor Company. Life was good. We moved several times, from 215 East Palmer to 574 Horton in Detroit, to Ypsilanti near Dearborn, and then to 111 East Willis, not far from Harper Hospital. In Ypsilanti, we had a new home; it was so beautiful. This was in 1943, and we had a victory garden in the back. Mother had all the labor-saving devices that a home economics major could desire—a mangle (while seated, you could iron clothes), a Kelvinator refrigerator, a Maytag washing machine, and a clothesline out back. The washing machine had a wringer on the top to get the water out of the clothes. Then she'd hang them on the line with clothespins to dry.

Mother baked cookies and served beautiful dinners. For breakfast, we ate hot cereal, such as Ralston cream of wheat or oatmeal, in cold months; in the summer, we ate cold cereals with fruit—Raisin Bran, cornflakes, and Grape-Nuts. On weekends, we had pancakes and pan sausage. When all the family was together for meals, it was the best of times.

In 1939, my sister, Carolyn, was born, and my brother was born in 1945. After moving back to town from Ypsilanti, we moved to a large three-story home on East Willis. Lots of company visited my parents, much the same as immigrants come to this country today. Friends and relatives came to our doors, carrying everything they owned in a brown paper bag; they would say, "Alzenia told me to go here." My folks took them in and helped them find work.

One very sophisticated woman, Mrs. Divine, was quite a memorable lady. She had worked in Alaska in the finest of homes and was a friend of my mother's mother, Rosie. She interviewed prospective employers, instead of the other way around, and only worked for wealthy people. She cooked with pure butter and made gourmet foods and was adored by her employers. We referred to them as "rich white people." They lived in Grosse Pointe, a suburb of Detroit. Her day off was Thursday, and she would visit us on that day and have dinner with our family. She was very proper and had strict manners for dining, based on etiquette. Thursdays were unique. Mrs. Divine kept us on our best manners at the table and did not allow us to drink liquids with our food, not until we finished eating.

She trusted my parents with her trunks of furs, jewelry, and collectibles from Alaska. She often brought hand-me-downs and clothing to my parents that had been given to her by her employers. When the lady of the house had a row with her husband, she would throw out all of his clothes and her clothes and make him buy them new ones until she felt better.

When the Arkansas State choir came to sing in Detroit, my parents housed many of them and had a dinner for them. Our home was always a center of activity. The things we lived through in Detroit are as vivid today as when we lived them.

Policymaking, the precursor of today's lottery, was commonplace. A typical day was like this: You woke up, wrote down your dream, and got the dream book out. You looked up the number and bet on it (policy making), while having coffee and reading the paper. If the number came out, you made money, and the policy writer made money. And everyone was happy. A man came by to pick up the numbers and bring the winnings. All I know is that a lot of dreaming occurred. I have dream books today that interpret dreams. I remember the three sixes as a hot number. I do not remember the odds?

In the 1940's I remember the race riots, food rationing, and how challenging it was to get bread, bacon, and other food. My mother still has a ration book, from which you used ration stamps to get food. My parents helped so many people all the time; people were always bringing things to them. Our home abounded with grains and vegetables, and Mother was such a great cook that she could make everything taste good. We ate a lot of beans with pigtails in them; we ate organ meats such as liver, kidneys, brains, chitterlings, hog maws, and tongue. In Louisiana, we ate raccoon, possum, rabbit, buffalo, and a lot of fish—gasper goo, gar. Pork chops, fried chicken, and meatloaf.

We had sweet potatoes, turnip greens, cornbread, watermelon, and pecans by the barrel. We had pecan trees, and the paper-shell pecans were all over the ground. We gathered them in baskets. We also had fig trees and persimmon trees. I never knew hunger.

Mom and Dad made a way for their children, as well as for many people who needed help. Dad partnered with a cousin, and they owned two billiard parlors. Dad also owned two gas stations in Detroit, running those businesses as well as his job with the union. The cold, damp weather of Michigan became a health hazard for my dad, forcing him to have a change of lifestyle. He developed pericarditis. The doctors said the cold was too much for him.

In those days, when a car drove up at the gas station, a gas station attendant (I worked there too) pumped the gas, checked under the hood, and wiped the windshield—in all kinds of weather. Imagine trying to service a car during those frigid Detroit winters. Passengers always stayed inside of the car. Detroit was really cold and damp.

We had one relative, Uncle John, in California. We went there to visit him when I was nearly thirteen years old. I already knew how to drive and had worked at a lot of jobs. My sister, Carolyn, was eleven, and my brother, Limuary Jr., was seven. After that trip, we decided to move to California, and it was like the heavens had opened up. The frigid winters were over, and jobs were everywhere in the early '50s.

Racism was evident but not overt, like in other places. My dad bought a house in Los Angeles.

1766 W.23rd Street. Dad worked night and day at Locheed Aircraft to get the down payment. He drove back to get us with a uhaul trailer in the back. A maytag washing machine and all our belongings. Our beginning in California. Bigmama was not pleased my Dad was gone for a new life other than Louisiana after Detroit.

We had our Sunday clothes, our school clothes, and our play clothes. Those were the times. You changed clothes dependent upon the activity. Play clothes, work or school clothes, Church or party clothes. Special ! the same for shoes. Contrasted to today, clothes are not as important. Comfort and easy care fabrics are the demand. Men wear hats for sport, rarely fedoras or brim hats. The same with women, maybe to church, the pill box hat was popular in the sixties and wide brim as well. Men have stopped wearing ties and women do not wear gloves. It is rare to see a sartorially resplendid man or woman today. Our culture has changed. Why not?.

What were we? The number of names assigned to us was incredible. We were colored; we were Negroes; we were to become black and then African Americans and, now multiracial, biracial—somewhere, maybe American. I remember the drinking fountains were marked either "colored" or "white." The waiting rooms and public accommodations signs read colored or white, and basically, our dreams were limited by what a colored reality might be. but thankfully for me my my parents said we are Americans. Think like Americans whatever that spirit is, do not think limitation.

When my parents came to Los Angeles with their hopes and talents and education in hand, they would become teachers, placed in "combat areas" of the city—ghetto schools that had crime problems so bad that white teachers did not want to teach there. Ultimately, combat pay was added for high-risk schools. Telephone operators jobs, telephones were big, employees wore expensive suits and had good diction. There was government service, like keypunch. (Remember those data cards that had information punched in? Where are they today? Technology passed them by.)

The cultural shifts were unusual, as neighborhoods were primarily ethnically formed by religious Jews living near synagogues. They had to walk to synagogue, as driving was work, and work was not allowed on the Sabbath. Catholics lived near cathedrals, and the Hispanics lived way on the other side of town. Jews followed white people into housing and neighborhoods, and Negros followed Jews into homes. Whites would rarely buy a home that Negros lived, in but Hispanics would. These trends are alive and well today. Racial sucession in housing.

In the fifties, we dressed in hats, gloves, and stockings with seams. Pantyhose were to come much later. We wore sensible shoes and had sensible hair and makeup. Most men wore hats and overcoats. Weather of course dictating clothing.

The hot water bottle in the bathroom is not seen today. Neither is the douche bag, diaphragm, or other dinosaurs of a time long past. Life was simple. School, homework, chores, Saturday laundry, house cleaning, yard work, movies with Dad on Saturday night, and church on Sunday. We joined Mount Sinai Baptist Church, Reverend H. B. Charles's church on LaSalle and Adams. The friends we made there are still friends today. Eddie Kendrix, Shirley Andrews Campbell, Calvin Norton, Aretta Hunt and her brother James, Marcia Arnold, Lonnie Farrell, Paul Persley and sister Val Joyce Toran Black, countless friends too many to name and I know I am in trouble because I have forgotten to name so many. Daddy was on the Trustee Board, I sang in the junior choir. Ms. Waters was our director. Good times then and now.

Years later, the family moved to Saint Paul Methodist, where I was married. On Sunday afternoons, we visited relatives and friends, or we entertained friends and family.

I was sixteen, a senior in high school, when I got my first car. I had been driving since I was eleven. This was a 1937 plymouth with a stick shift and a clutch. loved it!!

The beach was wonderful. Congressman Augustus Hawkins had fought a hard battle to desegregate the beaches in Los Angeles. He had begged my dad to be on his staff, but Dad did not want to go to Washington and uproot our family, thank God.

Mom and Dad persevered and kept moving up. They worked hard and became very successful in everything they did. They always had enough to help others. Mom and Dad were loved dearly by so many people. Their retirement parties and home-going celebrations gave witness to that fact. Everyone loved them and they were fun!

I learned from them that a job was a blessing and work was honorable, that education was the key to a good life, that you enrich your life when you give to others, that serving God and living his commandments is a recipe for a pleasant experience, and that people with prejudices are like everyone else, except they act out of fear and ignorance. It exists everywhere, even within one's own race. As people become educated about issues and are free of worry and concern for their own security and well-being, they lose their radical thinking and ease racial barriers.

My parents continued to be faith-based people and giving people. From my childhood until today, that has been a lasting legacy of their lives—the gift they have given their children and grandchildren. Our children and grandchildren continue the dreams of our ancestors— walking through doors they prayed would open and fulfilling prayers, much as did messengers sent by our praying ancestors. These prayers occurred everywhere, from the dinner table to bended knees by the bed. On Sunday, prayers were in the fellowship of God's houses— at Corinthian Baptist Church of Rosa and Joseph Wilson, at Zion Traveler Baptist Church of Alzenia Jordan, and at Mount Sinai Baptist Church,Saint Paul Methodist Church, and the Church of Christian Fellowship of Adeline and Limuary Jordan. A lasting memory of my Daddy is one of seeing him on his knees every night thanking God. In his quiet moments he gave God the glory. He knew hard work and he taught me hard work. He knew how to have fun and he taught that too. The Ironic thing is that after I was grown, wife and mother and lived near my parents we were such good friends. We traveled together, belonged to the Links together and truly enjoyed being in the company of each other. Many of my friends have teased me saying "I love Adeline and Limuary more than I love you" Beatrice will say "I miss Limuary", Marilyn (Birdie) called mother "Mrs. J." Some friends sought their advice, counsel and encouragement as their confidant and friend. Mom and Dad played bridge and poker, loved to cook and eat and swim and travel. They owned three motor homes over time and loved taking the grandchildren across country building dreams and loving on their Grandchildren. So, you see my Camp Shirleywhirls nick named that by Paula, my eldest daughter had a template from those experiences.

*All that I am or ever hope to be I owe to my parents.*

*—Abraham Lincoln*

# CHAPTER 4

## Ode to Mom and Dad: Wishes and Wisdom

*Fiftieth wedding anniversary*

I have often wondered why I was as motivated at such a young age; I was much more driven than just being inspired by people I admired. Maybe it was due to my father's faded dream of becoming a doctor or other hero. I wonder what instilled the strong work ethic in me that I have always possessed.

As the oldest child and being big and sturdy, it was my call to assist my dad with the chores and projects he had to do, including repairs and construction. We plastered walls, built cinder-block fences, and did the yard work—whatever the need. I slopped hogs in Louisiana, rode old mares in the field, dug potatoes, and cleaned and picked chicken feathers with hot water in a tin tub after the chickens were killed for dinner. We also ate possum, raccoon, squirrel, and rabbit that were shot in the woods. We fished in the Ouachita River, a few blocks from Big Mama's home, for perch, gar, and gasper goo, as well as crayfish.

But these were only my activities; there was more to it than that. It seems to be the voice of my little mother—diminutive in size at four foot nine, weighing under one hundred pounds, and wearing a size two shoe—in my brain, telling me, "Get your education. It's the key to a good life. It will mean true freedom." Maybe it's because she left Arkansas State University at age nineteen, and married at such a young age.

Dad was a six-foot, very fair, handsome man, whose father was a Caucasian doctor in Caldwell Parish, Louisiana. The doctor had two other Caucasian sons, found through Henry Louis Gates's roots work at Harvard University. The ancestry search led them to visit our family and verify that we have roots in England. Dad was thought to be a white man for most of his life, and it was so stated on his death certificate in 2002; the hospital did not ask us. We learned this later.

Both my parents, after dropping out of college to marry and start a family, later returned to college to get their degrees and then find good jobs. It was hard to do with a growing family, as two years later, my sister, Carolyn, was born, and seven years later, my brother, Limuary Jr. was born.

I was validated as being smart. I could learn almost anything to which I applied my mind. I was described as having a photographic memory and was double-promoted in school twice. I graduated high school in Los Angeles at age sixteen—I was among the top students in my class at Manual Arts High School—and completed Fisk University at age twenty.

The challenges I met in high school were all race- and gender-based. To obtain an academic major, my parents had to come to the school and insist that I be allowed to take algebra and geometry, as blacks were stereotyped as being suited to nonprofessional majors. For me, that was a dietician or a beautician.

Our doctor, Dr. Perry Beal, went to a historically black college and suggested that choice to my parents for me. After my first year at Los Angeles City College, I transferred to Fisk University. It was not commonplace for girls to have the opportunity to go to college, as the thinking was that they would soon marry, and the money would have been ill-spent. Boys' education was not as questioned, if they did not go into the military.

Thankfully, my enlightened parents were willing to make sacrifices for me to get an education. Tuition at Fisk was $750 a semester in 1955, which included room and board. That was a sacrifice, considering that our house only cost $7,500, and my goal for a dream home was priced at $35,000. Mother and Dad had the confidence in me to make those sacrifices. There were no Pell Grants or bank loans for this; you either had the money or you did not, which is why my dad had limited hope to become a Doctor.

Having started a family while still in college, those responsibilities were challenging to even completing college but he did. His Quest was lost for medical school as he soon had three children and a wife to take care of so he chose another path.

My mother gave me some additional advice that has stayed with me. I had severe trepidations about childbirth—the pain and the ability to actually deliver a child. She said, "Look at the millions of people in the world and in centuries before. If they could have children, you can have them too." I kept that belief and delivered four healthy children.

Mother also kept a simple scripture on her nightstand: "The Lord will provide." It now sits on my nightstand, tattered a bit but preserved.

My dad held similar positive affirmations on life subjects. He was a real dreamer. He visualized his success in much the same way. He and my mother were a good team, working together for their dreams. Dad would often drive to the top of the mountains and ask, "Can you visualize yourself as a successful American? Can you imagine anything you see down there as possible for you with hard work and trust in God?" Dad knew you had to believe first to accomplish things. Those moments of inspiration are buried in my mind, and I am grateful for them. I was young and as imperfect a kid as any other but, a good kid exploring life and relationships as my peers. But, at my core I had some deep values, big dreams and purpose driven motivation.

I believed my dad, I trusted my mother, and I thought my dreams were worthwhile. I also agreed that the Lord does provide.

*Know when to hold 'em and know when to fold 'em.*

*—"The Gambler" by Don Schlitz*

*Rosa E. Wilson, Maternal Grandmother*

*Joseph Wilson, Maternal Grandfather*

# CHAPTER 5

# Grandmother Rosie and Big Mama

It was only natural to dream of better days in the 1940s and 1950s. For so many, life was very hard, and for black people, even more so. The nation was segregated, including the military, and the southern states were visibly and overtly so. There were not many dreams to which black children could aspire, other than to be a minister, doctor, lawyer, businessman, nurse, or teacher. It took education and resources to achieve these goals, as there were few grants or scholarships. The achievements by blacks were not mentioned in books or the media, other than George Washington Carver and the abolitionist Frederick Douglass. Few knew of the accomplishments of black people, as they were not recognized, credited, or publicized.

What about the invention of the electric elevator by Alexander Miles, the automatic gear shift by Richard Spikes, the supercharger system for use with an internal combustion engine by Joseph Gamell, the three-position traffic signal by Garrett Morgan, the portable pencil sharpener by John Lee Love, an updated design of the fountain pen by William Purvis, a typewriter machine by Lee Burridge, an automatic refrigeration system by Frederick Jones, or a heating furnace by Alice Parker? There are hundreds more examples, some as simple as the mop by Thomas Steward, the dustpan by Lloyd Ray, improvements on the ironing board by Sarah Boone, and clothes dryer by George Sampson. That was not the information age; it was just the beginning of the Industrial Revolution. The postmarking and canceling machine, invented by William Barry, helped to transport letters in the mail, and Philip Downing invented the letter drop.

Most families were struggling to make expenses, and they had inadequate health care or income. People commonly died in their forties and fifties—shorter life spans—before many advances in health research, pharmaceuticals, and preventive information. For the average black family, dreams were deferred, or, worse, there was no dream. I am speaking of the period of 1920's to the 1960's here.

My grandmothers were extraordinary for their day. One from the North and one from the Deep South, their lives, as much as their personalities, laid the foundation, motivation, and inspiration for me and others in our family today.

It would be unholy to tell the story of my mother's mother and not begin with Corinthian Baptist Church, which is where Grandmother Rosie dedicated so much of her life. The church was and is a Des Moines, Iowa, institution for religious, social, and political change. Founded by twenty-two women in 1898 in a family dwelling, it grew so rapidly that it twice relocated to accommodate the burgeoning congregation that worships there today. Reverend Robinson, the minister of that church, encouraged Grandmother Rosie to send my mother, Adeline, south to college and had her apply for a scholarship to Arkansas State University.

Grandmother Rosie, a heavyset, black-skinned woman, whose stout legs were suited to low-heel shoes and stockings, routinely dressed in long skirts or dresses and was always on the move—"up and doing" or "out and being." She encouraged the pursuit of excellence. "Education is the key to a good life" was her mantra. As the mother of five children—Anna, McGilvery, Frances, Adeline, and Kermit—she showed them a path for living.

Anna and McGilvery, or "Mac," the eldest two children, attended Drake University and the University of Iowa and excelled academically. Mac intended to become a doctor, and Anna was the first black social worker in Des Moines. All the children were musical—singing and playing violin and drums—and were in the honor society. Tragedy struck the family when Mac was found drowned, and Anna died of a ruptured appendix.

Although Grandmother Rosie did everything that was needed at home, she never relished the homemaker role. She had big dreams for herself, as well as for her children. Travel, books, music, and culture occupied her thoughts, as well as her work at the church. She loved planting flowers at the church and making the grounds beautiful.

Grandfather, on the other hand, did not require much. As a father of five and someone who gave a hard day's labor in the coal mines, he wanted a hot bath, a hot meal, and rest. Grandmother Rosie, as one of thirteen children, had seen enough hard work to last her a lifetime. Her heart and spirit longed for broader intellectual outlets. She was extremely erudite and adept for someone of her limited formal education.

She was never limited, however, by her circumstances. She thought and lived like a philanthropist. She always helped others, and she did small things in grand fashion. She would send one handkerchief or one cupcake with red hearts to me at Fisk University on Valentine's Day, elegantly wrapped and shipped from Yonkers department store in Des Moines—the finest department store at that time. My memories of her are very sweet. She had a large heart and a large home on West Fifteenth Street. She often kept students from Drake University as roomers for extra income. This was a huge grand house with an attic and a basement. There were trunks and treasures from top to bottom. We always enjoyed our summers there. Grandmother was a woman of action. She did not sit and dream. She would say, "An idle mind is the devil's workshop." If you spilled something, she'd say, "Hasten, Jason, get the basin," or "Oops, slop, get the mop!"

The unforgettable thing about Grandmother Rosie is that she was courageous enough to embrace herself; she knew who she was. God knows she had enough tragedy and grief in her life, with the loss of two wonderful children in their moments of promise and the eventual divorce from Grandfather, as she could not be there for him and his simplest needs. Her younger children embraced her teachings

35

of excellence, and they escaped the bondage of a life of servitude and lack, to which so many black children succumbed, as they were not prepared to compete.

Frances married into a prominent Des Moines family, and Kermit became a professional musician, a drummer. Adeline, my mother, has most closely personified Grandmother Rosie's visions and dreams, as she raised her family and achieved renowned distinction in her career. She was Federal Woman of the Year, honored by Secretary of the Treasury Henry Fowler, and National President of the Urban League Guild for example … Links Inc. Legacy member. These are National Black Philanthropic,Civic and Social Organizations.

Mom was married to my father for sixty-three years. She really loved Dad, respected him as a family man, provider and help mate. She was a great cook and Dad loved her cooking. She said the way to a mans heart was through the stomach.

Mother was a philanthropist, with endowments and charitable giving as an integral part of her life going forward. At age ninety-seven, she was the last surviving member of her immediate family. Mom was 4'10" and about 100lbs all her life. she was a pound and a half at birth and wore a size two shoe. (childrens dept or sample shoes.)

Grandmother Rosie's life and work were never diminished by the challenges before her. Her heart must have been shattered, but her faith kept her strong and smiling. Her final resting place, under a sprawling oak tree in a serene Des Moines cemetery, is a place of peace and thanksgiving. When I visit there, I can almost hear the words, "Well done, my good and faithful servant."

## Alzenia "Big Mama" Collins Jordan

My father's mother was equally unforgettable. She lived in the Deep South all of her life, except for brief periods in Detroit and Los Angeles in her nineties, near the end of her life. She was a colorful, humorous woman who laughed often, loved deeply, and lived well. She was tall, heavyset, light-brown–skinned, independent, and stylish. She loved to wear big hats and colorful clothing. She was attractive to men and married seven times. Mr. Johnny Jordan, Mr. Emmett, Mr. Flowers, Mr. Kidd, Mr. Holliday, Mr. Hood were most memorable.

"Big Mama" took that name, in contrast to my mother, who was so small, so there would be a distinction between them after they became grandmothers. Her adult life began quite suddenly, as she was beset with the enormous responsibility of raising a sister and four brothers—Allene, Rob, Elbert, David, and John—after the death of their mother when she was only fourteen years old. She had two sons of her own, Leamon and Limuary (my dad), beginning at age sixteen. My dad became an only child when his brother died as a teenager from a sinus infection that spread. Big Mama's siblings were near Dad's age, so it was like he had older brothers and a sister.

Big Mama was a survivor. Failure was never a thought. Her first serious words to me, which are indelible in my memory, were daughter, "It takes wit, grit, and bullshit to make it. If you give out, don't give up."

She also would give you a long look and say, "Heap see, but few know." One of the ways she made it was that she seemingly could become anyone she needed to be. She was a beautician, a nurse, and a businesswoman who ran a tearoom. She owned rental houses, and she was a psychic called Madam Zenia. People came from everywhere to get a reading from her. She said, "It's simple. People are only interested in four things, health, love, work, and money. You can put almost everything into one of those categories." She studied her craft and was very successful at it.

She was very superstitious, and some things were never done because they were bad luck—no peanuts in the shells in or near the house; no umbrella raised in the house, and no hats on the bed. On Monday mornings, no woman could enter the home unless a man had entered first; otherwise, it would ruin your business for the week. Never sweep your feet, or you will get arrested. A black cat crossing your path is bad luck. While driving, don't make turns that tie a knot in your business. Card playing was not allowed on Sunday (the Sabbath). She also told us not to use the Lord's name in vain. Although she often cursed. A wayward man was a bastard and a wayward woman as a slut, but she never used God's name in all of her cursing. She would say, "You are worse than a coon eating yellow jackets!" She would call someone a baboon or an ignorant jackass, or she'd say, "Ah, hockey!" not the sport (that's yellow baby shit). When something went wrong, you knew how bad it was by her reaction.

She said if your right hand itched, money was on the way. If your nose itched, someone was coming. If your left hand itched, an important letter was on the way. She had a thousand sayings, and we had to obey them.

She is unforgettable because she had a presence, power, and confidence. She had smarts from experience. She was self-taught, very meticulous, and neat, and she wanted everyone around her to be that way. She lived on a paved street on Layton Avenue. Italians were her neighbors on the left, and on the right was Mr. Vic, a Jewish man and his family.

Integrated housing, unheard of for a black woman in Louisiana. White folks called her by her first name, Alzenia, and she called him by his first name, George. She had indoor plumbing, beautiful furniture, a lovely screened-in porch with a swing settee. It was a big, gorgeous white house, and her rental houses were a beautiful white with green trim. Years later, the city of Monroe bought her property for the city hall and municipal buildings.

She had a lovely home, by anyone's standards, there in Monroe, and they all lived peacefully and happily. Big Mama had two cars, both DeSotos, but occasionally, she liked to go to DeSiard Street on the bus. This was all of the town, one long street. If a young or new bus driver said to sit in the back, she would get off the bus and walk. She would not yield her dignity to the policies of segregation. After all it, made no sense. She had nursed Judge Harper's babies from her breast. Judge Harper was the most powerful white man in town, and Alzenia could get anything she wanted from him. She got men and women out of jail by telling the judge that their children needed them at home. She would say, "I'll see he doesn't do that again."

So what was a little bus driver gonna say to her? She wasn't afraid of anything or anyone. She took risks and worked hard. She cooked, she sewed, and she built houses. She had hogs, chickens, and hens laying eggs. She had pecan trees and fig trees and always was looking to expand her holdings. She loved money and what it could do.

She had silver dollars by the barrelful, and she saved money in jars and buckets. She collected everything from Tiffany lamps to china and crystal. She had a player piano with the paper rolls that filled the home with beautiful music.

There was plenty of food, prosperity with caution, tragedy, ambition, and always laughter. Our family was a food family, not a drinking one. No one seemed to care for whiskey or even wine, except at Christmas, and that was elderberry wine. In Detroit, at Uncle Elbert's, I once saw a pint bottle of Four Roses bourbon. That was rare; I never saw whiskey until I went to college. My father has never had a drink in his life. I heard that my dad saw his stepfather drink a full bottle of whiskey and pass out, which, over time, caused his death at age thirty-nine.

Big Mama found people to be very interesting, as well as animals. She loved her dogs. When she lost Billy, it was like a relative had passed; she grieved for months.

After a good meal, when the dishes were done and nothing was on the radio, we would sit on the porch in the swing and talk. The next morning, mosquito bites would be all over our legs and arms. How had they gotten through the screen?

The Ouachita River was only six blocks up the street, with a high levy. We would walk to the river, fish for gasper goo or gar, come home, scale the fish, and cook 'em up. Big Mama used lard, as Crisco was new, and I never saw olive oil as a child.

Big Mama described herself as a "poor widow woman." She loved understating herself. She never believed in revealing too much information, like her age. She said, "If a woman tells her age, she'll tell everything she knows." She also loved to say, "An empty wagon makes the most noise."

Her view on banks was that she didn't trust them. She buried money and sewed hundred-dollar bills in quilts. She bricked up money in the fireplace and kept it in barrels; some was in the bank. She said, "It's a poor rat that ain't got but one hole"—her version of diversification.

Her view on education was not as the end-all and be-all, as one might think. She said she had seen a lot of "educated fools." She banked on common sense, faith in God, and sheer wit and grit.

On love, her views were that "romance without finance is a nuisance," and "Daughter, never lose your head over a piece of tail." Big Mama found a way to raise all of her siblings and Dad, and they thrived. One became becoming a minister. Uncle David attended Union Theological Seminary and later was the pastor of a church in restored Williamsburg, Virginia. The Rockefeller family built his church and dedicated it. Uncle David was a friend of Martin Luther King Jr. and introduced me to him. I went to many rallies with Uncle David where Dr. King was speaking in the late '50s.

Uncle John had a restaurant in Los Angeles called Ivy's Chicken Shack, named after the entertainer Ivy Anderson. Nat King Cole and many entertainers frequented his restaurant at Vernon and Central Avenues. Uncle Elbert lived in Michigan and was an insurance man, and Uncle Rob was a businessman, who later contracted TB and was in a sanitarium for many years. Auntie, as we called her—pronounced "Ah-nee," was very attractive. She married a couple of times and became the mother of three daughters. Auntie was the only smoker in our family.

All of Big Mama sibling's left the South and went to Detroit, Michigan, following the northeast corridor of the industrial revolution, but she remained in Louisiana. She owned blocks of rental houses and wanted for nothing, materially. I am not sure if she ever found love, but it wasn't for a lack of searching. She had many wonderful friends. Ms. Henrietta Johnson lived down the street and was part of perhaps the most prominent black family in town. Her other friends included Ms. Shirley Davis, and Ms. Spears, to name a few. Her oldest tenants were Mr. Fred Grant and Ernest, who worked at the bakery.

Big Mama did what she needed to do by all means available. She would say, "Can do. Will do. No such thing as can't do." Her favorite scripture was the Psalm 121, adopted by my Dad and now our family scripture. Her church was Zion Traveler Baptist Church, then at Eleventh and Grammont. Architecturally, it was a total miss, as the stairs veered upward at a forty-five–degree angle to the second floor. There was no possibility of a handicapped individual ever getting to the sanctuary. To this day, I have never seen a building like it.

Big Mama sat in the middle left fourth pew, wearing her colorful hats encircled with tulle and flowers. Ms. Johnson was at the piano. I learned "The Old Rugged Cross" and "In the Garden" there.

Big Mama was laid to rest at age ninety-three at Garden Valley in Columbia, Louisiana, Caldwell Parish, near her birthplace. She lived the life she loved and loved the life she lived. When I think of her, I smile. She left us quite a lot.

A cortege of cars led by the Sherriff of Caldwell Parrish led Big Mama to Garden Valley Cemetary for burial by the fence behind the church. Columbia, the town where it all began for her. She was back home. My Dad took it so hard he cried and cried.

When she arrived at the pearly gates, I am sure God said, "Come on in, Alzenia."

*You never fail until you stop trying.*

*—Albert Einstein*

# C H A P T E R   6

## *The Sixties Cultural Revolution*

This was the most important decade of my life. I entered and graduated from dental school in the sixties. I married. I had four children. I bought my first home and moved to California. I experienced the assassination of civil rights leaders, the US attorney general, and our president.

What is next may appear as a blitz and a blurr because it was! All these things were symbols of the 1960's. One of the most eventful and transitional decades in history as well as my life for sure. The United States was hopeful, lets put a man on the moon says President Kennedy. Nonviolent protests of Dr. Martin L. King, The Vietnam war, then assasinations, war on poverty, great society programs all while I was in Dental school, marrying, four babies, internships fellowships, it was Yes, the names and voices of the times. There was big noise! so, roll through these headlines.

Change, crisis, civil rights movement, women's rights, gay rights, antiwar demonstrations, Abbie Hoffman, Allen Ginsberg, Andy Warhol, the Black Panther party, Bob Dylan, President John Kennedy, Robert Kennedy, Martin Luther King Jr., protests, shooting, death, funerals, the Vietnam war, the Democratic national convention, Jerry Rubin, activists, Bobby Seale, SNCC (the Student Nonviolent Coordinating Committee), James Baldwin, the Beatles, Lyndon Baines Johnson's Great Society programs, psychic Jeane Dixon, Neil Armstrong and Buzz Aldrin, Apollo 11, walking on the moon—the sky was no longer the limit. Voices and names of the day.

Shirley, dental school, friends, dating, intense studying, little sleep, true love, Dan, wedding, marriage, baby, baby sitter, car, bills, diapers, another baby, graduation, hospital internship, another baby, Group Health Pennsylvania Avenue (White House dentist), another baby, family moves to California, four children. Dr. Dan, MD degree, general surgeon, and Dr. Shirley, DDS degree, pediatric specialty. Life was a blurr!

Birth control pills hit the market—Enovid and Ortho-Novum. Dan related to his colleagues, "Shirley can write her own prescriptions now." I began daily chewing my enovid. I cannot swallow pills to this day. No more babies; family complete. We got the boy after three beautiful girls. Dan had wanted eight children. He was the oldest of seven. We were happy, at last, with four, thanks to birth control pills. Planned parenthood was born in the sixties, and I was first in line.

"Open up that Golden Gate" was our mission. My parents were in California, and that was home to me. We immediately actualized our plans and dreams and began to implement the tenets of the movements of equal opportunity in our country. We were prepared and thus able to walk through all the doors of opportunity. Dan did not wish to return to the oppressive South, to his home in Panama City, Florida, and chose California instead. He loved it there it too, until the first earthquake. Our pool shimmied with massive waves of water, our bed moved out three feet from the wall, and he sincerely reevaluated his decision to move to California. Dan was mortified. He was a Southern boy who had never experienced anything close to this kind of natural phenomenon.

Life had been a blur, moving fast, like a speeding locomotive going downhill. As a young woman in my twenties, I was beginning to evolve beyond the goal-setting I had done—getting married and having a family and a career. It was surreal. It was happening.

I was raised as a Christian. I loved the church, the Lord, and all that being a Christian represented. My spiritual journey had been little more than attending church and supporting ministries. I was looking for more, and through the music of the sixties, as well as the art, books, news, government, movements, and films, I was expecting more.

We had lived through a revolution of riots, assassinations of national figures, television funerals, grief, change, poverty programs, political malcontent, inequality, racism, and economic oppression. People were restless. America was at war and not winning. After the United States went to the moon, expectations of what could be accomplished soared. Progress, however, was slow.

Amid these rapid life changes, I was referred to a psychic reader named Mrs. Gladys McGruder. She was an old black woman who lived in southeast Washington, DC. I was sensitized to the phenomenon of predicting the future. My Louisiana, superstitious, wonder-woman, paternal grandmother, "Madam Zenia," was a psychic, so I thought I'd give it a try. Mrs. McGruder accurately predicted that my fourth child would be a son for my male-gender–starved husband after having three girls. She had a 50 percent chance of being right, but I was hooked. She described the beautiful home we had purchased in California, with the swimming pool, maids' quarters, and all, down to the shelves in the garage, before we ever saw it. I wish I could say I was making up this stuff, but I am not; it is all true.

On my first visit to Mrs. McGruder's home, there was a long black limousine with a chauffeur parked outside. When I walked inside this black woman's relatively upscale three-story attached brick walk-up, I was surprised to meet Lady Bird Johnson. I knew many Washington dignitaries visited Mrs. McGruder, but this was a particular delight for me. President Lyndon Baines Johnson was my favorite president. He accomplished much more than John Kennedy but didn't get the recognition. General Westmoreland's inaccurate assessments of the Vietnam War did not help. LBJ! Hooray!

Life in California was beautiful. Our children were in private school, and our careers were launched. I bought a medical building and had a podiatrist renting from me. I was a school dentist for six hours a day and built my practice. Dan was chief of surgery at the Watts Health Center and opened his private practice on Santa Rosalia Drive in the premier professional high-rise of the day. Dan barbequed on Saturdays, and the family swam and enjoyed family and friends. We lived on "Pill Hill," the community where mostly black doctors lived. Our neighbors are still friends to this day. It was a great time in our lives.

The itch returned to see a psychic. In the '70s, we had been attending the Church of Religious Science's Wednesday night sing-along—religion for the here and now, more than the afterlife. Practitioners would treat essentially the same as a reading after a prayer. Treatments were healing consultations with prayer.

I became a minister, ordained in the spiritual movement known as Religious Science, after attending classes and learning the doctrines of Ernest Holmes, the founder of Religious Science. The power of positive thinking, Norman Vincent Peale, teaching's and the Gatepost publications were all connected philosophies of thought.

I was evolving as a woman, spiritually searching, exploring, and reading. The challenges of life were mounting as well, but we were very blessed.

I was referred to an Orange County psychic, Rose Boike, a white woman on Willamette Place, and saw her for a few years. (John Wayne's supernatural, by the way—a little Hollywood trivia.) Rose gave us two dachshund puppies, Hans and Heide, and thus began our family's love of these beautiful dogs.

Rose could find lost items, and people sought her from far and near for this, as well as for seances with the dead. Rose was not the best psychic for me. I personally think she struggled with her skills, but she knew nothing else.

I do not remember how or when Alvina came into my life, but what an incredible woman and gift she was.

Alvina was a psychic astrologer. She made extensive astrological charts of your life from the date, time, and place of your birth and then explained them. I was attracted to the scientific aspects of the research she did. Astrologically speaking, my sun is in Libra. All my other houses are in Virgo. My moon is in Gemini, and I fall on the cusp, explaining my characteristics quite accurately, depicting my real signs.

She spoke of our son, Dan, saying he will always be fascinated by shiny jewelry and gems. She exclaimed, "Do not ask him to take out the trash or other menial things because he is from a royal family of privilege in another life. He will always desire a particular station in this life." Oh yes, there was so much more. Alvina was amazing. Most things she told me have come to pass. I wish I had kept accurate records, but my memory of these accounts is excellent. We enjoyed a great friendship for many years. Sadly, I recently learned that Alvina died. I'd googled her to try to locate her and found her obituary. She died the same year as my husband, 2012; she was seventy-eight.

A Chinese dentist who worked for me, Dr. Lee, referred me to perhaps the most spiritual and insightful psychic I ever encountered, Mrs. Agnes Scott, a black woman who lived in a large house on Westmoreland in Los Angeles. She was terrific. She possessed gifts like Mrs. McGruder. Board member colleagues and many other friends saw her as well. She was always worth the trip and time. She could tell me, for example, that my daughter had an earache in the left ear. She would pray and then speak. I said nothing.

After some years, she had a stroke and could not speak for almost a year. Her large Asian clientele missed her. When she finally regained her ability to speak, it was difficult for her to enunciate, but her dialogue was still sharp. Ultimately, about 25 years ago, Agnes told me that I did not need her or any other psychics anymore. She saw a vast field of tall corn that now was mature, ready to eat, and delicious.

I have not seen a psychic since that time or had any inclination to do so. (Her graphic message of the corn was one of prosperity and she said I no longer needed her as a spiritual guide. She affirmed for me my own spiritual capabilities and I never did see her again. (She was a season in my life and I am gratefjul for her).

Some years ago, after I retired, I took some college-level courses in Bible study fellowship. I studied books of the Bible from the King James Version and other teaching of Bibles. The mysteries of the unknown no longer intrigue me as they once did. Now, I know where those answers are. I have learned to listen as well as hear. All those psychic agents of the day served a real purpose. I reflect on each of them as guides in my rites of passage. Thankfully, I can smile when I look back at those times, as well as measuring my growth and remaining grateful.

Young people today are stirred up, much like in the sixties. They desire change and are feeling a revolution. They want things to be different, supporting various candidates who are not leaders, just different. I think we are beginning another cycle of significant change, but, of course, predicting the future is something I was so curious about. If you know the future, you can change the future.

*You reap what you sow.*

*—Galatians 6:7*

# CHAPTER 7

# *Growing Pains*

The nation's capital, Washington, DC, is a city whose beauty in the spring, with cherry blossoms around the tidal basin and the fragrances of Rock Creek Park along the trails through the center of the city, is majestic. As a student, when I looked at the monuments along Constitution Avenue, pristine like snow on the white alabaster structures that house our institutions of government, I knew this city was a magical place. It pulsated with news, speeches, electricity, rallies, and the business of the people.

It was 1960, an election year. John Fitzgerald Kennedy was elected the thirty-fifth president of the United States the previous November. Adults, young and old, were full of hope and enthusiasm to work toward the promises and visions that JFK had painted for our nation—a man on the moon, the Peace Corps, and VISTA, a national service corps.

Howard University, in northwest Washington, stood on a high hilltop as a post-Civil War university. It was founded in 1867 as an educational institution for ex-slaves and others, along with several other historical black colleges and universities. In 1960, Howard was a bustling university, with many colleges of higher learning—law school, medical school, architectural and engineering schools, dental schools, and many others. It had a descriptive nickname: the capstone of Negro education. Many black families aspired to send their children there to get an education but also to have their children exposed to other black families. This led to the creation and evolution of the black middle class. The graduate schools were a different story. These were purely academic and allowed little time for anything social. There were waiting lists for admission to the medical and dental schools, with alternates for each place.

The early 1960s also signaled the beginning of freedom for women, as Enovid, the first oral contraceptive approved by the FDA and developed by G.D. Searle & Company, was marketed in the United States. It reigned for twenty-seven years as the first generation of oral contraception. There were many skeptics, but it was the beginning.

My story is about a bright young woman from California who entered Howard University College of Dentistry in 1960 as the only woman in her class and one of thirteen women in the United States enrolled in one of the forty-seven dental schools. Dean Russell Dixon had recruited her away from medical school to enter dental school.

Not everyone on the faculty agreed with the dean. Dr. Percy Fitzgerald was chairman of the Department of Prosthodontics. A small man with wavy white hair and round gold-rimmed glasses, he was meticulous in his dress and manner. He wore individual loops on his forehead that magnified structures many times when he looked into the oral cavity. Dr. Fitzgerald had penetrating blue-gray eyes, and most students feared him. He was easily the most powerful man in the dental school after the dean. Dr. Fitzgerald was an icon in his profession, a lecturer at Georgetown and nationally. In his seventies, he remained resolute that women in dental school were taking the places of men, who would head households.

Shirley Jordan, at age twenty-two, had been in the graduate school of pharmacology for the last year on a scholarship from NIH, doing perfused heart studies. She met Dr. Dixon in Coral Gables, Florida, while presenting a research paper. That September, she enrolled as a dental student. The charm of Washington, Howard, and a young medical student all played into the marriage of Shirley and Dan by the end of her freshman year.

Shirley did well in the preclinical studies and was an officer of her class by the time she reached the clinics in her sophomore year, by which time she had given birth to her first child, Paula Lynn Bailey.

Dr. Fitzgerald was outraged. Never in the history of the school had a woman had a baby while enrolled. The faculty met and resolved that, academically, Shirley was sound. Clinically, she asked for no special favors and was a good student. She was married, so there was no issue.

For the crown and bridge clinic, Shirley asked Dr. Fitzgerald to be her instructor and courageously met her challenger face-to-face. Dr. Fitzgerald required Shirley to repeat cases over and over. Shirley had other instructors examine her work, and they found it highly acceptable. She had the laboratory assistant, Mr. Coles, with whom to discuss her work, and he found it highly satisfactory. Shirley responded to Dr. Fitzgerald with a smile each time and looked forward to any minuscule teaching point he offered. Finally, Dr. Fitzgerald saw that Shirley's spirit was to succeed and learn and that she was determined to know her profession well.

When graduation came, Shirley had two little girls; Pamela Anne Bailey was born in her junior year. Shirley was one of only thirty-six who graduated out of eighty-one who started in her class. She received one of the two internships in the course, pediatric dentistry; the other was oral surgery. Shirley was one of seven doctors to pass the DC board upon graduation from Howard. She enjoyed the exam, as she had done the castings many times with Dr. Fitzgerald and was confident in exhibiting her skills.

In her senior year, another phenomenon occurred. The Beatles, pop music icons, arrived in the United States from England. It was 1964. The country had been mourning the assassination of JFK in 1963, and the refreshing new sounds added to the joy of graduation.

The first Mustang by Ford came out in that year. Shirley and Dan bought a Mustang—a teal convertible—which later became a classic car. Life was great.

Shirley and Dan had their third daughter, Patricia Susan Bailey, during Shirley's internship at DC General Hospital. After that, Shirley and their family accompanied Dan to New York Sloan Kettering Memorial Hospital, where Dan was a surgery resident. It was the last resort hospital for patients who need heroic surgery and other treatments. It was a high honor for Dan to achieve this appointment as a junior resident. The training was the best in the United States.

Shirley became a Guggenheim fellow while in New York and quickly passed the New York State board. Returning to Washington, DC, Shirley worked at Group Health on Pennsylvania Avenue and took care of White House staff, among others. Shirley gave birth to her fourth child, a son, Henry Dan Bailey Jr., while there, and she worked until their family moved to California in 1967.

Dr. Russell Dixon's vision of women in dentistry and Dr. Fitzgerald's tenacity as a teacher led Shirley to a historic career with several firsts as a black woman dentist. Appointed to the California board by Governor Jerry Brown, Shirley rose to be president of the California State Board of Dental Examiners, Commissioner of the ADA, distinguished alumni of Howard University, and a Kellogg fellow, to name a few, for her service and accomplishments. Another honor includes election into the American College of Dentists as a fellow in 1984.

Shirley's four children all have become professionals in medicine or law and have produced eight beautiful grandchildren.

Today, women constitute nearly 50 percent of all enrollments in dental schools; this is up from 1.5 percent in 1964.

Dentistry allows women to control their hours so they can find a balance between family and their profession. I have been called a trailblazer and pioneer being among the first to arrive at many closed doors.

I am blessed to have lived long enough to be witness to hundreds if not thousands of Black Women Leaders who are amazing in every walk of life. Lets start with the United States Congress, Black women in the House and in the Senate. The President of the National Medical Association, President of the National Dental Association, President of the National Nurses Association, President of the National Pharmacy Association, Bar Associations, CEO's of Fortune Five Hundred companies and Vice Presidents and Leaders in the Legal and Financial world, and I could go on and on. I can say "We may not be where we ought to be, but we are definitely better than we used to be". For Black women and all women of color everywhere and all minorities, we must think of our journeys like a relay race and never lose hope. Hand that baton off to the runner behind and stay in the fight with the gains we have made.

Romance without finance is a nuisance. No money, no honey.

—Alzenia "Big Mama" Jordan

# CHAPTER 8

## All about Love

To define love, we might start with what we believe it is—an emotion that has an attachment to another. This is expressed in different terms, depending on with whom we have the attachment. The Greek view presents a clear delineation. *Philos* is philosophical love, not family; it can be brotherly love or friendship. *Eros* is passionate love—erotic, sexual. *Storge* is family love—mother, father, brother, sister; the old "blood is thicker than water" theory. And finally, agape is abstract love, the highest form of love that is the unconditional love for others, in spite of their character flaws or weaknesses. Agape love is best seen in the lives of Mother Teresa, Jesus, Martin Luther King Jr., Gandhi, and others whose lives have demonstrated this.

Most of us have experienced these kinds of attachments. Love is expressed in poetry, in the lyrics and music of songs, in the paintings of a beautiful woman or a bowl of fruit, and in books that use words to describe the search for love, the loss of love, the destruction of love, the beginning of love, or the end of love. We look at plays, movies, and dances, many of which are the expression of love in some form. There is the love of nature when you see a field of flowers, the blue sky, the waves of the ocean, a quiet lake, a flowing stream, a snow-capped mountain, beautiful rock formations, birds in flight, the greens of a manicured golf course, the sound of the human voice, a baby's cry, or a child's giggle.

I asked my mom what love was, and she said, "Sixty-five years with your father."

I asked my daughter Paula what love was, and she said, "Love is action. Love is not passive. It is doing."

I asked Courtney, my nine-year-old granddaughter, and she said, "That's easy, Grandma," and she began to recite 1 Corinthians 13:4–8: "Love is kind. Love is patient ..." She attended Legacy Christian Academy and had memorized verses since the first grade. She felt confident that she knew what love was.

I asked my best friend, Marilyn, what love was, and she said, "It's a bond that exists between two people and is a powerful force, like none other. Love is a commitment, loyalty, trust, and a longing to be in the company of that person as much as possible. It is free; it cannot be bought, sold, or traded."

For me, love is the most powerful force on earth. When you find it—or it finds you—in any form, you are exhilarated, numb, dumb, blind, and blessed. It is euphoric, exciting, active, overt, and expressive. If I light a candle under a blanket, it cannot be hidden for long. There is a glow, a smile, a twinkle in the eye, and a spirit in the walk; the heart is light and happy. You look and act differently. You are not the same as before love has entered into your life.

You may experience an intense feeling of deep affection—a deep romantic attachment that is unconditional through the invisible flaws of the person you love, and in time some great sacrifice is usually a hallmark of love.

Love speaks its own language. The Bible says you put your treasure where your heart is. We are extolled to love our neighbor as ourselves; do unto others as you would have them do unto you. I believe we must love ourselves and appreciate all the good things about ourselves. Celebrate the good you, the deserving self, which allows and creates a higher capacity to give of yourself. Learn to *just be* in the moment of your life as you are.

While the Bible extols love as the most significant thing of all, men and women lust for love, die for love, kill for love, sacrifice for love, and fall in and out of love; these are expressions of the way we react to attachments. Our great teachers from centuries past say that all accessories are suffering. To end suffering, end attachments. This is related to divorce. Love can be transient, forever, eternal, or platonic, or it can end. One makes new attachments, and the cycle begins again.

Deepak Chopra has spoken of influential studies on life and love, which I have become transformed enough to understand reasonably well through my studies in the age of wisdom.

If we can embrace the science of matter—that it is neither created nor destroyed—the concept that we are all connected through our DNA on this planet becomes logical. We are breathing the same air as did Julius Caesar, Moses, and Jesus, when he walked the earth. We see that the Bible really is a procedural manual for living. Having hatred and resentment is like poisoning oneself; we are all connected' We need to live in a meditative state. Learning about love and how to love is pretty much our mission in this life.

We can then change our relationship with time and realize that life is an energy field, full of possibilities and opportunities. Deepak became a monk and, in so doing, had to walk barefoot through a village and beg for food, as a part of the process, which also included shaving his head. He was asked if his feet hurt. As a cultured man of many years, having never walked on rocky, rough roads, he answered, "Yes, indeed it is tough."

A monk said to him, "Only one foot is on the ground to hurt you. Concentrate on the foot that is not." Recognize the impermanence of this body and the mind-body connection.

What is love?

Love is the ultimate truth of the beauty of creation, not a sentiment or emotion. We are all the same being.

We must love ourselves. We must learn to appreciate all the good things about ourselves instead of our apparent flaws. Our reality is what we perceive it is. What is right for me is my reality, not an illusion. When it ceases to be good, it is also my reality—my perception of what is not good.

You might see love as a risk or a path searched out, a rainbow followed, a song lyric as my broken heart, crazy for feeling so lonely, or for having given all of your love. Even if I didn't treat you well, you were always on my mind.

"The very thought of you, and I forget to do the little ordinary things that everyone ought to do."

"If I give my heart to you; will you handle it with care?"

"Can you feel the love tonight?"

I have also heard it said "People often fall in love with what they can't have"

There are countless lyrics of love, from "Unforgettable" to "Always," from "Please Release Me" to "Your Cheating Heart," Let It Be," "Love Me Tender," "Climb Ev'ry Mountain," and "The Glory of Love."

I genuinely think it's better to have loved and lost than never to have loved at all.

I have read some of the sermons of Dr. Martin L. King that speak methodically on the subject of love. I want to share a particular sermon from Sept 16, 1962 given at Ebeneezer Baptist Church in Atlanta Georgia. Through most of his speeches Dr. King lays out "loving your enemies" and has built his llife upon the premise that "love is creative" and that only love is capable of transforming hate into love. Therefore, to change the world love has to be extended to everyone, even our enemies.

Dr King lays out the levels of love from lowest forms of love to the highest form. The first and lowest form is "Utilitarian Love". One loves another for his usefullness to him based in selfishness. Plato spoke of true love as "eros", the yearning of the soul for the realms of the divine. We see that at "Romantic Love" something beautiful for sure, Romeo and Juliet, Anthony and Cleopatra, Edgar Allen Poe and "Annabel Lee". but this is not the highest form of love, Its selfish love too. I love you and you love me and jealousy is a part of this one on one romantic love.

A" Mothers Love", the loving care, the tender care, the patience of a real mother. This love never quite gives up a child whether one wanders to a foreign land for many years, no matter the mistake or how low a child sinks if its a real mother she is there waiting. But, even a mothers love is not the highest form of love as this is her child. This love has a degree of selfishness.

The Greek word "Philos" which is the intimate "affection between friends," this love moves even higher not because the love is deeper but because its scope is wider broader. A man can love a man, a woman can love a woman, it becomes one of the most beautiful things in the world. One can have five or ten friends, twenty, jealousy does not creep in. In romantic love jealousy always creeps in. Friendship is not based on sex. The level is one of standing side by side and united by common interests. There is a beauty that will always stand. But this is not the highest level of love because even friendship is selfish. You love people you like, though the circle is wider than romantic love and mothers love it is still a mutual concern.

"Humanitarian Love" is higher, it is inclusive. You rise to the saying that in every man there is something sacred so all humanity must be love. Danger points here are it is impersonal. Dostoyevsky the great Russian novelist said "I love humanity in general so much that I don't love anybody in particular. It is easy to love an abstraction and not a human being." Think of the millions of dollars sent by White churches to Africa for missionary efforts yet if they got the money to come to their church to worship on Sunday morning they would be kicked out."

The Greatness of God's love is that it is big enough to love everyone and small enough to love me.

"Agape Love" is higher than all the levels we have spoken of because it is"unmotivated" "spontaneous" "overflowing" asking nothing in return. It becomes the love of God operating in the human heart. You love every man not for your sake but for his sake becauses God loves him. It becomes all inclusive. Tall or short, black or white, ugly or pretty, rich or poor it is the love of God operating in the human heart and it comes to the point that you even love your enemy. You hate the deed that he does, but you love the person who does the evil deed.

The Only testing point for you to know if you fit into the category of christian love is to test your ability to love your enemy. This is what God has left for us as Christians. He has left us a love, he loved us, so let us love the brother. Love is the greatest power of all in the world. What is the "summum bonum of life" what is the highest good? Epicureans sought to answer, as did Plato and Aristotle. It is love,

God is light, God is love. He who hates does not know God, but he who loves at that moment rises to a knowlege of God. Thank you Dr. Martin Luther King again, for your life and work. I did get to meet him multiple times, As Chapel Convocation Speaker at Fisk University and on the bible belt tours with my Uncle the Reverend David Collins in Williamsburg,Virginia,Maryland and Washington, DC in the late 1950's.

*What you think of me is none of my business.*

*—Terry Cole-Whitaker*

*In the end, it is not the years in your life that counts; it's the experience in your years.*

*—Abraham Lincoln*

# CHAPTER 9

## *Capital City Memories*

*Howard University School of Medicine, 1960*

*Home—Hillcrest, Washington, DC*

Washington, DC, is a beautiful city. I lived in upper northwest Washington at the Hillcrest Center on Van Ness Avenue off Wisconsin Avenue. I spent many wonderful times in Rock Creek Park. I have some beautiful pictures of the fall foliage, the oranges and browns of the leaves changing colors. Walks in that park were a delightful respite from studying. Other fond memories are my brown-bag lunches and a day of studying at the Library of Congress. It is such an impressive library; I felt uplifted and almost like I was a member of Congress.

While I was a student, I landed a fantastic position as a counselor at the Hillcrest Center, a residential treatment center for children with behavioral issues who were emotionally disturbed (not mentally disturbed) and needed to be removed from the home environment so that the core problem for the child and parents could be diagnosed and treated.

The center traditionally hired graduate students from universities to serve as counselors to cover overnights and weekends with a rotating schedule, in exchange for a lovely room and bath, board, and maid service, plus a monthly cash stipend. This was a dream job. There was great camaraderie with the other students. Dan Graves was a foreign service major at Georgetown University. Joe Maxie was a student at American University. Fred was studying law at George Washington University. Ron was from Nepal, from a royal family there; his embassy got him the job. We learned a lot about Nepal from Ron, who had quite a sense of humor.

Hillcrest was beautiful. It covered about ten acres, with flowering trees and gardens. The primary residence resembled a massive mansion. Everything seemed brown—the floors were dark maple, and the walls were wood-paneled halfway and plaster and paint above. The windows had panes that were about twenty-four inches square, and we could look out on the grounds, as no shades covered them. In the Great room there were round tables of rich wood and comfortable chairs, but overall a barren feeling. A beautiful fireplace commanded one end of the great room, which was off the excellent galley-type kitchen. The kitchen had the longest butcher-block counter I had ever seen. It was easily a hundred feet long because everyone at the center could gather around this counter. It doubled as an eating space after all the prep work. The private rooms were upstairs; there were about sixteen rooms for children and four larger suites for the counselors. Across from the main house was a cottage residence with a piano and a rooftop patio also a reception room and caretaker's cottage. There were also counseling rooms for parents and children and a reception area for social gatherings and holiday celebrations. There were gardens and acres of land trees and beautiful green lawns in summer and snowy mounds in winter. There were plenty of circular drives for parking cars. The general look of a resort or a mansion was what you felt when you drove up. Very impressive. Inside less warmth than home and less color.

Perle Mesta, the "hostess with the mostest" of the day, lived across the street. Washington society was at her doorstep in a steady stream of parties and politics.

John Kennedy was president of the United States, and nothing seemed impossible. It was Camelot—at least it seemed so. This was my best life so far.

American University was down the street. I was a student at Howard University Dental School. Grover Dye was one of the psychologists, and Ms. Bluestein was the director. Dr. Yacoubian was the medical director.

I was so happy at that time of my life. I was pursuing my studies at the Dental school, my parents gifted me with a '57 Chevrolet in my sorority colors—crimson and cream. This car is still a classic today with the fins and iconic design. Wow I loved that car. I was literally living my dream on top of the world and I knew it !.

I was buying pretty clothes at Franklin and Simon, including wide hats. I was dating and meeting people from all cultures, as well as learning about children. One little girl, Laurie, was eight years old. She was very thin and pale, with red pimples and unattractive scratches all over her arms, face, and legs. She picked at her skin until it bled. At night, she would upset herself so much that she would provoke a life-threatening asthma attack and arouse all those sleeping. Her wheezing and heaving made her little body and chest appear as though she was taking her last breath. She was inconsolable, and other kids, who usually showed empathy to each other, would avoid her.

Laurie drew herself away from people, but I could feel she needed hugs and closeness. She had gotten worse while at home, and her parents did not know how to manage her, or maybe they were incapable. That was her issue. We counselors tried to implement the therapies that the doctors recommended, to make life more enjoyable for all of us. We involved Laurie in activities at night, teaching her how to make pizza and hot chocolate. I sat her in my lap and hugged her. We put ointment on her scratches and sores and told her she frightened us at night. We gave her responsibility on the weekends. We planted vegetable gardens and worked in the dirt and got her smiling a lot more. I saw Laurie improve, and she was able to return home, clear up her skin, and move to outpatient therapy. That is an excellent memory to this day.

I remember Stanley and Bobby and so many children for whom, for the most part, the home environment was toxic to their survival. Stanley lived with his grandmother, mother, and sister. He'd rarely been in the company of men since his birth, and he mimicked the mannerisms of women in hand, face, and walking gestures, which made public school impossible for him. His family was bewildered as to how to approach helping Stanley. In therapy, Stanley was not encouraged or persuaded to adopt a sexual identity but was given behavioral options from which to choose. At Hillcrest, he was supported for who he was.

It was terrific to see the children heal and thrive. They had setbacks when they visited home and would go back into treatment until they were stronger. The thing I remember most vividly is the love and admiration that the children gave to me. One small boy in particular, Johnathon, helped me overcome my fear of water. He said, "Just hold your hands under the water and put your face into your hands and blow, and pretty soon, you're not afraid anymore." He accomplished for me something I had not been able to overcome in my entire childhood—my fear of water. I swim today and have never forgotten this sweet boy.

My experience at Hillcrest is a beautiful memory because, on those same grounds, my love affair with a medical student led to a proposal of marriage. Dr. Dan Bailey did so on his knee while I was sitting in an apple tree.

Many beautiful friendships, advice, and wisdom were gleaned during my time at Hillcrest—a lasting memory of growth and development. Upon leaving, the psychologist who became my friend, Grover Dye, said to Dan and me, "You will find that when you strike a match to light the world that it is made of asbestos, but you have time to make several mistakes in your lives and recover."

Dr. Yacoubian tried to dissuade Dan from a surgery specialty and me from dentistry, encouraging us to go into psychiatry. We were offered a cottage on the Hillcrest grounds. I thanked him for all I had experienced and what I had learned.

I recommended a friend to take my dream job, Fisk University classmater Dr. Linzy Scott, who later became a brilliant orthopedic surgeon in Atlanta, Georgia. Dr. Scott was Ethel's old beau before she married Billy. Ethel is my old Fisk College friend and roommate in Washington, D.C. We attended Howard University in the Masters program in Pharmacology together. Billy is Dr. William Jackson who Ethel married.

Dan and I were married June 25,1961 in Los Angeles and became the parents of four beautiful children and eight amazing grandchildren.

*Shirley & Dan, Mid-Career with Kids in College*

*If it should befall your fate to be a streetsweeper,*
*be the best the world has ever known.*

*—Martin Luther King Jr.*

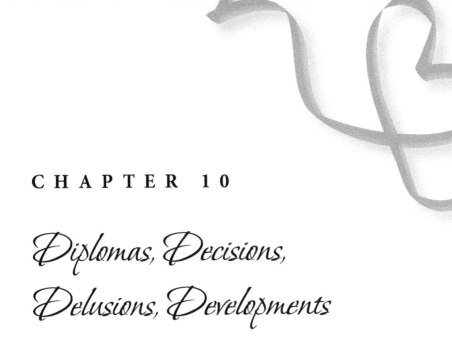

# CHAPTER 10

# *Diplomas, Decisions, Delusions, Developments*

Arriving in Washington, DC, at twenty years old in1958 was no picnic. I was armed with a grant to study pharmacology at Howard University Medical School. Money was limited, and housing, safety, transportation, and segregation were all issues.

Ethel Jackson, a classmate from Fisk University and fellow colleague in pharmacology, was to be my roommate. She had arranged uninspected housing for us, which our parents had approved in concept, in the private home of an upper northwest Washington family. While it was a safe residential area, with two twin beds in a small room, we knew it was just not going to work. We were a reasonable distance from the university as well, with no transportation except the Georgia Avenue bus.

By chance, we met an older, sophisticated dentist at a welcoming reception. He introduced himself to us and listened to our lament regarding accommodations. He said he had an efficiency apartment for rent at 920 T Street, within walking distance of the university, if we were interested. We were indeed, but we had to furnish it with our own beds and lamps and a chair.

We walked to the Hecht Company clearance department to look for bargains in the humid heat of a Washington, DC, summer. We found what we needed and arranged for delivery. We had blisters on our feet, as we'd worn sandals, which were not for that kind of walking. Transportation was next. I had owned a car since I was sixteen, and walking was the pits; our new neighborhood was not as safe as the upper Northwest Place we had moved from but was close to Howard University.

I bought my first car, a Model T, a beauty that ran very well. My association with Mr. Worthy who owned the auto garage where I purchased the car would grow over the next years, as every time a car failed mechanically, Mr. Worthy would take it back and give me the keys to another jalopy. He was a wonderful man and goes down as one of my unforgettables. Life was better but still very tight. I bought these used cars for fifty dollars never more than one hundred dollars, I muse because you cannot purchase a bike for that amount today.

The perfused heart study, using guinea pig hearts to test the structure,activity and the relationship of various types of drugs on the heart was our major focus of study. The research began at the Karolinsky Institute in Sweden. Dr. Walter Booker, head of the Department of Pharmacology, had been a recent fellow there. Dr. Booker, wanted these studies continued in the United States and obtained a grant for three students. Ethel Jackson, Victor Berman, and I were the graduate students selected for this study. A master's degree would be the academic completion after two years. All our classes were in the medical school at Howard with the freshman medical students. We studied gross anatomy, physiology, biochemistry, histology, bacteriology, and all basic sciences and labs. This was quite the place to be, with all those gifted, intelligent, and good-looking men of color in the medical school, who were the brightest and best to be found.

I was pursuing research and medicine from a different aspect than my original goals. My dreams were being encouraged at every turn. Accepting the grant was a fallback position for me because my application to the medical school was met with the reply that I was taking the place of a man who was head of a household, and why didn't I become a science teacher? Gender bias was overtly active, which was the male dominance in the professions. Women were not welcome. Far less than 1 percent of medical school class enrollments were women. "Persistence and patience" was the only way were the words of encouragement passed on to me.

While in graduate school, I met people who would become lifelong friends, such as Frances Johnson in the Department of Anatomy. She was the administrative assistant to the famed anthropologist and anatomist William Montague Cobb. He was an Amherst College graduate and head of the Department of Anatomy. He was a giant in academia—brilliant, inspiring, accomplished, and encouraging; a master in his field. Dr. Ruth Lord was an associate professor and well known as a woman professor of anatomy.

Many professors at Howard in those days distinguished themselves in their fields. They were giving their lifeblood and skills to the university. They trained the majority of the nation's African American doctors, as has been described in the annals of our profession. I was in the right place and worked hard to make the best of this opportunity.

I was in Coral Gables, Florida, presenting a research paper on the structure of catecholamines and their activity on and relationship to the heart, which caught the attention and impressed a distinguished audience member to the point of his requesting a meeting after my presentation. This gentleman happened to be the dean of the College of Dentistry at Howard University, Dr. Russell Dixon. He explained that he had just returned from Russia, where the profession of dentistry is dominated by women, and he wanted to attract talented women to his program. He offered me admittance on the spot, with the proviso that I would take the dental aptitude exam upon my return to Washington.

I was flabbergasted but excited. I had once worked for a dentist in Los Angeles, Dr. Theo Evans, and remembered the distinct, pungent smell of zinc oxide and eugenol (oil of cloves), which was used as a palliative dressing and temporary stopping for cavities. I then wondered what life would be like as a dentist instead of a physician. Dr. Dixon made his case, saying family life would be enhanced, with no night calls and scheduling of patients at my convenience. He further stated I would be one of thirteen freshmen women from forty-seven dental schools in the United States in 1960 and that I would be the only woman in my class of eighty-one men. *Wow!* I thought. *That is a lot.*

I accepted Dr. Russell Dixons offer, took the Dental Aptitude exam and was admitted to the Freshman class. WOW!

Remember that life in Washington was not easy. Ethel had opted out of the study and chose marriage to brilliant space physicist, Dr. William Jackson, only twenty-seven years old. I then had to leave T Street, and while looking at a school bulletin board, I found the live-in counselor position at Hillcrest. They took one student each from American University, Georgetown University, George Washington University, and Howard University; it was Joe Maxie, Fred, Dan Graves, and me. We had to be home by ten o'clock and take calls at night if the kids woke up and had issues.

This was a big break for me. Grover Dye was a weekend psychologist there and became a great friend. Mrs. Bluestein and Dr. Yacoubian were the hiring counselors and were very encouraging professionals. This marvelous facility was just across from the Howard Law School and not far from American University at Van Ness Avenue and Wisconsin Avenue. I was to remain there until I married.

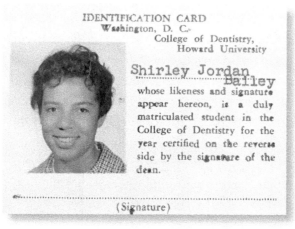

*Dental Student ID*

Life definitely improved with transportation, as did dating. These were my most exciting years of having friends of the opposite sex. House parties were popular—cooking a big steak with a nice bottle of wine and a great salad; playing cards or the like. Television was not the big thing; it was interaction with other people, conversation, books, people playing the piano or mixing gin and tonics, and talking about the future.

As I've mentioned, I met Dan at the medical school. He was tall, dark, and extremely handsome; shy, indeed, but the brilliant number-one in his class. My friend in anatomy staff, Frances, said he was the smartest guy in the class and very helpful. She said, "Shirley Ann, you should go out with this guy." You should say yes to a date with him.

Well, he was giving me the eye, but his best friend, John, was doing so as well and had allready asked me to go out. I knew if I went out with John, Dan and I would not become an item. Our first date moment arrived and was to go bowling; John finagled a double date out of it, and joined us. Dan and I went out alone after that. We fell in love and made plans to meet each other's families. We were both students with limited incomes. I was making money as a researcher with Dr. Harold Fleming in the College of Dentistry. Dan had a few stipends as well.

We decided to get married at the end of my freshman year in dental school; Dan was then a senior in the medical school. We married on June 25, 1961. John Anderson was the best man. Our California summer wedding was a big event, bringing both grandmothers to Los Angeles, as well as our families and our friends from college.

A dream became an actual event, with seven bridesmaids, hundreds of guests, and a thrilled bride and groom. We had a U-Haul trailer full of wedding gifts to help us get started. Our life was beginning, and it was unbelievable. Our friends said we had laid down the gauntlet, and they felt the pressure to get married too.

*Wedding day, 1961*

Our first apartment was 712 Marietta Place, a rental that will remain in family lore for years to come. (The rest of this story will be told in the pages to follow.)

Format Realty was our landlord; our rent was $89.50 a month. The apartment had parquet floors—a one-bedroom dream. Frances lived on the second floor, and Cary Booker lived below us in the basement. Seven months after we were married, I was pregnant. Dan selected the famous Dr. Harry Martin to be my doctor. He was my hero in more ways than one. He absolutely was one of the most handsome ob-gyns in the city and the most skilled.

As I was in dental school and uniquely a woman, I wanted to do well. Dr. Martin told me, "Pregnancy is not a disease. Go on with your education." So, through it all, I did. For morning sickness, I took my antiemetic. Dan dropped me off at school, and I went right into the women's lounge, upchucked, wiped my mouth, walked upstairs to class, and never said a word to anyone. I asked for no special favors, other than exemption from radiation exposure during my first trimester.

The faculty was outraged. Women in the dental school was enough, but now that I was pregnant, I was a target; I was suspect. My professors asked me to repeat lab exercises, asking for the highest standard of acceptance, rather than the acceptable. Dr. Fitzgerald, in crown and bridge, was the mastermind. He resented the fact I was a woman; he felt it demeaned the men somehow that a woman—a pregnant woman— might succeed when some men did not.

Dr. Russell Dixon called me in to tell me of the protests about me in faculty meetings. He defended me saying, "She is an honorably married woman. She is passing and excelling in her studies, and no regulations are prohibiting any of her activities." My attitude would be the determining factor.

*Dr. Russell Dixon, dean, College of Dentistry*

I was happy. I smiled through every transgression. If Dr. Fitzgerald wanted a frictional fit for a crown, he got it, no matter how times he made me do it again. I was determined to have my work checked by the heads of the department so they would know me, while most students avoided them like the plague and opted for accessible check instructors to move on through the clinics. We had stringent requirements for graduation; if we did not reach them, we did not graduate. We would have to finish in the summer or the following year.

Paula was born November 12, 1962. My classmates brought my work to me at home, and I was back in the clinic after the Thanksgiving break. I missed fewer than ten days of school. Pamela arrived the following year on November 13, 1963. It wasn't my plan but Dan's, hoping I would quit. Now, all gloves were off, and it was clear this infuriated the faculty members. I had another caution from Dr. Russell Dixon. "Shirley," he said when I was making the case about family life, "I did not mean during dental school."

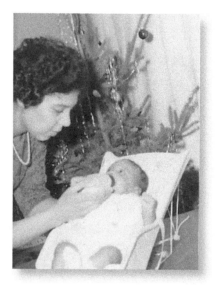

*New mother with baby Paula, 1962*

I continued, more determined than ever, because I loved what I was doing. I rocked the babies and read the books. Dan washed diapers and folded clothes as he read as well. He loved being a father; he loved children. He wanted seven or eight, I was soon to learn. Attitude is everything, so I did everything with a smile and respect. I did respect my professors, but having a woman come in, have two babies, and still meet her requirements for graduation was a little hard for them to swallow. Out of my class of eighty-one, only thirty-six of us who started out together graduated on time. The staff, mostly women, came to the front steps of the dental school and cheered me. It was quite a moment, but that was not the best. More was to come.

The District of Columbia licensure boards were among the toughest. I passed my boards with flying colors. Only seven from Howard University passed, and two of my instructors did not move. Our names were published in the paper, and the pediatric internship at DC General Hospital was awarded to me. Dr. Russell Dixon was so proud of me. We had another conference, where he said, "Whatever you do, do not come back here to teach. Go out into the world. You can do more for Howard that way than any other."

*Howard University College of Dentistry*

Dr. Rusell Dixon was honored in 1981 when they added two floors to the dental school and named the dental school after him, it was same the year I was honored as a distinguished alumnus of Howard University because of my career accomplishments and barrier-breaking appointment to the California State Board of Dental Examiners. I was the first black woman dentist in the United States appointed to a state board. A board that examines more Dentists and regulates a population of citizens larger than fifteen northeastern states. The Board licenses, regulates and disciplines Dentists and Auxilliaries, supports and defends legislation impacting the profession, Accreditation studies of Dental schools, Regulates Dentists, Offices, Quality Assurance and Quality assessment. Continuing Education, Consumer input, to name a few.

I was later appointed by Dr. Collins et al. to the Northeast Regional Board of Examiners. We met at the famed Watergate Hotel in Washington, DC. Attitude and perseverance was the key to my moving forward continually; I said that to the countless young women and men whom I mentored.

My internship at DC General Hospital was another unique experience. The third miracle of life, Patricia, was born during that time. I was performing full-mouth dental rehabilitation treatment under general anesthesia, Dr. Tantoco was the chief of dental anesthesia. I did rotations through the hospital and also administered general anesthesia. My first patient to whom I gave anesthesia was a woman undergoing a brain tumor.

I routinely identified bodies taken from the Anacostia River or the Potomac or elsewhere, and I'd take Dental impressions (molds of the dental arches) after rigor mortis, identify x-rays and do forensic reports on the findings. I learned how to make all kinds of pedodontic appliances. Thumb-sucking devices were huge in the 1960s, and prevention of protruding crooked teeth was the goal. Metal palatal wire appliances were constructed and cemented in via orthodontic bands. We constructed tongue-thrusting appliances as well. Baby bottle nipple design contributed to harmful muscular habits during sucking that caused protrusion of the anterior teeth. These appliances restrained muscles like the tongue and intervened to break the harmful habit.

You might wonder how I found time for everything and childcare, but I did. Wherever I could take the babies, I would. This was a time before seat belts. I used to drive with Patricia in my lap, facing me, with the steering wheel at her back, and the other girls in the front seat next to me. This was summer. In winter, it was snowsuits, boots, hoods, mittens, and whatever else to keep warm before we could go out. Daily challenges were on every front, but somehow, I kept pushing forward. Physically, I felt strong and determined fortunate and happy.

I am about to tell you of an experience that is uncomfortable for me, yet it's a chapter or more in my life and in the lives of Paula and Pamela, in particular. My aunt Eleanor came from Williamsburg, Virginia, to stay with us in Washington, DC, just after Pamela's birth in 1963. It also was just after President Kennedy was killed. Pamela was ten days old when we experienced that national tragedy.

Aunt Eleanor was accompanied by my uncle David and their six-year-old daughter, Linda. Uncle David drove them there, with considerable concern regarding Linda's development. He was the minister of the First Baptist Church of Williamsburg in the sector restored by the Rockefellers, and it was a beautiful edifice. Uncle David, a graduate of Union Theological Seminary, was a friend of Dr. Martin Luther King Jr. We had visited with him many times on his speaking trails before I was married.

Uncle David was a very handsome, lovable man; he was my grandmother's youngest brother, and she raised him along with my father. Their parents died and left her to raise Robert, Elbert, Alenia, John, and David. Uncle David was proud of his success, and after dating Aunt Lelah (girl friend) for many years, he met and married Aunt Eleanor, who was a beautiful, Detroit society woman. Attractive by any standards, she was of medium height and fair-skinned, with a shapely figure and very sociable. Some might say she was loquacious; some might say flighty, with unpredictable, loud outbursts of laughter or exclamations. She was a character by any measure, causing his brother John to remark, "David can really pick them."

Because I was at dental school all day, and Dan was at the hospital, responsible childcare was our primary concern. We had been taking Paula to Mrs. White's, a friend of Marcia, a bridesmaid in my wedding's mother whom we felt we could trust with our new born. That had worked well and been good, but now, with two babies, we were exploring new options. Aunt Eleanor proposed taking care of the girls, and she also would explore some therapeutic options for Linda that might be available in Washington that weren't in Williamsburg. In the limited vernacular of developmental disabilities of 1963, Linda would have been described as *slow, retarded,* or *mentally deficient.* She could not perform tasks routinely performed by six-year-olds, just as she hadn't met developmental milestones at ages two and four. Eleanor and David had been living in benign denial of their daughter's deficiency. She was a late-age baby; Aunt Eleanor had been at least forty plus when Linda was conceived.

In addition to being Uncle David's "trophy wife," Aunt Eleanor kept a spotless home as the first lady of the church—almost too spotless; she was cleaning all the time, but if anyone noticed it, no one remarked too much on it. I often took college friends to Williamsburg to visit, and Aunt Eleanor would make us Jell-O, made with delicious wine, but we always noticed the immaculate appearance of the house.

Aunt Eleanor and Linda arrived, and a routine was established for us to make it all work. Dan and I had been sharing the duties of diaper washing. No disposable diapers were on the market yet. There were diaper services that picked up soiled diapers and brought clean ones, but we could not afford that service, so we used the laundry machines in the basement and did our own laundry.

The building at 712 Marietta Place was a lovely building that still stands today, much as it did over fifty years ago when we were there. The Building was a Three-story walk-up with one- and two-bedroom apartments, upper northwest Washington near Military Road and Georgia Avenue. This apartment building was to become a historic landmark in our family. Frances one of my besties lived on the third floor, I lived on the first floor and Cary Booker lived in the basement whom my sister married.

After some months of cohabitation and teamwork, we were alarmed when a tragic accident occurred. We do not know why Aunt Eleanor left Linda unattended for some time, or maybe she was there but did not notice Linda playing with matches. Linda managed to strike a match while sitting on the side of her bed. The mattress was smoldering, but the sheets did not burst into flame; if they had, the whole apartment would have burned down. Paula and Pamela could have been killed, as well as Linda.

Linda sat on the hot mattress as if to smother the flame and received third-degree burns on both legs; she never moved. No flight-or-fight reflex ever kicked in. We never knew for sure what happened, but we supposed that Aunt Eleanor might have been in the laundry room downstairs when this occurred, although she never admitted that to be so.

This was a seminal event. All attention was definitely now on Linda, as her burns were horrendous. She and Aunt Eleanor moved to other living accommodations and did not return to Williamsburg. A series of medical operations and full-time care of Linda consumed Aunt Eleanor. After Linda healed, which took more than a year, she developed painful contractions that limited her gait, and she underwent multiple operations.

Apparently, Uncle David and Aunt Eleanor had other issues in their marriage, and a child that had catastrophic effects did not bring them closer. Aunt Eleanor had total care of Linda. I do not know if guilt, sadness, despair, or desperation drove her, but her whole world became the care of Linda throughout her many surgeries, with some attention to education. Linda was always cheerful and maintained an interest in fire.

Aunt Eleanor and Uncle David no longer had a relationship. It is difficult to know if he blamed Aunt Eleanor for the accident or if she took on the blame and Linda's care to distance herself from Uncle David. Whatever it was, it was painful for all to see—total disintegration of a family; my family, who had come to help me.

Dan and I did all we could to find doctors and to offer support, but her child, her husband, and her life as she knew it was over.

After a period, Uncle David remarried and became the father of a son—a new home, new wife, new baby, new life, new church. He left Williamsburg and moved to a church in Roanoke, Virginia. A couple of years later, after getting up in the night to eat some vanilla ice cream, he succumbed to a heart attack. Shock waves went through the family, for this was not the first uncle to die after eating a milk product. Uncle Elbert in Flint, Michigan, had eaten a biscuit and a glass of cold milk, had a heart attack, and died, leaving Aunt Cora and two children.

I wondered if the condition was genetic. After a certain age, some enzymes that break down milk molecules are minimal or nonexistent in some people. Regardless, Uncle David was gone.

Aunt Eleanor faded into another life, as I graduated and ultimately moved home to California. Keeping contact with her became more and more difficult. Child Services had enrolled Linda in a vocational program, where she learned to do some repetitive things. She met a boy named Freddy, who had similar challenges, and they learned to ride the bus to the center and do a few tasks. Eventually, Linda became Aunt Eleanor's caregiver, as Aunt Eleanor would not leave the house and would not allow anyone in. In the beginning, Child Services would come by for inspections, and Aunt Eleanor resented that. Linda's fascination with fire and matches continued, and she had multiple burns on her hands and the side of her face.

I found them on a visit to Washington, and Aunt Eleanor tried to talk to me through the window. I told her I had come a long way and to please let me in. This was the turn-about. Aunt Eleanor had become the opposite of who she used to be. She was now a hoarder. The apartment was packed, floor to ceiling, with paper tied in bundles and clothes. She liked to walk around naked, and she tasked Linda to do everything. I found checks that had not been cashed. She did not bank; I do not know how they ate or paid bills. It was the saddest thing I have ever seen. The falsetto and overly dramatic, exaggerated speech were still there. The crazy laughter was still there. She told me things about Linda, and Linda told me things about her.

A lawyer became involved to be Linda's guardian at some point. I last saw Aunt Eleanor in a nursing home; she had breast cancer and succumbed to that. The lawyer would not tell us where Linda was. Her half-brother was asking about her, and his mother was trying to help. After Pamela moved to Washington, DC, we tried to find Linda but could not. What a sad chapter in my life—sorrow and joy in a family; two sides of the same coin.

When Dan was in his third year of his residency in surgery at Howard University under Dr. Syfax, again being at the top of his class, he was selected to go to Sloan Kettering Memorial Hospital in New York to do a one-year fellowship. I was just finishing my internship at DC General Hospital.

It was 1965. Patricia had been born on May 25, and they made arrangements for all of us to go with Dan. Our apartment was beautiful and spacious. A nursery school was in the building, and there was a parking lot on East Sixty-Seventh Street and First Avenue, right at FDR Drive.

I was awarded a Guggenheim fellowship at the Murray and Leoni Guggenheim Clinic on East Seventy-Second Street. This was mass dentistry; school children were bussed there, and we screened them, took x-rays, and performed operative dentistry—pulpotomies by the hundreds and tooth extractions, when necessary. I took the New York boards. After combing through files at New York University's patient files to find a case, I climbed a walk-up in Queens to find a woman who needed a full upper and a partial lower. What an experience.

I passed my boards and was welcomed to the state of New York after oral exams in pathology and a variety of other subjects and clinical exams of prosthodontia with my lady from Queens in New York

I went to work at 115th and Seventh Avenue in Harlem, part-time, when I wasn't at the clinic. What an experience that was—the best and brightest of Harlem Hospital all practiced at that prestigious African American office. I got a lot of excellent knowledge. Every extraction was done with a general anesthetic. This did not make me comfortable and was the footprint of my platform of changes that I made in California when Governor Brown appointed me to the Board with the title as "Member" This appointment came only after I was vetted by the Democratic Black Caucus, including Speaker Willie Brown and Assemblywoman Gwen Moore. But my experiences in that New York clinic framed my vision for improved safety for patients. Twilight sleep was the order of the day back in the sixties, but if bronchospasm occurred, most dentists were ill-prepared to handle the emergency. Patients died; patients were at risk. Dental supply companies sold nitrous oxide and oxygen machines to dental offices at an extra profit. Extraction was one fee; anesthesia was a separate fee. If there were an emergency, they would use100 percent oxygen and hope for the best.

If oral surgery was needed, that was a justification for anesthesia. Beyond other surgical indications, however, I did not feel the risk was justified. We did not even have 911 services until 1967. AT&T worked with the FCC to try to establish a universal emergency number. This happened in 1968.

My mission was accomplished, but not without a fight to require a general anesthesia permit with educational requirements for renewal. I was on the board from 1981 until 1985.

My New York experience brought that risk to light. I also had done a lot of general anesthesia in the hospital in my internship at DC General Hospital but with a nurse anesthetist administering the anesthesia while I did the dentistry. To accurately monitor a patient while performing the operative procedure is not the ideal or best approach to making a patient comfortable or to delivering the safest-quality dentistry. While Dan was having the highest academic experience of his professional life, I was as well.

Dan performed surgical hemicorporectomies, which involved dissecting the body in half and placing an obturator in the body cavity to protect vital organs. When cancer ravaged the body of some people, they wanted another year of life and could get it many times.

We were there when the Shah of Iran arrived for treatment and demanded to be saved. This was a hospital of last resort. The rich and mighty from all over the world came there for the most excellent treatment imaginable and paid thousands of dollars for whatever might work. Chefs prepared lobster and the finest of foods and wine; it was gourmet dining. It was a hospital only in the sense of the procedures that were done and the recuperation afterward.

Dan was a very emotional man, and this was a lot for him. I am not sure if surgery was the best specialty for him, even though he excelled at it. He was a doctor's doctor in Los Angeles. He took the losses to heart and felt for the patients' families.

Frances Johnson, my dear and lifelong friend (she's now eighty-nine) married Dr. Colden Raines, a good-looking and good man, who wooed Frances. She fell in love with him. He badly needed a wife, as he had lost the mother of his three children to breast cancer when she was just thirty. Frances married him and moved to Teaneck, New Jersey, to a lovely home, and she became a helpmate to Colden in his office in Newark. For the next forty years or so, she was a wonderful mother to his children. Their daughter passed away from breast cancer at age thirty, the same as her mother. The sons have done well; one is heir apparent—dentist Colden Jr.—and one is a lawyer. They each have children, Crystal and Jade, and Romney has Brittany. Frances has befriended my family as well. She is an excellent cook and always told me, "If you can read, you can cook."

*Colden and Frances Raines*

Frances is the older sister I never had. She is considered as much a part of my family as anyone. We are sorority sisters—Deltas—and attended a national convention in Las Vegas together. We're both affiliated with Howard University, both in dentistry. Colden sponsored me into the American College of Dentists, a fellowship of the highest order. We are both members of the Links Inc., a national and international philanthropic, service, and social organization. We both have enjoyed gaming in casinos and sports. Frances follows basketball and football, just like I do, and we have always loved going to church together. We are sisters in the Lord.

Frances's family took me in as one of the family as well. She has seven brothers and sisters and many nieces and nephews. Our salmon cakes and fried apples, grits, and eggs recipes and menus came from Frances. Oh my, how we enjoyed that excellent food. Then we'd get into the kitchen and clean everything up. Frances said, "Never go to bed with dirty dishes in the sink."

While living in New York, one of the great blessings was visiting Frances and Colden on the weekends with the babies. Frances is Paula's godmother. She would cook, and the kids would run on the lawn. After a full day, we'd put them in the back seat to go to sleep for the drive back to New York. We crossed the George Washington Bridge over the Hudson River into New York via the Harlem River Drive, down to the Eastside to Sixty-Seventh street.

If we did not go to Frances's house, we went to South Orange, New Jersey, to Aunt Edna and Uncle Orlando's, or "Uncle Lens," as he was known. He was Dan's father's brother. They loved us coming over, and Aunt Edna could cook up a storm. We enjoyed visiting them too.

By the time we'd been married four years, we had three children. Dan never asked me directly to give up my profession, but he hinted indirectly. I was inspired by my work, my success, and I never entertained stopping work. I also knew Ethel, my colleague and former roommate, had regretted not continuing her quest. She eventually returned to Howard University and received a doctor of dental surgery degree as well.

Dan was a bit bewildered that the children were cared for and that I was doing well. He was doing well too, but he was a pessimist and kept thinking it couldn't last. The thing he admired about me was my optimism and positive thinking. We both were Christians but not as faithful as we should have been or as we became in later life. We were grateful for our blessings, but success was something Dan had never known; he was ill prepared to be an investor or wealth builder and was too stubborn to admit it or talk about things as a family. He badly wanted to hit a home run for his family and was a dedicated provider and a good man, but his vices were his Southern-macho-man, provider-in-chief approach. I was not adept enough to know how to penetrate that exterior. He firmly believed firmly that women had a place and specific duties, and men had theirs, and he was steadfast in his beliefs.

This was what I had been hearing from men in power all my adult life—application to medical school, matriculating in dental school, bias from my professors when pregnant, no pass for being legally married and in a family way while studying. My father was told not to waste money educating a girl—"All they will do is get married and have babies."

Maybe the record playing in my brain was so immune to this mantra that Dan, with all his efforts, had no chance of halting me. When we returned to Washington, DC, after this year of achievement and introspection, Dan was chief of surgery, with all his new experience from New York. I was to become a member of the pediatric dental staff of Group Health on Pennsylvania Avenue. My associate dentist was Dr. Irey. I made a high salary of $12,400 a year; my professors at Howard University, by comparison, were making $7,500 a year.

I was treating families of the White House staff and Congress. It was an enjoyable experience. Paula and Pamela attended the private Barrie School. Patricia was just a year old, and I was pregnant with Dan Jr. We only had one car, so I took a bus to work because transportation was direct. Standing at the bus stop was very difficult in the cold. I could never keep my hands warm enough, even with the best of gloves. But life was moving.

Washington was in the throes of President Lyndon Baines Johnson's Great Society programs, in the aftermath of John Kennedy's death. The War on Poverty was in full force. If ever we had a chance to rise out of poverty, that was the time—at least, it seemed so, but no. Both of us had advanced degrees and a good income, but the conservative Riggs Bank would not lend Dan money. I was a purist and wanted to build something good. I asked Dan earnestly if he wished to go back to Florida, where we could open a clinic together. He vehemently declared that the racism there had been too strong for him.

Washington weather was not for me, nor was the conservative restrictions on opportunities. Dan and I both agreed our best chances would be in California. He was still a front-row pessimist. He said, "What do you think will happen in California? You will open your briefcase and money will fall in?"

I said, "No, Dan, we will both take out an Interns and Residents loan, and move and settle the loan, and take jobs in California until we qualify for a home."

I got a job at a clinic for $16,500 a year, and Dan got the position at the Watts Health Foundation that he would keep for his entire career. As chief of surgery, he was paid $25,000 a year. This was enough income to qualify us for a loan for the dream home we'd picked out at 4216 Enero Drive. It was everything we wanted, including quarters for a live-in maid.

My parents helped with the down payment, which Dan paid back quickly, as we both wanted to open our private practices and did. I took my five-thousand-dollar loan and walked up to a medical building that had two wings and was near our home and asked if they had thought about selling. I loved the building and location at 5831 Overhill Drive.

The doctor's wife, Mrs. Epstein, said to me, "Yes, we are very interested in selling. My husband is not well. I am from Canada and wish to return there."

I said, "I have only a down payment and a dream. Will you accept a note?"

She said, "Yes. We want $45,000, with five thousand down and payments of four hundred a month for ten years."

"Great!" I said.

The Epsteins drew up the papers. Dr. Epstein rented a small office in Westchester for the next couple of years, and I paid them off early.

I rented one unit to a foot doctor named Jeffrey Widen, who paid me $165 per month, so almost half my note was in income. This was 1967. Dan Jr. was born earlier that year; I now was the mother of four children. I was thirty years old, had my own medical building with a paying tenant, and was five minutes from home. I could set my hours and manage my home and family. I immediately quit the clinic job and took a job fulfilling an earlier dream as a school dentist. I had to get teaching credentials with a specialization in health. I only worked until two o'clock and had time to build my dental practice for a few hours a day. I operated a mobile dental unit with an assistant and hygienist. Pauline Louque, my hygienist, was a great friend and colleague. We fluoridated entire grades in the elementary schools, and we did operative dentistry on first molars. We did a lot of education on prevention to students and teachers, and we worked with school nurses.

My practice became very successful in less than two years. The Los Angeles Unified School District offered me the position of head of the department. (The head of the department had been involved in the fatal Tenerife airport disaster, leaving the department suddenly without a leader.) I had to decline. I needed to devote full time to my practice.

My parents moved a few blocks from Dan and me on Monteith Drive. This gave our children the excellent benefit of extended family close by and the ability to get to know and love their grandparents.

Dan and I continued to build our practices. Dan opened his office in a professional building on Santa Rosalia Drive, where he would see patients after his day at the Watts Health Center. We had a live-in maid, Maria, from Morelia, Mexico, in the first years, who had begun sewing in a factory in Mexico at nine years of age.

The kids would climb into bed with us at night, and we would cookout on the weekends in the backyard and swim. The kids all learned to swim at Crystal Scarborough Swim School on Robertson Boulevard. She was famous for teaching babies to swim and was swim teacher to the Hollywood stars' children. When our kids learned to swim, we eventually were able to take down the safety gate that surrounded the swimming pool.

Dan was happiest on weekends, with all the children in the pool while he smoked ribs and sausage with unique woods that he prided himself on finding. I'd get the salads ready and keep careful watch over everything. We'd listen to records—Aretha Franklin, Sam Cook, Nat King Cole, Frank Sinatra, Dinah Washington, and let's not forget Al Green with "Love and Happiness"; just great music blaring and fun, fun, fun.

Into the seventies, the men wore dashikis, metal chains around their necks, and natural hairdos. After that came the leisure suit. Not everyone looked good in these fashions, but there we were.

We had two dachshunds, Heide and Hans, who had litters of puppies, and we had a cat named Pepper. But as happy as we were with the children at Pilgrim School and the integration battles, there was racism. Patricia and Danny were the first blacks to attend the nursery school, and Paula and Pamela were among the earliest to enroll in Pilgrim School after Dr. Dotson a (Black Doctor) filed a lawsuit for the admission of his children to this private church school called the Pilgrim School. Money was donated by the Seaver family who had also donated heavily to Pepperdine University in Malibu.

Patricia and Danny were the first Blacks to attend the Nursery School. Adjustments and compromise were of the first order as the teachers did not know how to receive black children. They did not want to touch two year olds in assisting with going to the bath room. One's first instinct is to enroll the children somewhere else. This is what Dr. Dotson did after winning the lawsuit for admission. We decided to enroll our children, because of the quality of the faculty, core curriculum and daily chapel and bible learning. I was daily checking on my children as well. It was far superior to public school. There were adjustments and compromises for sure.

For example, I had to buy only elastic-waist pants for Danny at two years old so the teacher could pull his pants down without touching him when it was time to go to the bathroom.

We complied and did fine, until the John Birch Society got control of the church and the school. They had disdain for diversity; they cut out the hot-lunch program. These conservative Christians seemed anything but Christian. A parents commission countered many of the power changes, but ultimately, there were losses as well as gains. The school, however, has prevailed to this day—it still stands tall—and I have seen my grandchildren attend there.

I moved all the children to the Isabel Buckley private school in the valley from the sixth grade on. Testing for admission to the school was a gateway to the best colleges, with a proven track record. One of my purposes in working was to give our children the best education. I knew that education was the key to a good life.

I did not have a lot of confidence in public school. I had attended public schools; that was my only option. Over the years, however, public schools have suffered a continuous decline. Many factors are involved— the influx of thousands of English-as-a-second-language students in some parts of the country, failed property tax increases, and inadequate compensation and benefits for teachers, prompting the gifted teachers to seek other occupations.

It was always a quest to find and secure the best opportunities for our children. Dan supported these ideals as well and loved our children completely. While his misogyny never disappeared, he stopped expressing it as often.

When Patricia was just three years old in 1968, Dan lost his sister Louria in a car accident when she hit a tree. His world was tossed upside down. He did not handle it well, and he was seemingly angry with God. Dan was in such a state.

A few weeks later, I lost my maternal grandmother, Grandmother Rosa, in Iowa, and then Grandfather, who was living with my parents, was never the same. I had to get my grandfather and father ready for the funeral. My mother was out of town when the call came, so she went from Mississippi, where she was attending a meeting, straight home to Des Moines. I could not participate in Grandmother Rosa's service; I stayed with the children. Our family was taking hits that left permanent change. Joy and sorrow were here again.

Our marriage was being tested as well. Dan was not very communicative and brooded a lot. It was necessary for me to be there for him, and keeping our traditions and routines seemed most helpful and gave the best opportunities for talking about pain and disappointment. Fortunately, we both had our work, which we loved, and we had a lot of people around us—staff, colleagues, friends—as buffers. We had our doctors and ministers. We were attending Founders Church of Religious Science on Berendo Street at the time. Danny never liked to go to the children's classes, always opting to stay with me and never making a sound in the pew. We loved the Wednesday night sing-along, with Reverend Hornaday playing the marimba. We followed the philosophy of Ernest Holmes and the power of positive thinking of Norman Vincent Peale, and we read *Guideposts* magazine. I ultimately left the Church of Religious Science because I did not hear the name Jesus enough or the teachings of Jesus. When we arrived in California, Religious Science was the latest thinking for many educated souls, looking at tools for living in the here and now. Heaven was a goal but problems and challenges were at my fingertips. Positive thinking is definitely a tool. loved the Wednesday night sing a longs and feeling uplifted. I loved the teachings and the songs. Let there be peace on earth and let it begin with me, for example. I returned to my roots after a few years. Protestant fire and brimstone preaching and teaching.

I was still a seeker, Having many challenges and many questions. I was finding few answers and solutions from leaders but I always felt better about the problem aafter service and by continuing to evolve spiritually. I was busy as a wife, mother, heallth care professional, employer of a large staff, later a Dental Examiner and regulator, volunteer, homemaker, friend and all the hats a woman wears, add in all the school activities for four children, followup, afterschool activities, taking children to school and picking them up. Believe me my soul looks back in wonder. That is why I am so grateful to so many hands and hearts that have helped me, I was never alone.

*You will never change your life unless you change something you do daily.*

*—John C. Maxwell*

# CHAPTER 11

## My Father Always Treated Me Lovingly

*Limuary Alja Jordan*

When I think of my father, I always smile, and soon after, I chuckle, and then I am in a full grin or laughing out loud. He was so funny; he always had a story and many times would laugh before he could finish the story. He was a Southern man, born in Louisiana of a single Creole mother and a white father who was a physician and coroner of a small town, Columbia, in Caldwell Parish, Louisiana. My father knew hard times, hard work, and even hard luck. Through it all, he had a sense of humor. He was a visionary and dreamer, a possibility thinker, and he would try anything. He believed in himself and his abilities to conquer any challenge. He nurtured and taught his children to dream big dreams. My father always treated me, his firstborn child, as someone special—his pride and joy, his helper, and his buddy, as I grew older.

We spent a lot of time together, mostly outdoors. I was healthy and active, and he introduced me to everything he did, from slopping hogs to carpentry, plastering, painting, bricklaying, yard work, riding horses, and repairing cars—hard work, which is what he knew best.

I was driving a car by eleven years old and doing it well. There was nothing he liked better than to work hard and get complimented on the job by my mom, have a great dinner, and go to the movies. It was years before I realized Glenn Ford there were movies other than westerns. Dad loved Randolph Scott, Hopalong Cassidy, Glenn Ford, the Lone Ranger, the Vigilantes, and so on, so that is what we saw. (Daddy used to say, "He who has the gold, rules.") The lesson was: be sure to get some gold. Mother never cared much about movies, but Shirley Temple was the child star of the day, and I was named for her.

Those hot and humid Louisiana days and nights are a vivid memory to me, as there was no air conditioning when I was a child. We had one electric oscillating fan that we used in times of desperation only, as it raised the electric bill. Screen porches and screen doors were vital necessities as mosquitoes seemed to be our mortal enemies. We would sit on the porch in a swing and talk and enjoy sweet tea or watermelon in the summer.

Rain is another powerful memory, as it was an element of nature that made everything come to a stop. The rain was not a mist, like you might experience in Hawaii; it rained buckets in Louisiana. The skies parted with lightning and roared with cracks of thunder, so loud that it sent us cowering under cover. The river and bayous would rise and streets flooded. It rained so hard that it would beat the paint off the houses. Many houses would catch fire when struck by the fierce lightning.

The sound of the rain was ominous. People walked everywhere, and they took refuge indoors; animals went under the house. God was seemingly speaking. Those times in Louisiana are unforgettable. Dad was there to take care of us all.

In the winter, it got freezing. Monroe is in the northeast boot of Louisiana. The house was warmed by gas heaters that had to be turned off at night, due to the danger of fire or gas escaping. The first ones up in the morning lit the heater and turned on the oven in the kitchen to warm it up for making biscuits for breakfast. How well I remember standing by the heater and being told to move over by someone else who wanted to get warm.

The house sat upon concrete pillars, about a foot and a half off the ground. Chickens and ducks walked freely around the grounds during the day, pecking at chinaberries and other findings, along with the dogs and cats, who would crawl under the house for refuge. They chickens would go back to their coop at night and lay their eggs.

There were all kinds of sounds that I remember so well—the rooster's crow at the break of day; the clucking of the hens as they strutted around, pecking and looking; the dogs chasing cats or scratching at fleas and mosquitos, while lying around lazily in the heat. Pecan trees, with tasty paper-shell pecans, surrounded the white-paneled house with green trim, as well as chinaberries, fig trees, and beautiful hibiscus bushes.

Resting against the sides of the house were thirty-foot bamboo fishing poles, with lines and hooks, as we were only six blocks from the Ouachita River, bounded by high levies. We fished often, and the Friday fish fry was the catch of the day—gasper goo, gar, perch, or the favorite, catfish, with those big whiskers, looking pretty formidable to eat.

Cooking and the enjoyment of food and friends and family was a massive part of our culture when I was growing up. Sweets were big cakes and cookies and soft drinks and tea.

We played cards, except on Sunday, and games and listened to the radio—*Mr. Keen, The Shadow, Dr. Christian*. But come Sunday morning, everyone went to Zion Traveler Baptist Church and visited or entertained relatives afterward. Visiting your kinfolk and eating some cake at their homes was the ritual of the day. We always had something good on hand in the eventuality that someone would stop by. If alcohol was served, it was usually homemade wine.

Daddy taught me to work hard, overcome adversity, do a good job, and then have fun. That work ethic has been a mainstay in my life, as well as my teachings to my children and grandchildren, and it works. As proud as Dad was of me, I am that proud of my children's work ethic. It has to be taught, and we were taught well.

We moved a lot, leaving the South, where opportunities were limited. We followed the northeast corridor migration to Detroit, Michigan. Dad worked for Henry Ford at the Ford Motor Company and helped found the UAW CIO union. The assembly line production of automobiles was a national phenomenon, and Dad was very successful there. The stick shift and clutch were replaced by automatic transmissions—Dynaflow in the Buick and Hydra-Matic in the Oldsmobile. Automation was advancing. It was 1949. I was twelve. We had a new car every year, and a vacation in the car was a family tradition. By the time I left for college, we had seen 90 percent of the United States. Both parents had us kids as a captive audience, and they taught us values and educated us on each state.

Mom and Dad owned two gas stations and other businesses that did well, until Dad became ill with a heart ailment, pericarditis, which is inflammation of the pericardial sac around the heart. The doctor advised him that the damp, cold weather of Detroit was not good for him. I remember the ambulance taking Daddy to the hospital and how frightened I was when I saw him placed inside.

Dad looked to the West, to California. Within a year, we were on our way to Los Angeles, after considering San Francisco as well. How did life change after moving west? In California, Mother, who had been mainly a homemaker, went to work; we kids were all in school, and Daddy was building a new life and new home for us. Our family quickly made a success of the move. Daddy never had the heart issue again.

All of Daddy and Mother's teachings were indelible in my life, as I finished high school in California at age sixteen and college at age twenty, aiming for a career in medicine. Few of my high school friends took the path I did—to go away to college. How grateful I was that I could face any challenge squarely, knowing I had the security and support of loving parents and a dad who believed in sacrifice for the education of a girl, who likely would marry, as was said in the day. In the 1950s, life was still pretty tricky. Tuition was $750 a year, and there were no student loans. Many of my friends' parents could not afford the cost of sending the children away to college; they went to city college, as I did for my freshman year.

I never will forget the hard work I did while growing up. I would be tired yet happy, and I enjoyed the company of others, laughing and playing. As I write this, tears fall upon my cheeks, as my emotions are getting the best of me, remembering how much I cherish the way my father treated me. It was as if he knew I would need all that he could give me and that I would be able to use.

When I arrived at dental school, working with the plaster of paris was nothing new for me; I had plastered walls. What was making a mold of the mouth? Being the only woman in my class was not difficult. As I met barriers and challenges, I had that same sense of invincibility that I saw in my dad, and I knew it could be done and done well. That I would become president of the Board of Dental Examiners for all of California and a commissioner of the American Dental Association— historic firsts—were not even a dream, not even imaginable.

Daddy was thrifty with money, never overspending. When he would give us money, he would hold the money as he said, "Just because you have this money does not mean you need to spend it." Later in life, Dad became quite wealthy. He and Mother amassed real estate and stocks to millionaire status and established endowments and gifts, as this was his greatest joy. His mantra was, "It's not how much you make. It's how much you keep." Also, "A fool and his money are soon parted."

Every time I tell a story, I think of Dad. I know he is smiling—no, he is laughing—because he always loved a good story. He would say, "That reminds me of another story. Did I tell you about the time ..."

Most times, he had us working while he told these stories. He was a great man. I hope he knew that.

My father, Limuary Alja Jordan, was a kind, good-hearted, generous, talented, gifted, funny man. He was courageous and adventurous and would try to accomplish anything. He would right any wrong and fix anything broken. He worked hard and wasted nothing. He was an enormous dreamer for a country boy from Louisiana, whose mother was raising her five sisters and brothers when she had my dad at age fourteen. He had uncles and aunts younger than him. What is most indelible are the principles and values that built a remarkable family and have sustained our family.

My father always wanted to be a physician, but there were no grants or government loans available. His mother struggled to provide for her parents and the ready-made family left behind after their early deaths that she had to raise. My father learned early on that the lack of money and resources was equal to the lack of options and freedom. Money, while only a medium of exchange, has a far different meaning when there is none.

My father met my mother in college, and they both became teachers. They continued to look for opportunities in the industrial revolution that was emerging in the United States in the early thirties. They left the South and went to Detroit, Michigan, and their lives began to prosper. My dad worked at Ford Motor Company, and the UAW CIO union guaranteed wages and opportunities for the American dream—home ownership, automobile ownership, good neighborhoods, and good schools for the children.

My dad went further and opened gas stations, in addition to his job. He was learning how to be an entrepreneur as well as an executive and a leader. Early on, Dad knew the pain of not being able to accomplish something when obstacles of lack appeared. My dad determined that he would work to become independent of those early lessons and that America was the land of opportunity, where values and principles translated into the fulfillment of dreams. My dad's story is a success story.

Dad told jokes continually and saw the humor in life, as well as the pain and suffering of those unwilling to keep trying. Daddy was profoundly spiritual, but other than the obedience to his Christian faith and our rituals of weekly church attendance, I did not know why he was so devoted to Christ. No matter where we were on vacation or visiting, Dad was on his knees every night of his life, thanking God for one more day. After his death, I found a letter Dad left me, recounting the "miracle of faith" and the appearance of the presence of God in his life in a hospital room in Michigan. I read this letter in January 2012.

Dad had been in Harper Hospital for over a month with an infection called pericarditis; *peri*, meaning "around," and *carditis*, meaning "the heart." The damp cold of Detroit and working at his gas stations after his day job had taken a toll. There was a new drug out called penicillin, but it was not working. One night, the doctors told my mom and dad that nothing was working. My dad had terrible pain with each breath he took because there was so much pus and fluid that the pericardial sac was stuck to the rib cage.

The next morning, the doctors said that they would have to open his chest to let the pus out, or he would die of septic infection. This was in the forties, and medical advances were in their infancy; as we know medicine today, it actually rather primitive. My dad knew there was a huge possibility that he was not going to live. That is when his faith prayer began. After my mother left the hospital, my dad said he prayed and prayed for all the dreams he had for his family, for the purpose of his life, and for his promise to God to serve him all the days of his life. A very bright light appeared at the foot of his bed and thrust him into a peaceful sleep without pain. My dad said it was the best sleep, and when he awoke the next morning, his temperature was normal. He had no pain on breathing, and the doctors could find no fluid.

Dad sat up and got up, and the doctors said, "You do not need an operation. There is no sign of infection. You may go home." This was after thirty days of no progress. My dad received a miracle of healing and has been a reverent servant since that time. He never shared that event until he was enjoying everlasting life with God. He spoke on life, love, and religion.

Dad said love and hate are the two most potent forces in the world. "Walk gently!" On life, he said, "What am I living for?" He knew clearly and kept the reasons in front of us daily—family, the family unit. He said, "Can you imagine the holidays without family? If a family member is a bastard of a human being, he or she is still a part of the family."

On religion, he believed in the "faith experience," not just faith. "You need a testimony of faith to show your belief. God performs miracles from moment to moment." Dad taught me to drive a car at eleven years old, and I had a permit in Louisiana.

When a woman makes a vow of love to her husband, that man is obviously a significant man or, more appropriately, her greatest love. I made such a vow to Dan and was blessed with great love and four children. I knew love because my father showed me love. I watched my father care for my mother and our family.

A man such as my father was so significant because he took nothing and made something through sheer determination. He grew up without a father, a man he saw only once, and a mother who was only fourteen years old when she birthed him, while raising her five brothers and sister.

Dad's dreams for his family and his miracle of faith have all come full circle. Dad was a great man, setting a bar that was very high for any man to surpass. My dad and Dan were great friends; Dad thought Dan was a good man, a good husband, and a good father. I thought my dad was the greatest man in the world. I loved him and loved being with him. I speak of him daily as though he were here. A "Limuaryism." Friends will call up and say, "I miss Limuary." You know what he would have said about that.

*The secret of getting ahead is getting started.*

*—Mark Twain*

# CHAPTER 12

## Mother

Sunrise, sunset.
Is this the little girl I carried?
Is this the little boy at play?
I don't remember growing older.
When did they?
When did she get to be a beauty?
When did he grow to be this tall?
Wasn't it yesterday?

The table in the lobby of the assisted-living facility at Las Ventanas was beautifully decorated with ninety-five roses this Friday morning. I included four floor vases of roses with red ribbons, linking them together. The *Review Journal* on Saturday morning, January 19, under "Celebrations," had her picture and an announcement to mark the milestone birthday of Adeline Jordan, my mother.

After some months of anticipation, the day for family arrival had come. Grandma GiGi's birthday was here, ninety-five wonderful years. Carolyn, my sister in Atlanta, began the idea for this party. Mother had received many other big parties, at age eighty and at age ninety, with a few hundred people at each. But this was to be a small family celebration because my mother had been through a year of questionable health challenges, and I already had been planning Camp Shirleywhirl since the previous year. CampShirleywhirl is the term of reference for bringing all eight Grandchildren and their parents together for a trip adventure that has been planned.

The song lyrics, above, seemed to describe my emotions as I welcomed the caravans of my children, nieces, nephews, and extended family—Dan Jr.'s mother-in-law and sister-in-law (his wife, Marcela's sister), motoring in from California.

There were arrivals in rental cars from the airport, and I greeted them in the Red Rock Hotel lobby. The suites and rooms were ready, and the bellman took up the goodie cart of Costco's finest fruits, cheeses, beer and wine, juices, water, chips, and cookies for snacking, meeting, and greeting. Everyone was quickly settled, happy with their accommodations and elated to see each other.

I returned to Las Ventanas after everyone was comfortable and told them of the plans for the evening and beyond. We were to meet at Vintner's Grill at six thirty for dinner. My sister had a later flight and would come directly to the restaurant. This was to be Mother's first contact with everyone. I got her there, seated in her wheelchair and comfortable at a center table. As they arrived, I know she felt the words to the song, as I did:

Swiftly flow the days
Seedlings turn overnight to sunflowers
Blossoming even as we gaze

She received kiss after kiss, hug after hug. This was a perfect venue. Even though we were in a private room, there were roaring firepits outside, music, and a packed house, with a buzz of ultra-excitement. Everyone was dressed up and felt special.

We had wonderful waiters, who were also caught up in the excitement of our celebrations and made every act of presentation special. Flatbread hors d'oeuvres, crab cakes, and cocktails were the first course. Dinner and tributes continued into the night. Tyrone flew in from University of California, San Diego. Later, my sister, Carolyn, and Cary arrived. It was a memorable evening.

On Saturday morning, I'd scheduled an executive breakfast meeting at eight thirty with my investment adviser. Since all my children were together, we seized the opportunity to discuss my portfolio with them. This worked out well.

We returned to the Red Rock for workouts, rest, and family time; the big day was here. A day of celebration, a luncheon and an evening of theater at the Smith Center. Flemings restaurant at 2:00. Videographer, gift presentation, luncheon and birthday cake, speeches, and sharing.

Carolyn presented Mother with a charm bracelet from all of us. Each family had purchased a charm from Pandora, and the bracelet had been preassembled.

Limuary Jr. was the master of ceremonies, and each family told why they had selected a certain charm and then told a favorite memory of a time with Grandma Gigi. My charm was called "A Piece of My Heart"—a red, heart-shaped charm. Others' charms expressed their memories with Mother. She really loved the bracelet and wore it continuously, never seeming to take it off.

This was special and quite a trip down memory lane. Mother closed the day with her thank-you and words of wisdom: "We are a blessed family." She said how proud she was of each and every one of us. Then we were off to the Smith Center's Reynolds Hall for a night of entertainment, and what a show it was—Strike up the band for Drumline this was the live show of Marching bands and entertainment.

For Mother and everyone, this was entertainment extraordinaire. There was a cast of at least sixty who danced and sang from significant band eras—'30s, '40s, '50s, on up to marching bands, swing, hip-hop, Motown, jive, blues. You name it; they did it. Beautiful costumes, fantastic music—the center was sold out. We had box seats and preferred center seats and enjoyed every number. What a show! Everyone was impressed, and there was rousing applause.

Then it was home and to bed for most. At the Red Rock, they were up and out for late-night fun, but on Sunday morning, we went to Desert Spring Church for services, where ninety-five roses were on the altar, to the glory of God and to celebrate motherhood. When Pastor Devereaux announced Mother's birthday, the church applauded. There was an announcement in the church bulletin of our celebration of our mother.

After church, everyone checked out of the Red Rock Hotel. We all met at the feast buffet at the Red Rock for our goodbyes and thanks. Airlines and highways awaited as we prayed for the safe return of all to their homes. What a time—the humor, love, sharing, caring, the happiness of belonging, and knowing your place in the family and that each one is a unique family member.

Many people never see ninety, but there was Mother at ninety-five. She never had been really sick in her entire life, but that year, she was very ill with pneumonia and took a long time to recover. So her celebration also was a time for rejoicing. Her children were so grateful for a loving mother. The grandchildren felt blessed for a loving and extraordinary family that recognized family milestones. We make a big deal out of love, respect for our parents, and teaching the importance of family and every member of it. The Grandchilden, all of moms children's children related that the best of times for them is when they are together with their family.

Mother received many calls and cards from the newspaper announcement, sending good wishes as well.

> Swiftly fly the years
> One season following another
> Laden with happiness and tears

As a young girl, I did not spend a lot of time with my mother; it was mostly with Daddy. After my marriage, children, and becoming a homemaker, Mom was everything to me. She was a peacemaker and a compromiser, always. I learned so much from her, just watching her manage her booming career with the federal government, travel, and my father and grandfather. Mom and I were in the Links, Inc., together, which is a national social and philanthropic organization. We enjoyed going to meetings and conventions together and with the family as well. We became such close friends in adult life. I am so grateful for all that Mom taught me in her subtle way. She was a mentor and teacher to her friends and coworkers and to my friends as well, a tiny but mighty woman who was the great matriarch of our family, after Daddy died in 2002, until she passed in 2015. In addition to all that, she was my dearest love and friend, and she is missed every day.

> Is this the little girl I carried?
> Is this the little boy at play?
> I don't remember growing older
> When did they?
> Sunrise, sunset

That was Mom's big day. She was a friend for all my life and one of my most cherished blessings. God has smiled on us.

*No one ever attains eminent success by only doing what is required. It is the amount of excellence that is over and above that determines the greatness of ultimate distinction.*

—Charles Kendall Adams

# CHAPTER 13

# The Pursuit of Happiness

Long before I experienced much about life and personal responsibility, I had dreams! I had adolescent images in my mind of what I wanted my life to be. I didn't visualize many obstacles, nor did I give attention to the usual blockades I saw in the struggles of others. I just had visions of a beautiful home, lots of children, my own Prince Charming, and a successful career. Being a naive teenager, just having the dream seemed to be the necessary qualifier. I had simple thoughts.

Let me tell you a story about my journey to find happiness. From the time I got on the train, the Sunset Limited, in Los Angeles and headed to college, my life unfolded before me like a precious treasure map. That map has been folded many times and opened a section at a time. It was all there in my mind. Bang, hot ziggety, wow, whoopee—I was sixteen; it was preparation meeting opportunity. I had strength and fortitude. I never questioned where it came from; it was just there when I needed it.

From the beginning, it was never easy. Nothing was automatic; the smallest things could derail me, and sometimes, they did. Many times, it was teachers or peers who did not believe I was serious about my lofty ambitions. I had dedication, such as wanting to carry eighteen units—a heavy course load, including challenging science courses—and persistence and patience paid off.

I had success from my actions. I knocked on doors that opened. I worked hard and with purpose. After college, I received a scholarship to study on an NIH grant at Howard University School of Medicine, Department of Pharmacology. I received tuition and a stipend. It was my first total independence as I made the transition from college girl to college woman.

Not unlike a map, plans sometimes take detours that allow you to move on through, and that's what mine did. I loved dental school and thrived. My only prior experience was a summer job in a dental office as a receptionist and my personal dental visits as a patient. I knew the smell of zinc oxide and eugenol (oil of cloves) used in dental medicaments. I was an officer in my freshman class and the only woman; I was doing well.

The courses I had in the first year of dental school were the same as those I had studied in graduate school. This took a lot of pressure off me. I liked it. I was one of only thirteen women in the freshmen classes of forty-seven dental schools in the United States—Dr. Russell Dixon's reason in looking for women to enter the profession and his persistence in recruiting me.

I had a '57 Chevy that was red and white and is today a classic. Daddy had gotten it for me, and I really loved that car. This was after a series of fifty-dollar cars I had gotten from Mr. Clarence Worthy. He was a fantastic mechanic and used-car dealer. When one car stopped working, he took it in, gave me another, and said, "Drive this one." I have many stories about those cars, from a Model T to old ones with floorboards through which the ground was visible.

Red and white were the colors of Delta Sigma Theta.my sorority. What else in the world could a girl want? I was friends with many special guys. Dan Graves was a student at Georgetown, studying to enter the Foreign Service. Lawrence Phillips, my Fisk University boyfriend, became an engineer in Chicago. A few others were medical students, but one, in particular, Henry Dan Bailey, was exceptional indeed.

I fell in love with this very handsome medical student. After a courtship of more than a year, he sat me in a tree on the grounds of Hillcrest, got on his knee, and asked to marry me. I said yes.

Dan often spoke about having a family. He was the oldest of seven children. I wanted children also, in due time—maybe not seven. I never visualized marriage as compromising any of my personal aspirations, my career. I was in love, and I saw nothing else.

We were married at the end of my freshman year in dental school. It was a beautiful June wedding with eight bridesmaids. I wore the loveliest gown I had ever seen, which had been on the cover of Seventeen magazine the popular publication. Being home in Los Angeles was heavenly. My parents had given us a memorable summer wedding with hundreds of guests. Too soon, it was back to school, books, apartment hunting, and a U-Haul full of wedding gifts—linens, crystal, and beautiful things we needed and used.

I became the mother of four children in the next few years—1962, '63, '65, '67. I was happy, loving my babies, loving school, reading, and working. There were diapers, Similac, laundry, and school. There was never enough sleep. If this was the plan, it was not in this order. It was exhausting.

Dan graduated in 1962 and in 1964. Thank God for birth control pills that came on to the market—Enovid. I was still among the top students. I got one of the two internships in our class, pediatric dentistry at DC General Hospital, and I was one of seven from our school to pass the District of Columbia dental boards the first time.

Later, I got a fellowship and a job treating White House staff as a dentist at Group Health. Dan had finished his surgery residency, and we lived in New York while he did his study at Sloan Kettering Memorial Hospital. I accepted the Guggenheim fellowship in 1965.

Lyndon Baines Johnson was the president; he was a great one. He launched his Great Society programs of equal opportunity for everyone. The war was going on in Vietnam, a terrible war. Things were chaotic in the United States and abroad. Unlike Iraq, we all felt we were a part of the Vietnam War—the cruelty, torture, loss of life, and the feeling we didn't know how to win the war. General Westmoreland making calculations that were off the mark.

The hope America had for accelerated space programs was uncertain. The War on Poverty, as well as improved education, were also in peril.

President Johnson was not widely liked because he was doing what he knew was right on the domestic front, and that was not what many wanted. General Westmoreland's advice on the Vietnam War was the sinker.

The president also forced the states to obey federal regulations. He pushed for the War on Poverty. Equal opportunity programs surfaced. The attorney general of the United States was doing landmark work for the poor and oppressed.

LBJ was such a seasoned politician from Texas that he had a way with Congress to get passed what he needed. He could buttonhole congressmen and get his way. He had been in Washington long enough to know where all the skeletons were. My interest in politics was born with LBJ and Lady Bird Johnson, and that interest has never wavered. Dan and I and our family of four children left Washington, DC, in 1967, right after Danny, our son, was born that August.

Riggs Bank was very conservative. We found it hard to get a start as a young family. I was making $12,400 a year as a dentist at Group Health, and Dan was a surgeon, and we could not get a starter loan at Riggs Bank. Unlike many young people today, we had no debt, no student loans. We had worked our way through school, and our parents had helped. Dan was also a captain in the National Guard medical evacuation unit. We wanted to go to California anyway, so now seemed like the time. What a difference.

We took out loans from the Interns and Residents Association and got jobs at health centers in Los Angeles until we could start our own practices. Our parents cosigned additional investments for us, and we bought our beautiful home in California within months of moving there—three massive steps up to a beautiful swimming pool, fire pit, and green grassy knoll.

The kitchen was beautiful, with a walk-through pantry, built-in grill, cove base floors, and patio. There was a unique door for milk delivery, built-in mixers, pull-out drawers, and a stove hood with a vent. The master suite overlooked the pool, and there were side yards for the dogs, a sunken living room, counter space, terrazzo floors and carpet, an intercom, music speakers, and a maid's quarters for taking care of the children. This was really the dream.

We were at home, all in a few months after moving to Los Angeles. Just a few miles away, I bought a medial building on a personal note that was financed by the doctor who owned the building. With five thousand dollars down, I had a tenant, a foot doctor, Dr. Jeffrey Widen, who paid me $165 a month rent, and I was off to the races.

The office was close to our home. Dan moved into a high-rise medical building, as his business would be referred to as a surgeon. Also close to home, he was down one side of the hill, and I was over the other side of the mountain.

We were young doctors, beginning our practices and raising our children. Life was good! Danny less than a year, Patsy was two, Pam was four, and Paula was five.

The society programs were also a realization come true. I utilized the CETA (Comprehensive Employment and Training Act) program and the WIN (Whip Inflation Now) program in my office, doing job training for auxiliaries. I used investment tax credits to buy dental equipment, notably a panorex machine that took a full mouth picture of the oral cavity, jaws, and teeth. I ran a mobile dental unit for the Los Angeles City Unified School District, going to underserved areas, delivering care. I obtained a lifetime teaching credential with a specialization in health Services.

My private practice prospered, and I not only hired hygienists but other dentists to work in my office. Dan was doing well as chief of surgery at the Watts Health Center, performing surgery in his private practice and keeping his health center position, which he held until he retired. We felt we were living the good life and placed our children in private schools so we could replicate providing an excellent education for them, which we knew was the key to our success.

Everything about our lives was positive—social success in medical circles, living in an affluent part of the city with other professionals. The hills where we lived were jokingly called Pill Hill. Most of the black professionals lived in View Park and Ladera Hills. Our neighbors were Tina Turner, Ray Charles, prominent business figures, ministers, lawyers, and so forth. Coming home was beautiful—the backyard parties, coffees, and get-togethers. Our neighbors were our friends as well. Our children swam in each other's pools and had great playtimes. This was another daily validation of seeing we had made the right choices and had landed in the right place.

Black people who were prepared had walked through the doors of opportunity, at least in California. People were moving there by the thousands each month. It was not all about what we had but who we were. We were professional people, helping to build our community. We were parents raising our children. For Dan, this was another unbelievable dream. As the oldest of seven children, he grew up in a house built by his father in Panama City, Florida, where the white-sand beaches took years to integrate for black folks.

Segregation had been so painful that Dan could only bear an occasional visit to see his parents. It was as difficult for him to be comfortable among whites as it was for whites to feel safe around minorities. Atlanta and Washington, DC, had been the farthest he had traveled. California was something he wanted his folks to see. And they did; our families visited and shared and bonded. For Dan and me, life was busy. I was always an early riser, getting up about 5:00 a.m. This bode well for the active growth I had designed.

Dan helped where he could. He usually cooked on the grill on weekends as the children swam. We had live-in help who went home on Friday evening and returned on Sunday evening. My morning meeting with Maria was to plan dinner, see what she needed, and let her get it.

I had been smart in school and average socially. I had lots of friends wherever we lived and that was three major cities: Monroe, Louisiana; Detroit, Michigan; and Los Angeles, California. To this day, I am still in touch with friends from all three cities. I was double-promoted, as skipping grades was called, and graduated from high school two years early.

From the fifth grade, I had crushes on boys and wrote love letters to Isaac, and I liked Jimmy Haywood, who used to put my long pigtails into the inkwells in his desk behind me. Jimmy had a broad smile and loved my reaction to his mischief. But even though I liked him, he was silly. Isaac was more serious; he had beautiful green eyes, played the cornet in the band, and was, as they said in the day, cool. Another girl, who was far less attractive than me, Roylene Ellis, had a crush on Isaac too. I was a bit worried, however, and avoided her like the plague.

Isaac and I liked each other a lot. He never said "a lot," but I loved his manner and all his talents. He was a natural cartoonist. He could draw anything. I learned early that I really liked good-looking boys and smart ones. Later, I would learn that this judgment-value approach was equivalent to deciding on a book by the cover, but these appraisals would continue to be a part of me and influence my life decisions.

In high school, I saw many of my boyfriends get into all kinds of trouble, seeking fun, making poor decisions, testing the limits, and seeking thrills. Seeing them was enough of reality check and never quite a temptation for me.

Smoking and the use of alcohol was not an issue, as my parents did not use those things. The worst thing a girl could do in the fifties was be promiscuous with sex before marriage and taint her reputation as a young lady; that would be the end of her personal dreams, along with being socially ostracized and bringing shame to her family. For me, fun was school and church friends, singing in the choir, volleyball and basketball games in a league, school dances, board games, and cards. Track and field were big—the hundred-yard dash. Comic books were really fun; everyone collected them. Veronica and Archie were two of my favorite comic book characters, as well as Marvel comics. I enjoyed the movies and the beach—oh, the beach. We lived at the beach after choir practice or games. There were bonfires and beach parties. The fellas loved their cars and to take the girls to the beach and then to Dairy Queen afterward. My parents felt there was safety in numbers and, for the most part, there was.

I also spent a lot of time in my friends' homes, and they in mine. Leaving home to go away to college was a sad time for me. It was an ending to a great chapter in my life—and a goodbye

I left on the Sunset Limited train, going to Nashville, Tennessee. I was to meet my grandmother along the way; she would take me the last part of the journey. I left all my high school friends, and although we would remain in touch, my world began to change instantly. I was a woman now, a college woman, not a girl. I saw sororities and fraternities and soon knew I wanted to join Delta Sigma Theta. I admired the women who were Deltas—the school leaders, best of the best. I saw the biology and chemistry labs and knew I was on my way to realizing my dreams.

I met friends from all over the United States and Africa, England, and many other countries through the exchange program at Fisk University. I was impressed. Everyone there was smart and, like me, had been either the salutatorian or valedictorian of their classes and had goals and dreams similar to mine. Obviously, we were Honor Society students who were focused on the future. Our parents and families struggled to send us to college. Most of the students recognized the sacrifices that were made for them, and they were not going to blow it. Money was not easy to come by in 1954.

Segregation and racism were ever present in Nashville. I was surprised that I could not try on clothes in department stores, for fear some of my blackness would rub off on to the clothes. I could buy the item but not try it on or return it. Coming from California, I thought the people were ignorant—in the Bible Belt, at that.

Fortunately, ignorance is reversible for everyone, and anyone can be enlightened. College, for me, was the beginning of wisdom. I knew making good decisions was important. I knew ambition and hard work were important. I also knew the competition was evident and that sometimes there was only one prize for the winner. I found some doors were closed for women and many were closed for race but that being outstanding was always good for pushing the doors open. I believed in myself. My parents' encouragement was to tell me, "Remember who you are. This is America. You can succeed with hard work."

I learned to work hard at home. We had chores to do before we could go to the beach or go out with our friends; we had to earn that allowance. The result of our chores had to be excellent as well because from my grandmothers, I'd learned that "cleanliness is next to godliness." We cleaned the house and the yard. We did the laundry, folded the clothes, and ironed our clothes; this was before permanent-press items and polyester. If we were behind on anything, our friends would help us out so we could get out because we had curfews. I had to be home by eleven on Saturday night. I had to go to church on Sunday morning and Sunday school before that. My chores had to be finished, and my clothes had to be ready. Those early habits served me well, as I knew how to organize my time, keep my dorm room neat, get to the library, dance at the Coop, have fun, and succeed. To make a sorority, one needed a B grade point average and one needed to have something unique about them, be known, and be invited to join.

That meant keeping my grades high and getting known. I joined the dorm council, biology club, and German club, and I was friendly to everyone. When the letter of invitation came, I was so happy. I felt that I had reached my first college goal.

> Oh, when a Delta girl walks down the street
> She looks 100 per from head to feet
> She has a word, a smile, a winning way
> And when you see her, boy, you'll recognize her and you'll say
> Now there's a girl I'd like to know
> She has a word, a way, that Delta glow
> And when you see her, boy, its sure a treat
> It's hard to beat a Delta girl

My dad and husband are both Omega Psi Phi fraternity members, a brotherly bond for sure. The fun and parties and beer in college are fond memories. We worked hard and played hard. Beer was served in quarts in college, so after exams, we went to a beer garden filled with college students, and the Quarts of beer were lined up on the table. The joint was called Colliers, and there was one theater, the Ritz, but we put the F in *fun*.

Graduation was brutal if you did not have all your credits. You did not march. The saying was, "Study hard or you won't be here when the magnolias bloom." I made it.

The ceremony was impressive. Fisk University is a historical Black college, where Martin Luther King Jr. was a frequent visitor to our chapel. John Hope Franklin and Dr. W E.B DuBois led the march at my graduation. I was twenty years old and heading to Washington, DC, to Howard University, with a scholarship. My quest was just beginning. There were many goodbyes and tears of leaving.

Ethel Barnes, my friend and classmate, and I both got the NIH scholarship and planned to live together in Washington, renting space at someone's home. That was acceptable to our parents, who felt that was safe. Ethel and I found the home pleasant, but we did not feel it would work. We met a dentist at the school who had an apartment for lease, and we took it. We walked to town, looking for beds and furniture, until we got blisters on our feet. This was brutal. I needed a car. I had owned one in high school, a 1937 Plymouth, and walking in Washington was not good. I found an alley mechanic and bought my first car for fifty dollars, a Model T Ford.

Mr. Clarence Worthy, a wonderful older gentleman, played a major role in my transportation fortunes; he would keep me rolling. I had a monthly stipend and tuition paid, and my parents sent me fifty dollars a month. Times were tough, but the studies were in the medical school. That is where I wanted to be, but few women were accepted. The school felt men deserved the places, as they were heads of households. My presenting a research paper in Florida was a turning point for me. The dean of Dental School, having just been in Russia, wanted women in the dental school and was impressed with me. He asked me to apply to dental school on my return. I did, and it was a fantastic decision.

In physiology class, I met Henry Dan Bailey—smart, tall, handsome, and a Q member of Omega Psi Phi fraternity. He was the top student in his class. He was shy but asked me out, and we dated a year before he proposed marriage.

Those years of reading books and rocking the babies were difficult. I thought I would never get enough sleep. It was diapers, washing and housekeeping, school, baby care, and trying to get some sleep. Whatever the challenge, I was not going to quit dental school.

George Burns and Gracie Allen were popular in those days. Mom and Dad sent us two black poodle puppies to add to the madness, and I named them George and Gracie. I took solace in Dean Martin on Thursday nights and Judy Garland. Dan would help with the chores, reading while drying clothes at the Laundromat, shopping, and doing some of the cooking. We had one car and took the babies to a sitter for the hours I was in school. Babies kept coming until—voila! Birth control pills came out, and I could write my own prescriptions. Four children would be the final number. It was not the same number as Dan had in mind; I think he had wanted to surpass his dad.

I graduated as the only woman in my class. I had delivered two babies while in school, got the pediatric internship at DC General Hospital, and was one of eight Howard graduates to pass the DC boards. I had met my goal. I was to learn soon that it was only the beginning. Dean Russell Dixon, my mentor, gave me some sage advice: "Go out into the world. That is what will make Howard better."

We moved to California, and seventeen years later, I was summoned by the board of trustees to return to Howard University as an honoree as a distinguished alumnus of Howard University for my career work in California. The governor's appointment of me to the board and my election by my peers to the presidency of the Board of Dental Examiners for the twenty-three million people of the state of California was a first in the history of any state board in the country for a black woman dentist. Thanks to Dean Dixon and to my parents, that was opening a door.

My work in quality assurance and quality assessment, the revision of the fifty-year-old Dental Practice Act, the addition of the periodontal examination to the licensure process, and expansion of duties for dental auxiliaries was most of what I was privileged and humbled to have a leadership role in for California. I would go on to open more doors as a member of the American Dental Association's Joint Commission on National Board Exams.

My daughter Paula was at Harvard now, Pamela was at Yale, and Patricia and Dan were still at Buckley in Sherman Oaks, California. Life was good, busy, and bustling.

A Fisk University graduation was always a memorable academic marching procession of dignitaries and celebrities of the day. It was known, in jest, as a most auspicious occasion. On the first Monday in May 1958, I, Shirley Ann Jordan, was marching in my resplendent cap and gown, with my classmates of those recent years, to the joyful strains of "Pomp and Circumstance." I had earned my bachelor of science degree in biology. I would, within minutes, be clutching this sought-after diploma. I was twenty years old and filled with the inspiration of Dr. Martin Luther King Jr., a frequent visitor to our campus. I was motivated to build my best life from my parents and from the promise of America that if I worked hard and persisted toward my dreams, I could have my dreams come true. Life was beautiful, the day was beautiful, and everything was in front of me. I saw the only opportunity.

Dr. William Edward Burghardt Du Bois led the processional of my graduation. Born in 1893, he walked with the limp body of one carrying the weight of a people. He was a distinctive man, the first African American man to earn a doctorate degree from Harvard University. He was one of the founders of the NAACP, a noted civil rights leader, sociologist, and author. Dr. Du Bois was the author of such works as *The Souls of Black Folk* and *The Talented Tenth*. Countless other of his contributions to American society lent to the occasion all the dignity and solemnity of the day. It was, indeed, a commencement. He, along with Fisk University president Charles Spurgeon Johnson, with their colorful hoods on their robes denoting their major studies, made a vibrant and everlasting memory of achievement.

In 1958, I was headed to Washington, DC. Ethel and I were going to be roommates as we had goals of becoming medical doctors. We had met our first obstacle in the rejection from medical school, even though we were excellent students who had passed the MCATs. We met sexual discrimination before it had a name. We were told we were wonderful girls but that admitting us would take a career away from a man and an entire family. We were offered scholarships to NIH and were enrolled in the graduate school of pharmacology. This placed us in the medical school for our classes with medical students. We were paid a monthly stipend as postgraduate students. We accepted this opportunity and were encouraged to reapply, if still so inclined.

Ethel had pledged a rival sorority, AKA, and I was a member of Delta Sigma Theta, quite different in many ways, but we held mutual respect for each other. Different sororities did not matter to us; Ethel and I considered ourselves good friends. Washington, DC, and the country were very much segregated in 1958. Money was also scarce and challenging to attain. Ethel had secured housing for us in upper northwest Washington in a woman's home, which proved too confining. We were now in a real dilemma, as our parents trusted that we would be living in the safety of a home in a crime-free, safe neighborhood. We knew we needed something else immediately. As luck would have it, we attended a university reception event at the medical school, where I met Dr. Norris, a dentist. He was strikingly handsome—very fair-skinned and tall—a personable, genteel, soft-spoken professional man and very well-heeled. He came up to me and offered a welcome to Howard University. Dr. Norris was an obviously mixed-race gentleman of white and African heritage. He was a property owner and wealthy by conventional standards. In Washington, DC, it was unquestionable that you were either in society or out of it—the haves and have-nots.

His welcome and warm acceptance let me know the first door had been opened. Howard University was known to attract the best and the brightest and was coined "the capstone of Negro education." Seventy-five percent of the nation's black professionals had graduated from Howard University, including the first African American Supreme Court justice, Thurgood Marshall.

The educational community of the university fostered prestige, coupled with the elite of the government community, there was an A-list, even in black society. In other words Washington, D.C. was a special place to be studying. Dr. Norris offered us an apartment on T Street, 920 T, for a small rent. It was within walking distance of the school. The apartment was in the middle of the block in a red-brick attached building, meaning walls touching the adjacent building. It was a second-story, walk-up efficiency with refrigerator, stove, and counters all built in. It was a large open space. Ethel and I were thrilled. We could come and go at any hour and get to school fairly quickly. The neighborhood was settled owners but not the best; it was old. We later found it housed many university people. We had made a wise decision.

It was unfurnished, so that meant buying basic furniture—bed, lamps to study, and a desk. Walking was suitable for us, so I looked for a used car to purchase and found the garage of Mr. Clarence Worthy, a kindly gentleman who helped me buy my first car, a Model T Ford. It became the first of eight cars over the next few years, all for only fifty dollars each.

Our parents cautiously went along with the changes and hoped for the best. Of course, they were spared many of the intricate details.

Our housing dilemma was solved, transportation was addressed, and now it was on to our studies. It was exciting to study in the medical school, with so many handsome, young black doctors. It was almost a total distraction, but our perfused heart studies of the guinea pig had begun. Dr. Walter Booker, chairman of the Department of Pharmacology, and Dr. Tureman had studied at the Karolinska Institute in Sweden. They studied the effect of certain drugs on the heart and wrote a grant, which NIH approved and funded. We were the graduate students who were there to do the actual work. We took academic courses in anatomy, physiology, biochemistry, bacteriology, and medicine, right along with the medical students. We began to form contacts with people. This was a good thing. Also, we traveled, delivering research results in academic papers all over the country.

Life was excellent from my perspective, but Ethel opted out of this quest after one year when she fell madly in love and married Dr. William Jackson, a physicist, and began her family. This left me alone, so I looked for other opportunities. It is incredible how every good thing you do can become important later. A previous volunteer effort, bathing and helping impoverished children, was about to turn to gold. A bulletin advertised a position for a student, experienced with children, to live at a residential treatment center for emotionally disturbed children. This was the ad I answered, which turned out to be the biggest blessing yet.

In the exclusive upper northwest area of Wisconsin Avenue and Van Ness, a mansion and grounds of about twelve acres of prime real estate, called Hillcrest, became my new home.

I was to learn that the notice I read was posted at Georgetown, American University, George Washington University, and Howard University. They sought four students. I now had my own quarters, maid service, and free room and board, and the only requirement was to be there by ten o'clock at night and work with the children for a few hours on the weekends. I had great fraternization with the other counselors—Fred, Bob, and Maxie—and with the psychologist and psychiatrist, Dan Graves and Grover Dye

I was the only woman selected of the four.

The children who came to Hillcrest were better off away from their home situations until therapy had reached a point where home residency could be resumed. We saw extreme asthma attacks, stuttering, nervous kids, early issues with identity, bullying, and untenable home situations that either contributed to the child's condition or did not support it.

For me, life was fantastic. My parents gifted me with a 1957 Chevy. It was red and white, my sorority colors. My transportation had improved up from my fifty-dollar cars. It was the best of times. I was meeting and dating some adorable guys. We enjoyed embassy parties, Georgetown attractions, and fine dining, and I loved all of it. I had not dated that much before this point. (Tiny had been my college boyfriend for almost my entire time at Fisk.)

I enjoyed the beautiful city of Washington's summer evenings at Hains Point or Rock Creek Park; the Library of Congress, where I loved to study; the cherry blossoms in April or May, depending on the weather; and the autumn foliage—the orange, red, and yellow leaves. All are wonders to behold.

I was accepted to dental school during one of my speaking lectures in Coral Gables, Florida. The dean just walked up to me and said, "If you will come to dental school, you will be accepted on the spot. You will have to take the dental aptitude test; otherwise, you are set." He wanted to attract women into dentistry. I was the only woman in my class of eighty-one.

I lived at Hillcrest until I married one of those handsome medical students, Henry Dan Bailey. Dan proposed to me on bended knee under a tree at Hillcrest.

*Push, pull, shove—if you give out, don't give up.*

*—Alzenia "Big Mama" Jordan*

# CHAPTER 14

*Family Values*

Most of us have a family. no matter how small or how large—mother and father, brother, sister, grandparent, aunt, uncle, cousin, adoptive parent, and so on. We spend our entire lives relating to family or being estranged from family, trying to find new families, or running away from our families, if we are not fortunate to have a loving, nurturing family. These are our basic beginnings. We didn't get here by ourselves. Our lives are the dreams and hopes of others or the fear and uncertainty of the unprepared and unexpected, but nevertheless, we got here.

Rocky, bumpy, stable, smooth—we all got here. Someone fed us and cared for us until we could care for ourselves. That is the cycle of nature with mammals, taking care of their young until they are independent.

This story is about the building and nurturing of great families. Matriarchs and patriarchs, as symbols of age, wisdom, and experience, are important and valuable because family values, character, and principles of living are clearly defined in the lives and actions of these figures. Most families can be described with adjectives that vary vastly, from humble and stable with generations of stability, to the rich and famous, notorious, and criminal. Families may have leaders, farmers, fishermen, hunters, politicians, teachers, ministers, business people and so forth. Most families either embrace the family business and want the children to follow, or they want something better for the next generation. You will know all about the family business by the time you decide on your life's work.

For our family, the first major value learned was the importance of education—the key to a good life. Ignorance is correctable; knowledge is power. Dad used to say, "The tassel is worth the hassle."

Education can be found in formal universities—our children matriculated at our nation's most renowned: Harvard, Yale, Notre Dame, Amherst, Stanford—or it can be found in the gutter, sitting on a curb, talking with an alcoholic or addict of days and years lost to idleness despair, and depression and life that has lost its meaning, and for many, lost hope. Education is sought to prepare you make a good life for yourself and your family but also for your community and the world. Be ever mindful that no one does anything alone. Be your best self; learn to work well with others; learn how to learn from others.

We spend the early preparatory years completing high school, college, graduate school, internships, first jobs, fitting in, learning how to be happy and satisfied, yet always striving to be better. But education can be found from the desert to the sea, from the bluest sky to the meteor storms of outer space, in a simple conversation with a friend or in a plan that did not succeed. Our mission is to find it and embrace it as a life force. Education is learned.

The second major value system for our family is togetherness. If families do not spend quality time together and visit with one another, they cannot know one another well or love each other and forgive each other. All families have to adjust to marriages, divorces, children, new people, people you are not fond of, people you do not admire at all. Planned time together is very important. Some in-laws act strangely, and you find it easier to just bake that turkey and invite others, but we must make the effort.

Dad used to say, "If he or she is a bastard or a bitch, they're *our* bastard and bitch." Holidays are not holidays without family; not the same. I can say, "Sure, you can cruise to the other side of the world during the holidays and avoid the hustle and bustle," but it's different. Knowing your family and knowing your place in the family is largely up to you; it's up to you to establish your identity. There is a sense of belonging, a sense of security. Your self-image is somewhat shaped by your place in the family—the baby boy or the oldest daughter.

My mother always taught us, "Know who you are. Define yourself! Then, when you are away from the family, you will know who you are."

Your biggest job is learning to love yourself and then to love others. The old saying—"Have you been introduced to yourself?"—is quite noteworthy. Do you have a grip on your identity? Do you know your importance to the family? Do you provide the laughter, the wit, the smarts, the encouragement? What is your spiritual gift? What are your spiritual fruits? What does the family give you? A sense of pride? A reason for living? A meaning to your short life? The importance of time together is huge.

Family ties need constant nurturing. You don't get to choose your family; God chose you and put you into this family.

The last value for our family is to remember that to whom much is given, much is expected. This is expressed as our treasures being stored up on this earth and leaving something to your family.

I once had a friend who aptly said, "We are just passing through." Looking at rocks and mountains that are hundreds of millions of years old, we recognize in a life span of one hundred or fewer years for us humans is almost an instant. But what we have gathered, we should share with those coming after us. That is the way to build great families and great wealth.

Each generation should have pass-through financial wealth through the vehicles of trusts and subtrusts, irrevocably recognized in our capitalistic society as assets. After religious giving and other charitable institutions, we have been taught to not spend everything we have amassed on this earth but to pay it forward. These values have been taught and lived by our matriarch and patriarch as well, as they believed it was necessary for esteem and security.

It is a blessing to be a member of a family that accepts others on the merits of the character of that person, cheers for family members in great endeavors, feels the pain of each other's losses and disappointments, sustains one another, and sends energy to one another. In every family, there are those who are stronger than others; there are those whose stars shine brighter, but inside the family, you are still just you. It's a safe haven of love and acceptance not found anywhere else.

We need to build and nurture the family. Remember birthdays, remember anniversaries, remember them. Anthropologist Margaret Mead spoke of the family unit as the strength of America. Today, the traditional family, for many, looks quite different. Our society now recognizes that freedom reaches to whomever you can love, without gender being an issue.

The values will not change, even though change will always be a part of the family. Let us strive to be sensitive to the importance of this institution of our lives; to be caring, loving, and kind, as our very lives depend on our ability to do so.

*Make every setback a stepping stone.*

—*unknown*

# CHAPTER 15

## *Rites of Passage*

I was awkward, clumsy, and in a great deal of pain as I tried to walk in my first red high-heeled shoes on Easter Sunday morning, going to church. I was thirteen and experiencing the new challenges of dressing up as a young lady. There was little natural about it. It was just a family tradition, I think.

We had just moved to Los Angeles by way of Louisiana and Detroit, Michigan. New clothes for Easter was a ritual of spring in our family and especially new shoes, ever since I could remember. Straw hats and patent leather purses were also among the necessities of this time of year and were adorned happily on Easter.

The year 1950 was different for me. My father had gone shopping with us, driving my mother downtown to a department store where my Aunt Lelah was working. We were going to get her assistance in shopping and use her 30 percent employee discount. Daddy was well invested in this jaunt, as well as having the realization that his oldest daughter was growing up and needed dress-up things.

For me, this was less than exciting, to say the least. I still loved everything outdoors—baseball, volleyball, bikes, riding horses—and I was already driving a car; I'd learned on the country roads when I was eleven. Being all fussy was something I could wait for, but that was not to be.

High-heeled shoes meant more than high-heeled shoes. To my mother, it meant a girdle, a slip, and silk stockings. Most stockings had seams up the back that looked crooked on many people, and the stockings ran easily if you were not gentle in putting them on. I was thinking, *How am I going to manage all of this? And by Sunday?*

I was tall at five foot seven, active, well-liked, and smart in high school. I was looking at boys and had a few crushes and many pals, but I did not fall in love until fifteen. Two years after all of these beginnings, to dress up as a young lady was expected.

Easter Sunday came. I was outfitted in a navy-blue linen suit, white blouse, and red leather pumps—the most comfortable I could find and walk in without falling down. Even though they were only about two inches high, they seemed like stilts to me—a girl who had never worn on a pair. Obedience was the only emotion I knew at the time.

After breakfast, it was back upstairs to do my hair and get dressed. The girdle was the first hurdle. It was tight, and I could barely breathe. The stockings, or hose, attached to clips that hung down from the girdle, so I carefully pulled on the hose. They had a fine seam in the same color as the stocking, but it was barely visible, and I got them on without tearing them. Mother was still clearing the kitchen, and time was of the essence. I needed to be ready when Dad called, "Let's go, everybody." I carried my shoes with my purse and gloves downstairs— walking down the stairs in those shoes was not an option. I went into the dining room to put on my shoes and stand up.

My father gave me a glance that made me think this might not be going well, and he called my mother. She asked if everything was all right. I, of course, said determinedly, "Yes, Mother dear."

As we made our way to the car, there was silence, until I heard Dad say, "Happy Easter! Everyone looks so beautiful!"

Entering the church, I could feel a thousand eyes upon me as I tried to glide without notice to our pew. Feeling conspicuous and dressed up, I drew attention, but I could only respond with smiles and half nods.

*Unless you try to do something beyond what you have already mastered, you will never grow.*

*—Ralph Waldo Emerson*

# CHAPTER 16

## *An Unforgettable Professor*

*Dr. Fitzgerald at his desk, June 1962*

My experience as a dental student with Dr. Percy Fitzgerald was born of concern from the dean of the dental school, Dr. Russell Dixon, who had recruited me as the only woman in my class in 1960. He further told me that I was one of thirteen women in the forty-seven US dental schools. He did not want me to fall short and offered this sage advice: "Shirley, a lot of our faculty are not ready for women to enter this profession, so

I suggest you make sure the chairman of all the departments work with you to see your work and provide you the assistance you need."

I respected the dean and took his advice, even if it meant waiting for a day or so or rescheduling my patients so that Dr. Fitzgerald could examine my work. We had clinical requirements and timelines in each department, and there was a tiny margin for lost time with qualifications in all clinical departments.

The particular case that has been the hallmark of my experience was an anterior six-unit bridge, a highly esthetic prosthesis that spans from cuspid to cuspid, including both central and lateral incisors. Shape, form, embrasures, protection of the periodontium, fit, contacts, occlusion, shading, and patient satisfaction are just a few of the parameters of the mechanics of making this prosthesis. Impressions, wax-up, sprucing, casting, finishing, and fitting are a few of the others. Each time I saw my patient, fitted in the bridge, and then presented it in Dr. Fitzgerald's clinic, he would say, "It seems good, but I would like a frictional fit." He'd tell me to try another type of impression material or use a different temperature when casting.

When I showed my case to other professors on the floor, I received high praise but not from Dr. Fitzgerald; he kept looking for additional parameters of fit for me to achieve. I made the bridge three times, each time with a smile and thanks to Dr. Fitzgerald and my apologies to my patient. I knew my attitude was as important as my clinical skills and that "good enough" should not be my final goal but the beginning goal. Only the best I could achieve would give me the ultimate satisfaction with myself and my work and my patients.

Those days in his lab and his demand for only the best are etched in my memory with a smile. At graduation, I was one of thirty-six (of the original eighty-one in our class) who graduated on time, and I received one of the two internships. Also, I was one of only eight to pass the boards for the District of Columbia.

I was so comfortable doing my bridge for the board that I actually enjoyed the experience. My test had come long before this, while working under the direct supervision of Dr. Fitzgerald.

Years later, I became an examiner for the Northeast Regional Board of Dental Examiners, as well as president of the California State Board of Dental Examiners from 1981 to 1985. I presided over the board, regulating twenty-three thousand dentists for licensure and enforcement. My peers voted me as commissioner of the American Dental Association in Chicago, where I served on the national board as exams commissioner for five years. Can one person make a difference? I think Dr. Percy A. Fitzgerald did.

Very few problems cannot be helped by coffee, wine, or chocolate.

If severe, call upon Jack Daniel's.

# CHAPTER 17

## *Shirley in Five Minutes*

*Newly wedded, newly graduated*

Shirley Bailey is a five-foot-eight, confident, attractive, and easily approachable woman. She usually wears a smile or moves purposely to her destination. Shirley is highly intellectual, well educated, and conversant in most subjects of the day. Shirley is a leader and has held the office of president in many organizations. Some of these are professional or as chairman of boards or charitable and philanthropic organizations.

No shrinking violet, Shirley will not hesitate to share her views, whether asked or not. Shirley is the oldest of three, born in Monroe, Louisiana. Shirley lived in Detroit, Michigan, for about ten years until her family moved to California when she was in her teens. Shirley attended two historical black colleges: Fisk University and Howard University College of Dentistry. Shirley married a surgeon, Dr. Henry Dan Bailey, and they became parents of four amazing children. Their children are all successful professionals. Her children and grandchildren are a great joy and an integral part of her retirement activities. Shirley enjoys her trips and times with the family. A world traveler, she has taken dozens of cruises and hosts Camp Shirleywhirl for her grandchildren every two years, with some planned trips of adventure.

Shirley's career has been historical as a black woman dentist, the only woman in her class of eighty-one. She was elected by her peers the other officers of the board to the presidency of the California State Board of Dental Examiners, one is appointed by the Governor(Jerry Brown) to membership on the Board. Officers are elected. and was voted a commissioner of the American Dental Association in Chicago (joint commission on national board exams) by her peers. She was the founder of the Association of Black Women Dentists, a Kellogg fellow to the National Roundtable on Quality Assurance, and a distinguished alumni of Howard University, as well as receiving many civic and professional honors and awards. She is proud to have had the privilege to serve her community.

Shirley is full of appreciation for her loving parents and for their sacrifices for her education and cultural development. Shirley believes happiness is a choice, and she chooses to be happy. Does she have challenges? Absolutely. Is her bucket list complete? Not at all; there are many more things she would like to do.

Who is Shirley? Depending on who you are, she may be Dr. Shirley Bailey or a licensed real estate broker in California and Nevada—she may be called broker Shirley Bailey. To her best friend and classmate,

Shirley is Birdie. To her grandchildren, she is Shirleywhirl or G-ma. To her Southern friends, she is Shirley Anne. At Las Ventanas, she was Adeline's daughter, and to her children, she is Mom.

Who is she? She is a blessed servant of Almighty God, Jesus Christ. The teachings of the scriptures and gospel have given her the security to know she can do all things through Christ, who strengthens her. Shirley knows God has a plan for her life. She embraces lifelong learning and meeting and enjoying people.

Music and playing the piano, watching sports, dogs, good food, and wine are also fun pastimes for her. Her passions are old friends, old movies, and early music. Necessities for balance are travel, some time alone, and time with her family. For Shirley, there is always room for the company of good people.

Other times are spent on the computer, taking pictures, reading, and playing bridge, poker, or board games. Shirley has discovered a great church. Being a part of that Christian community is an integral part of her life. Being active and trying to stay well—that's Shirley.

Raise your words, not your voice. It's the rain that
makes the flowers grow, not the thunder.

—Rumi

# CHAPTER 18

## Married Life, Communication, and Challenges

*Henry Dan Bailey, MD*

While our lives as a family and our careers as professionals were progressing rapidly, time together, getting enough sleep and rest, and talking were not as easy to grasp. Four children growing up and our busy lives of school and shopping, meals, and relaxation seemed harder to lasso. Even with a live-in maid and help on the weekends from Allie Smith, getting everyone together became a challenge. Everyone had a life, activities, friends, hobbies, family, and holidays, which sometimes seemed too much for Dan. Sometimes it seemed too much for the children and me too.

Dan was not verbal about his feelings, even in the most intimate of situations or most casual of communications. He let his emotions build up, and then he would blow. He would hit a wall or punch a door. When we were first married, I had never experienced this type of behavior or seen any display of emotions such as this, and I called my parents. It was frightening—I thought he was having a seizure. If not that, then I thought he was mentally ill. Not a lot was known about depression in the sixties.

My father spoke to Dan in terms of his managing himself in a safe and sane manner: "Take a walk. Think things over. Talk about your pain or displeasure. See our minister. See a doctor, but keep it out of your marital relationship because your wife is frightened."

Get help! Mind you, this was 1961. We knew little to nothing about mental health, anger management, or any of the parameters of mental illness.

Dan believed that actions spoke louder than words, and he used symbols of gifts and flowers. He was generous to a fault. His florist bills averaged hundreds of dollars; he'd send me roses as an apology for his often-unexplainable behavior. Likewise, gifts to the children were to account for his absence at dinner or his need to sleep or have quiet and downtime. Dan relied on gifts of expensive jewelry to express affection and love, where he seemed to think he could not make those expressions himself.

At many points, it became difficult for me to manage Dan and the children. When Dan arrived home, there was a tension around him, and his problems became everyone's problems. He could not sleep; he needed all the lights in the house on at night. He acted out of impulse, not reason, and he was perplexed a lot. He loved his family, and he loved me; he made sure we knew that. We loved Dan as well, and we made sure he knew we all loved him. But Dan seemingly had a deep well of sadness, a pit that could not be filled. It got to the point that I felt like I was walking on eggshells when he was home, as his emotional stability was so fragile.

Help was needed. We went to counseling but to no avail. Dan could not take it seriously. He was a brilliant surgeon and would not accept that he had a problem that he could not take care of. He had great pride in having a family and in providing for his family. He had to adjust to my parents and others giving me gifts; he'd say, "Don't they realize I can take care of you? You don't need anything from your family or anyone else." These were difficult times!

His mother was a Jehovah's Witness, and gifts were not exchanged. Our family backgrounds were different, for sure. I knew he was not happy as a young man and had left home at age fifteen, but I viewed him as an extremely brilliant person. Dan graduated at the top of his medical school class and was so smart that he might be a bit eccentric but not to this extent.

Dan wanted me to give up dental school and a career and to be pleased to be solely his wife. When married me after I'd completed my first year in dental school, he knew I was excited about my career and family. My life and career were not responsible for Dan's issues. This was about him—his background, his undiagnosed depression, and unknown depression. Love or religion was not a cure. Did we need a lot more? We were smart, young, and hopeful, and we loved each other.

The phenomenon that was emerging in the sixties was pharmacological—a pill for every ailment. Stay awake with Dexedrine. Go to sleep with sleeping pills. Lose weight with Eskatrol. For headache or anxiety, take Valium. As soon as birth control pills (Ortho-Novum) came out, I was all for it. Dan wanted seven or eight children, but thanks to that pill, we stopped at four children. He used to joke that once I graduated, I was able to write my own prescriptions for birth control pills, so we had only four children. After we got the longed-for son after three beautiful girls, that was it. I hated pills and cannot swallow them to this day (due to a traumatic fish-bone issue as a child), I would chew these. They did the job.

Because of Dan's long hours—surgery in the morning, the clinic during the day, office hours in the evening, little sleep—he began taking amphetamines. He took them in residency training for the long shifts and now was taking them again. But for every action of a drug, there is a reaction—side effects.

As a girl growing up, I only knew of a few remedies for things. Castor oil was number one, Vicks salve was next, and turpentine on a spoonful of sugar was next, a cure all for phlegm and coughs and congestion.

Iodine was swabbed on my tonsils often. I wore an *asphidity bag* (a leather pouch filled with pungent herbs) around my neck to keep away colds. (These were Grandmother Big Mama's remedies.) Bayer aspirin was the wonder drug, as well as cough syrup and cough drops.

I knew little to nothing about depression at the time. I had studied schizophrenia in school and thought I was quite learned about the types: simple, hebephrenic, paranoia, and catatonic. But what I was seeing in Dan was the regular storm of a helpless person who needed help and could not and would not receive it.

For Dan, marriage was children, as many as we could have, and enough to eat—the refrigerator was a testament to success and home. He was not a motivated social being. He could tolerate short spurts of social activity, but it was a sacrifice for the children and me. He knew it was vital for him to be there because he remembered how he felt when his parents had not shown up, even to his graduation from medical school. That seminal event was harrowing for him. His classmate and friend John and I tried to comfort him, but this triumphant occasion turned sad. That memory—the lack of recognition—did not fade away.

His mother was a Jehovah's Witness, and his father was a Christian. They loved Dan, but something had happened in his home life that was far less than pleasant. I do not know and do not want to know. I heard many stories, but Dan never spoke of it.

Dan enjoyed cooking, I bought him the *New York Times* cookbook, and he made a brown sauce and many others, including bearnaise and white sauces. He loved to cook duck with orange sauce and lobster and, of course, barbecue. He worked as a bartender at Norbeck Country

Club outside of Washington, DC, as a student and learned to make all kinds of drinks. Whiskey sours with egg whites were a favorite; he also enjoyed and collected wines. He loved doing all kinds of flaming dishes as well. To entertain the family, he made many different courses and changed table linens in between. He even made his own sorbets for palate cleansing between courses. As grand a time as we enjoyed having like a great holiday, as low a time we could have. The lows of depression would arrive with Dan and neither of us knew what it was. Not even that name depression. We saw it as irritation, exhaution, tired, bored etc.

When Dan was in his twenties, he suffered from hypertension and took medication for that, but his anger outbursts were routine. He did not suffer fools well. He could be funny, loving, fatherly, and happy in the backyard, grilling or smoking meat with his mesquite wood chips that he soaked and placed on the coals. He was extremely patient in cooking, less so in dealing with people. He was so very proud of his children and family. He approved of my choices for their private schooling and education and involvement in social circles for the children's enrichment.

He never could figure out how this all happened, with me working in dentistry and being successful at that as well. I was a professional leader in women's dentistry, appointed by the governor to the state board. Dan told people, "I am the husband of Dr. Shirley," as his way of introducing himself. He was a board-certified surgeon, a great man in his own right, but he seemed not to know it. He had that bottomless pit no one could fill; no amount of recognition would ever be enough. He felt dwarfed by my success, and his way of coping was to make a statement identifying who he was; he felt the necessity to identify himself as my husband to feel comfortable about himself. He was trying to be humorous, but it never came off like that. We just went forward until we saw a therapist. He was expressing a need for a void that was a bottomless pit.

Dan drove a Cadillac with a big trunk to hold his guns and hunting equipment. He would glide down the freeway with a big cigar in his mouth and Joe Cocker on the radio, playing "With a Little Help from My Friends." Dan was perfectly content with the simple things in life—food, family, and home. He was amazed by the success of his children. All were admitted to the best schools—Paula to Harvard, Pam to Yale, Patricia to Yale, and Dan Jr. to Notre Dame.

All his trepidations about my career, All his efforts to stop me from going forward in my career, now his daughters were on the brink of careers. They grew up so fast. He was consistent; he did not encourage them to go into medicine or law or other professions. He harbored professional disdain for women, as did many males of the day, expecting them not to do anything but raise babies and be dependent on their husbands for support. Two-income homes were the new thing of the sixties, and that ushered in a cultural change in the world. What happens when the income of the wife equals or exceeds that of the husband? I can tell you, A lot happens to a Southern man especially who believe a womans place is in the home. Was the economic infusion a weapon or a tool? Was the extra money the root of all evil? Was it the source that made private school and opportunities for our family possible? Yes.

Private school for four was a lot of money, and two incomes certainly made that possible, as did two incomes for vacations and many pleasures of life. This was a life that our grandmothers never experienced. Neither of my grandparents ever left the United States. Our children had summer study and travel in Europe and opportunities like Jerry West basketball camp for Danny while in high school.

These thoughts and beliefs about women in the workplace continue to exist; abortion rights as well. Not only are they insipid in the thinking about wives but daughters as well. I know you can love and respect a man for who he is, the authenticity of self, without knowing the balance of his checkbook. Hopefully, that will happen one day for women as well. This battle is not just cultural; it is real. It hits our daily lives, and our daughters have to be prepared for it—and our sons as well.

Optimism towards oppressive behavioral responses and attitudes is important; but difficult. My independence was always understated, never flaunted, as that was not my way. I valued family life as much as Dan did, having come from a structured, loving family life with stated values and a family willing to support a woman and her dreams for education and beyond. After twenty years Dan had not altered his views of Professional women and now had daughters. He was perplexed and proud at the same time.

I have maybe only one regret: we could have achieved so much more by working together as husband and wife. Dan wanted to hit a home run, rather than methodically and reasonably looking at investing and wealth-building as a team. His ego would not allow that. He saw himself, anthropologically speaking, as the hunter and the gatherer, the provider. I know there was no other template for him, so this is not a finger-pointing session. He felt love was doing everything for me and it was difficult to adapt to a sharing of that load.

In one sense, I can admire him for that. I can say he was a good man. His heart was a great one; his mind was another thing. This was a mountain he had to climb alone, and he was not prepared for it. He was a victim of slicksters who saw a doctor with expendable income, looking to increase it with flawed schemes of investing—this included mobile homes, post offices, you name it. He got letters of tax write-offs and never saw any of those paper dreams. One even absconded to Africa with $800,000. It is no consolation that Dan was only one of many of his medical chums who was caught in flawed banking ventures that never materialized. They knew that busy doctors had the money but not the time to explore the nuances of the offers.

If you take the time to get educated and take the time to make money, you must take the time to manage your resources. Again, Dan's love for our family and me was never in question. His pride and mind set up a destroyer. His need for validation and creating opposing forces was higher than the values we shared, and it became a constant source of stress for him personally and for me.

He had increased mood swings, side effects, and severe hypertension. He took medicine and mood-altering drugs. He drank a bit of whiskey—not much but regularly—and smoked cigars. He ate more and more poorly, coming home after family dinner hour except on weekends. He'd say he wasn't hungry then, as he'd eaten something quick earlier. So "life was getting more and more complicated, it was a bit of a mess." as I observed it. As a surgeon managing life itself daily it was too painful for him to believe he could be helped by a health professional such as a Psychologist etc. or we could be helped.

Counseling produced no verbal crystallization of his feelings or his desire to work on issues—silence, disbelief. And we tried more than one source of help.

My epiphany came in church. When the boat gets heavy, to save those on board from drowning, something has to go overboard. I was listening to Adele Rogers St. John, a guest theologian at the Church of Religious Science in Los Angeles, and on that day, I thought she was speaking only to me.

For the children's and my own sake, I knew I had to separate from Dan, as painful as that was. Everyone was overweight. Dr. Burack, their pediatrician, was concerned and had spoken to me. Dan was getting more and more extreme, and nothing was working.

A few years after we got a legal separation, Dan had a cardiac code in the hospital. If not for his being a few feet from the ER, he probably would have succumbed. He was resuscitated, and after a long period of stabilization, he was told he had to attend anger management for six weeks. This attack occurred after a board meeting, in which he got angry and stormed out of the meeting about discussions of under staffing of the hospital. This was a typical response to a problem for him, and finally, he saw a need for change, if he wanted to live.

The kids went to the completion ceremony for Dan's anger management course and saw their dad do a lot of crying as he stood before the group.

I do know that I loved Dan and tried to show him that I did. I know that he knows I did and considered me a friend, long after our marriage ended. Our family relationship continued for years afterward because of the children. He never stopped sending gifts and flowers to my mother and me. I was the mother of his children, and that was special to him forever. He considered the gift of children the most significant thing to ever happen to him, and he was a perfect father by being there, showing up for important things, and showing his love as best he could. He knew the importance of this because, for many reasons—(some justifiable; he had a brother with cerebral palsy)—he did not have that in his life.

He did not want his children to experience that pain. For example, His parents did not come to his graduation from Medical school which was so painful for him. We were expecting our first child. They had thought being a teacher would have been well enough for him. Dan left his home in Florida at age 15 on a tuba scholarship to Clarke college in Atlanta, Geogia.

Some years later after out divorce, Dan married a Filipino nurse, Marty—her name is also Shirley, but she was nicknamed Marty, as her last name was Martinez. Dan found happiness and love with her, until he was confined with a long illness and succumbed at age seventy-five in 2012. Marty is admired by me and all the family for her love and devotion to Dan during his life, illness, and beyond.

*Our Children*

*From Left to Right: Dan Jr., Patricia, Pamela, and Paula*

*Well done is better than well said.*

*—Benjamin Franklin*

# CHAPTER 19

## *Our Children*

I am blessed to have been born into a loving family. On my mother's side of the family, her parents set many traditions, customs, and standards. My mother was one of five children born to Rosa and Joseph Wilson. Mother's family—the MacDonalds and Wilsons, with large families of twelve to fourteen children—came from Alabama and migrated to Des Moines, years before my mother was born. Her upbringing was all in Iowa. Northern cold weather, snow survival, and preparation for the long, cold winters always was a consideration.

My father was just the opposite. He was born in Louisiana, the Deep South, into a small family. Dad had one brother, Leamon, but his mother cared for her five sisters and brothers. His traditions were different, but the dreams and hopes for a better future were similar. Making the best of segregation and oppression was instinctive, real in-your-face racism in the South at every turn. There were whites-only drinking fountains, lunch counters, and waiting rooms at bus stations and train stations. The colored waiting rooms and restrooms were far inferior to those for whites.

No one in our family had flown in an airplane when I was a child, so I never knew much about airports. I am sure it was the same there, as segregation was the law. I did, however, become the first in our family to fly. It was on a TWA flight from Nashville to Los Angeles when I was a college student, going home in the fifties. It took a lot of pleading to get my dad to allow me to do it, but he did. The Sunset Limited train that I'd taken to school and usually rode home would have taken three to four days, with a stop in St. Louis and a change of trains.

I recall this now because our children received the benefit of our dreams to find a better life, and when the doors of opportunity opened, they were more than ready and prepared. Paula went to Harvard University, Pamela to Yale University, Patricia to Yale University, and Danny to Notre Dame University, all noted as among the best universities in the nation. Our kids were pioneers as much as we had been. They forged toward new horizons and had no template of their predecessors. They faced different challenges than my siblings or I ever met.

## Paula Lynn Bailey-Walton, November 12, 1962

Paula is the firstborn child of four children. She is a poised, elegant woman. Paula is slender and walks gracefully, with exceptional posture. She is highly intelligent and possesses enormous faith and fortitude. She is a specialist in internal medicine and a generous humanitarian, beloved by her patients and her peers. She is the mother of three daughters, Sofia, Sydney, and Shelby. Paula resides in Santa Clarita, California.

As the eldest in any family, there is that unique commonality to all, which is the mantle of being first at everything. Paula has worn it well.

When Dan and I married in June 1961, we were medical and dental students at Howard University in Washington, DC. We welcomed our firstborn, Paula, into the world at 5:19 p.m. on November 12, 1962. She was 8 pounds 5 ounces, a beautiful baby girl with a round face, big brown eyes that focused right on you, and a playful smile that made you think she knew something you didn't. She was the joyful bundle we rushed home to hold and cuddle at day's end. A friend's grandmother, Mrs. White, came to our two-bedroom apartment on Marietta Place in northwest Washington to take care of Paula. Dan was interning at the time, and I was a sophomore in dental school.

Within a year and one day, Paula had a baby sister, Pamela, born on November 13, 1963.

By the time Paula was two years old, she was boarding a school bus on those cold winter mornings in Washington to attend the Barrie School, an excellent private preparatory for Sidwell Friends School. Paula thrived there and enjoyed it. We soon welcomed two more children: Patricia, born May 25, 1965, and Dan Jr. on August 5, 1967.

Our plan was to be moved and settled by the time Paula began school. We were closing in on this plan. Dan was now a general surgeon, and I was a dentist; we had passed our boards and were ready to begin our careers. We found a beautiful home—maid's quarters, a swimming pool, lots of built-ins, travertine floors, beautiful neighborhoods, and everything we were looking for and more. A trip to the neighborhood school and examination of the curriculum revealed that Paula had read all the books and course material offered at Windsor Hills School at the Barrie School in Washington, not only for the first grade but for the second grade as well, so public school was no longer an option.

Our search for a private school first led to thoughts of church schools. Traits of good character, faith, confidence, and respect for others would be reinforced in this type of environment, and that was something we highly valued.

After weeks of exhaustive searching and inquiries, we found Pilgrim School. This was the school of the First Congregational Church of Los

Angeles. As the years went by, we were grateful for the education and values our children acquired, as they all attended through the sixth grade. The Buckley School in San Fernando Valley was to be the middle and high school for our children. Founded by Dr. Isabel Buckley; she held a strong belief and offerings in a core curriculum, with all the arts and humanities, assuring the students' admission to the finest colleges in the nation.

Paula was able to spread her wings at Buckley, a campus-type of school much larger than Pilgrim, with a football team and sports and a large art department. With her orthodontic braces, and a tall, five-foot-nine,frame she was a thin, graceful girl with impeccable posture. She walked tall, although inside, she did not always feel as strong as she appeared. A very caring, humble spirit, she was likable and friendly and could play the piano. She played volleyball, loved music, and liked to dance. Paula was on the cheerleading squad, was an honor student, and was elected as student body president. But her most significant high school accolades came not from graduating magna cum laude or getting accepted into every school she applied to—Harvard, Yale, Brown, Stanford, University of California at Berkeley, and Princeton. It was her starring role in *Hello, Dolly* as Dolly Levi. She was sensational! A portrait of Paula hung in the school foyer for some years. Carol Channing attended the show, and the costumes were from New York at the cost of over $78,000 in the seventies. Merv Griffin's son and countless other Hollywood celebrities' children were in the production, as well as Pamela, Patricia, and Danny. This production was a huge success. This was Paula's big year. She was top of the heap, a number one!

This all followed her presentation as a Links debutante in the annual cotillion at the Century Plaza Hotel in Century City. She was presented by her father and to her mother. She took her first dance with her father and then with her escort. We dined and danced the night away; this presentation was the culmination of months of volunteer work done by the debs in places such as the Junior Blind and nursing homes, to assist those in need and to learn about service to others.

Paula selected Harvard as her college of choice. She majored in English, even though she knew she was going to become a physician, because she wanted a well-rounded education, not just the sciences of a pre-med curriculum. Paula danced through Harvard, earning a scholarship to the Royal Academy of Dance in London and a silver medal at graduation. She enjoyed full campus life and studied many subjects.

King Juan Carlos of Spain was a commencement speaker, and upon conferring degrees to the graduates, the president of the university said, "Welcome into the company of educated people"—a new and memorable comment.

Paula was recruited to medical school at Bowman Gray Medical School in North Carolina, and after graduation, she interned at Kaiser Permanente Hospital at Hollywood Sunset. She then opted for private practice after becoming board certified in internal medicine. She joined a group practice for a couple of years before opening a practice in Beverly Hills with a colleague, where she practiced for the next fifteen years.

Paula married Les Walton in 1994, and they became the parents of three beautiful daughters: Sofia, Sydney, and Shelby. The marriage did not last.

Sofia, their eldest daughter, graduated from Spelman College in 2018, Sydney graduated from Spelman College in 2020 and Shelby is currently a Sophomore.

Paula's relationship with her family and extended family has always been important to her. She regularly keeps tabs with old friends, and she values family. She cherishes the family values she grew up with and teaches them to her children: appreciation, thanksgiving, love of God, respect for others, and being the best "you" that you can be.

In 2004, Paula was stricken with a debilitating medical condition. She was attending a wedding with her family in Atlanta, and while crossing the street, her leg and foot gave way without provocation, and she fell in the road. She was treated for a sprained ankle and foot, and a boot was placed on her. It took two years, and many theories before a correct diagnosis was finally made.

The condition manifested itself next in both feet, making driving impossible, so hand controls were installed in her car. Medications were administered to alleviate symptoms, but still there was no diagnosis. She went to Cedars Sinai and UCLA and saw the best-recommended specialist, yet none gave a definitive diagnosis, just a series of changes.

Then she had intolerable pain in her elbows. It was finally determined that the myelin sheath of her nerves was being destroyed, leaving the nerve exposed and painful. Various medications were tried, and additional complications were apparent. Paula was in a wheel chair for months and crutches.

Paula was very ill and thought of giving up, but something within her kept fighting. Of course, she had the love and support of her family, friends, and children, but she also had pain and fears and thoughts of life in a wheelchair, multiple sclerosis, lupus, and many other dreaded things that attack women and men in their forties. There were dark days, doubts, and fear of the unknown, as none of the doctors seemed resolute in their diagnoses. But, here again, as that eldest child, leading in her way, she somehow held on and was determined to make it through. Few know the complete trials of her journey. Paula could only muster a faint smile at most; laughter had disappeared. There was a realistic gloom of the unknown, what was next, and real fear. Because doctors know all the good and the bad, being a patient is challenging.

She endured three surgeries, months of hospitalization, agonizing pain, and giving up her private practice after fifteen years, but she continued to practice medicine in group-practice settings with a schedule compatible with her tolerance.

I share Paula's story because she is a woman I have loved and nurtured since that evening in 1962 when she came into my life as my firstborn child. She is a dear friend as well as a daughter and a woman I admire for her courage and tenacity and for her love and devotion to God and her family through her determination and faith. She is showing her daughters and others that challenges may come, but you have a choice to keep going or stop.

Paula does not claim to be exceptional, near perfect, or anything close. She does consider herself blessed, in the favor of God, and a woman of faith. She believes her best days are still ahead, and she is grateful for all her blessings and the beautiful life she has. She has the sacred privilege of helping her patients as a physician, understanding with compassion the condition of those seeking her help. Paula has love a wonderful man, Attorney Raleigh Saddler and friendship in her life. With the health that she is grateful for, she knows life could be much worse. There are bumps in the road, but no journey is complete without them.

Today, Paula functions normally. She drives without aids. She has adapted to multiple pain-management techniques, as well as medications. But most wonderfully, Paula is smiling and laughing again because her neurological challenges have been managed. She works out, swims, and is physically active. She loves her medical practice and patients in Santa Clarita at Heritage Sierra Medical Group, where she has been for the last four years. She has to take care of herself, but life is good again for her. Paula continues to help her patients live their best lives with whatever medical challenges they are facing, and she is a blessing to her family. Her children are thriving and preparing for their futures,even in this unprecedented time of Covid 19.

### Pamela Ann Herbert, November 13, 1963

Pamela, our second-born, arrived on November 13, 1963, after we had Paula's first birthday party. I delivered Pamela the following morning, one year and one day after Paula.

Pamela was a gorgeous baby girl with big, soulful eyes and curly black hair.

The year before, after giving birth to Paula, I stayed home until the Thanksgiving break and returned to classes at Howard University Dental School after that. I did the same with Pamela, although on the tenth day and my first day out of our home, the world was turned upside down with the tragic assassination of President John F. Kennedy in Dallas, Texas. The nation's hopes and imaginations of great things with this president vanished in an instant, and the world fell into deep mourning.

Dr. Harry Martin, my obstetrician, had been so encouraging to me as a student mother in professional school, saying, "Pregnancy is not a disease. Continue—you are healthy." My husband, Dan, as loving and supportive as he was, wanted me to quit dental school and be a full-time mother. My leaving school was not to be.

Pamela was a sweet and good baby, she had a few formula difficulties with Similac. We changed the formula—some with iron, some without—until she was able to enjoy her formula comfortably. We used to drop Paula off at a sitter's home and pick her up after school. Two babies were a bit much, but we were fortunate to have Aunt Eleanor come to stay with us, along with her small child, Linda, and she cared for both babies during the day. She came from Williamsburg, Virginia, where Uncle David was a minister.

Linda was not developing typically, so Aunt Eleanor was hopeful that better medical attention was available in the large District of Columbia area. The arrangement worked well—until it didn't—the accounts of Aunt Eleanor are written elsewhere in this book.

Aunt Eleanor adored Pamela and called her "my baby." She did an excellent service for our family in caring for Paula and Pamela at a critical time in my life. I will always be grateful to Aunt Eleanor and Uncle David for the lift we received at that time.

Growing up, Pamela and Paula were mentioned in the same breath as they was so close in age. Years later, Pamela expressed her need to have her independence and to be considered more individually. She has built her adult life in that manner as an emergency room physician, wife, and mother.

Looking back, I know it was complex all around. My dreams were to complete my education and have a family but in that order. That was not my husband's plan. Before I knew it, we had four children—"The children" were for better or worse grouped. Activities were planned for all of them, little individuality was ever thought about until their teen years and Jack and Jill, a national organization we joined where they were grouped by age again. So Pamela was always paired with her older sister.

Pamela enjoyed horseback riding, which was introduced as a Jack and Jill activity. We continued private lessons. Pamela excelled at horse shows, with jumping and dressage. She had the jodhpurs, boots, and helmet needed for these skills. The stables were in Sunland, where Elisabeth Taylor rode while making her movies involving horses, *National Velvet* in particular.

Pamela was a beautiful Debutante in the Links Cotillion with her voluntary service and community work hours. All the family came to see her presentation by her father to me and see her take her first dance with her Dad before joining her escort who was Stephen Frazier. It was a beautiul event. friendships were made with about 30 other girls as well through their volunteer work, meeting and rehearsals.

Pamela was a good swimmer, was on the swim team at Buckley She was also a cheerleader at Buckley. The exposure to as many activities as possible was the benefit I could give our children by working and having the extra income for the perks.

Pam did a summer study in London and traveled to Paris, Spain, and Italy while in high school. Pamela graduated cum laude with honors from the Buckley School. She served as the Student body President and was accepted by all the schools to which she applied. She chose Yale University, where she prepared herself for medical school. She graduated and succeeded. Pam was heavily recruited for medical school and chose one in North Carolina, the Bowman Gray Medical School, associated with Wake Forest University, because it was a great university and offered her an attractive financial package.

Each of our daughters had unique Wedding's. Pam's was no exception, her wedding vows and ceremony were at the Beverly Hills

Presbyterian Church on Santa Monica Blvd and Rodeo Dr. The church was a beautifully decorated sanctuary creating a life time memory of beauty and elegance. Each Aisle had lighted candlelabras which illuminated when the beautiful bride walked down the isle on her fathers arm. Pastor Charles Blake married all three girls. Pam and Allen Herbert rode down Rodeo Dr. in a horse drawn carriage to the Beverly Wilshire Hotel for their reception dinner and dancing until they departed for the honeymoon. Pam and Allen an engineer from USC went shortly therafter to South Africa for their honeymoon and for Allen to enter into busines ventures involving energy with South Africans.

Pamela knew immediately, after doing her first rotation in the emergency room, that she wanted to do that specialty, and she has done that to this day. Pamela loves the All in approach to saving lives,making decisions, Helping people at their most vulnerable moment in their life times.

As her mom, I was most proud when she was in Washington, DC, and a massive snowstorm blanketed the city. As an ER doctor, her services were badly needed. They sent the National Guard to escort Pam to a hospital for her assistance in this snow-stormed city that had a number of accident victims. Standard travel was impossible. My little Pamela impacted the city with her skills and came to the rescue. She worked continuously until the matters were manaaged 24 hours later.

After some years, Pamela joined a travel team of ER physicians that flies to deliver care over several states, with a certain number of shifts per month. She has enjoyed that variety and has continued this travel practice. Today she is on the front lines of service fighting the Corona Virus as is Paula. All we can do is pray for their work and the safety of them and their teams. I have missed hugs and kisses.

Pamela is held in high esteem for the work she has done over many years in her communities. She has traveled to Nigeria, delivering volunteer health care services. She has bought, packed, and shipped hundreds of pounds of clothing and food to underserved countries through religious organizations and has stood tall when called upon.

In addition to her profession as an emergency room physician, she has been a proactive mother in seeking the best educational opportunities for Natalie, Nathan, and Noah.

Homeschooling was an experience and experiment that had positives and less than positives, but she tried it. It worked well for Natalie, leading to admittance to West Point Military Academy, from which Natalie graduated in 2017. What an impressive experience that graduation ceremony was. Natalie had an amazing experience there.

Natalie spent the next two years pursuing two master's degrees, one in Paris, France, and one in London. As of this writing, she has just returned stateside.

Homeschooling was not as suited for Nathan and Noah, so a return to a traditional model of school worked better and afforded them admission to the ideal universities for their desires and aspirations.

Nathan, interested in writing, filmmaking, and acting, is at Belmont College. As of this writing, he's doing an exchange in Shanghai, China, and is living with a Chinese family that speaks no English. He is studying Chinese and should be proficient after this immersion. He is also attending the university in Shanghai while there.

Noah, interested in designing race cars, wanted only one school, Purdue University, where he interned for two summers. He had been the summer commencement speaker, extolling the excitement of education and life at Purdue. He would only apply to Purdue, his dream school, against the sage advice of all who wanted him to have some safety schools. Prayers and blessings abounded and triumphed, as Noah is joyously attending Purdue University in engineering and is now in his sophomore year. Am I a proud grandmother? You might well say yes. Pamela and Allen job well done ! Pamela and Allen have been very supportive parents.

Pamela's achievements, recounted above, might be badges of honor alone, but there is more. Pamela has followed her passions, personally and professionally. She enjoys winter sports. This prompted her membership in the Four Seasons Ski Club. She enjoys regions around Park City, Utah. As an international traveler, she has traveled extensively around the world. She has taken study courses in life coaching, She consulted with and has helpfed many. This is possibly a consideration for life after the ER.

Pamela keeps in touch with family from the East Coast. She never misses recognizing birthdays, Mother's Day, and other times of celebration. I have enjoyed the cymbidium orchids she has sent over the years, gifts from Shari's Berries, and visits, no matter where I have been in the world. She was also devoted to her grandparents Adeline and Limuary, who she made a point to visit at least each year.

Pamela is a strong Christian woman who is blessed beyond measure. She is healthy and wise and independent. Why is it important to say this? Because every day, she meets a double-standard in society. On the job at the hospital, with the patients, she has comes to understand that she is not just working and practicing her profession but that she is on performance. This often unseen and rarely heard pressure is nevertheless present. Racism can be subtle but present. Nevettheless she has been blessed with an extraordinary career, professional experiences, life in South Africa and Virginia and Washingon,DC. Pamela, sis a proponent of designing the life you want.

For example, as a Black Woman Physician a patient might be heard asking,Is she a real Doctor? Many patients do not believe she could be a doctor—how could she be? She is black. Society is evolving but not as rapidly as you might think in some parts of the country. That is just the way it is. Pamela—and all of my children—deal with the reality of life. Racism and stereotyping are natural phenomena in our world. Accomplishing what my children have, what Pamela has is the exception, not a norm.

Therefore, they have learned to take each day at a time, and the same for people, until they give you a reason to see them differently. I'm not complaining; these experiences are basic survival instincts for people of color in America.

Pamela has always had a brilliant mind for medicine but also an instinct for business as well. What is ahead for Pamela? I believe it's whatever she seeks. She is comfortable in real estate development and has prepared herself as a life coach counselor with certified training.

I feel blessed to have raised a beautiful, talented daughter who is a strong and independent as a black woman, one who is making a difference in her community every day. Pamela is also a passionate mother with strong family values and enjoys unique and loving relationships with each of her children. I am also blessed to have a relationship with each of my childen that is thoughtful, loving, rewarding and caring.

We used different yet common values in raising our children, while providing them with the best educational start and support possible. We showed how we view the world, how we have personal relationships with God, and common Christian values. Today, we are all friends; we sometimes travel together and enjoy visits and holidays, but we have separate lives, to be sure. Like a garden, each flower has a unique color, texture, bloom, fragrance, and desire for growth and development.

Pamela is a beautiful flower that has come to full bloom. Her forecast appears to predict everything sunny and bright with little wind. Pamela's journey has been incredible, and I know that other than a storm here and a hurricane there, she is pleased with her journey thus far. I know that I am. I have great admiration for Pamela, as her Mother. She has faced the challenges in her life headon and took them on squarely working hard and leaning on her faith and family support. Pamela thanks God for her blessings, her work and her life which is abundant with love and gratitude.

Pamela is another blessing from God to all of us who love and treasure her.

If I picked a song to speak for Pamela it would be:

On the road Again
I just cant't wait to get on the road again
The life I love is making music with my friends
And I can't wait to get on the road again

Pamela is a servant of God in her dedication to her work and life and community. Her family and I love, admire and adore Pamela. To God be the Glory!

## Patricia Susan Cannon, May 25, 1965

Third-born daughter and our youngest girl, Patricia was a beautiful baby, with long hair and a cherubic face, arriving joyfully and smiling. She quickly asserted herself as a happy baby. She had a bit of curvature of her feet inward and had to wear a filaris splint for many hours each day. This was designed to direct her foot and leg growth to the correct position. She did not mind at all; she took it in stride. After the first year, she walked regularly.

From that sibling position, Patricia and her baby brother, Danny, who was to arrive two years later, had a vantage point of watching two older sisters go through triumphs and stumbles. I always used to reference the famous Clydesdale horses when talking to my children. The lead horses (Oldest children) have a challenging path, untrod before, while the horses behind (younger children)have the view of only the horses in front of them all the time. Or more simply put watch them and find out how to do it or how not to do it…what ever lesson was there It was not to be a template for the future for Patricia or Dan Jr. They would each take paths not trod before as well. The older two entered medical careers and the younger two said Law.

Patricia is a brilliant woman. I admire her character and qualities so much. She is a very sweet daughter and friend. Patricia's mind is like a steel trap—sharp and decisive. She is a quick wit, bored by the mundane and inspired by the greats. She does things well. Patricia is effervescent with her smiles, and her personality. She is adored by those who know and love her. She knows this too, as she is the life of the party, dancing and singing Michael Jackson songs knowing all the words. A believer in education, Her children Christopher and Coutnery attended Legacy academy and Sierra Canyon High School where both children have excelled in these pursuits of academics and in sports. Christopher, a football standout was offered a 4 year scholarship to Amherst college opting for Morehouse College in Atlanta where he is a Sophomore. Christopher is fascinated with finance and looks for a career in this field. Courtney, Patricias and Roberts daughter is a Senior in High school at Sierra Canyon.

Courtney, is like a clone of her mother in physical and intellectual characteristics. It is incredible to observe. Patricia is a funny, confident Christian servant, who practices her beliefs and knows how to count her blessings. She works in her church and has been a Sunday school teacher and evangelist, calling others to Christ. (You will hear more of this later.) Patricia and Courtney think of others primarily first. They are selfless.

Only a few years ago, I learned of one of Patricia's selfless acts that occurred in high school at the Buckley School.

Paula had been student body president, as had Pamela, Patricia active in student affairs also was approached by the mother of a student who asked her to not run for student body president because her daughter needed it more. Patricia said, "Sure, no problem" and she ran for student body secretary instead. She won; she was self-confident and did not mind stepping aside for another. (I was appalled when I heard this from my fifty-plus-year-old daughter only recentlly like it was nothing.) My immediate thought when she told me, after all these years, was, *That mother had some gall to put that pressure on my child.* But to Patricia, it was "no problem," and she was on to the next thing. Yale University and UCLA for Law School.

Kids knew little about the battles and the fight it took to overcome all the challenges just to have her at the Buckley School. For example, after Patricia took the entrance exam for Buckley, I went to the school to meet with Mr. Baumhoff. He wanted to speak to me about Patricia's admission.

"The problem is," he said, "you have two children here already."

"Yes," I said.

"How will you be able to afford a third child?"

"Tell me, Mr. Baumhoff," I said, "are the tuition bills paid for Paula and Pamela?"

"Well, yes."

"Then my next question is, did Patricia pass the entrance exam?" I asked.

"Well, yes. She did very well."

"Then, Mr. Baumhoff, what is the problem?"

"None," he said. "I will get your admissions packet."

I was in pre-primed fight mode, as Patricia and Danny had integrated the Pilgrim School nursery school of the First Congregational Church at Sixth and Commonwealth in Los Angeles. They were the first black children to ever attend. Dr. Dotson, a black doctor, had sued the school before our arrival. He won the suit but withheld his children from attending after the battle.

We had gone through hoops and loops to make this work. I wanted my children to have a Christian education, a hot lunch, and quality core-curriculum training versus the then-popular Montessori method. I wanted them to learn how to have respect for themselves and others in early education.

Well, this took some persistence and patience. Danny had to wear pants with elasticized waistbands only, so in assisting him at the potty, the teacher would not have to touch him. You pull the pants down on each side, and he could have a go. He was two years old. Patricia was four. Paula and Pamela were in the Seaver Building of the Pilgrim School and made many other adjustments as minorities.

The headmistress, Evalina Clark, was beautiful, very approachable, and very keen on being accessible and discussing educational options.

I had lunch with her before she left after some years, going to Orange County to assist Robert Schuller in building the Crystal Cathedral. It was an attractive offer for her, but I am sure her work at Pilgrim school and her efforts with Rev Schuler will stand and remain a testament to her achievements spiritual depth and beliefs.

Robert Schuller broadcast the *Hour of Power* for many years until his decline and death. His children and grandchildren have continued the ministry. The campus of the cathedral is a popular attraction at Christmas and Easter, with live camels and donkeys, as well as angels on wires, flying through the skies. The sheer beauty of the cathedral is a popular wedding venue as well.

Headmistress Clark cemented for me what I was looking for in early education for my children, and she made all the challenges softer. She has my appreciation for all time.

That interlude back to Pilgrim is a reference to the persistent fight and motivation it took for Patricia and all my children to obtain the excellent education they received. Then Buckley, where I transferred each child after the sixth grade, was about to give me grief with Patricia. I met with the headmaster, and I had that heart-to-heart. My dad used to say, "It's not the destination; it is the journey."

This memoir is recounting my need to remember the fight at every level for a quality education for our children. To our next generation, You need to know it takes everything you have within you but the journey and rewards are worth it.

One of the funniest and most memorable stories is about my granddaughter Shelby, Paula's youngest daughter, who attended Pilgrim years later.

I was living in Las Vegas and cherished driving my grandkids to school when I visited them. We would pray and sing the same songs I'd sung to my children—"A, you're adorable; B, you're so beautiful." Somehow we started talking about nationality and novellas on Spanish TV—Paula's live-in housekeeper was Spanish. Shelby, who was four at the time, learned a lot of Spanish by watching TV with Bere and speaking in Spanish to her.

Shelby was remarking about a Spanish soap opera actress, and I said to her, "Well, Shelby, thats wonderful but what nationality do you think you are?"

She replied, "Oh, me? I'm Korean."

She had no concept of herself other than the nationality of the majority of children she was in school with. She was the only black in her class; 75 percent were Asian, and she just naturally assumed she was one as well. That is a child's mind.

All of this is to tell of the racial influence in urban Los Angeles in the late sixties to the present time. I faced the same fights after the children left the Pilgrim School, each after the sixth grade, to attend the Buckley School. Now we were enrolling our third-born there and having to justify her admission because of race and stereotypes. Never mind that her father was a successful general surgeon and her mother a successful dentist. all our bills were current and paid. Our occupations were on the application.

The privileges our children enjoy today came with a fight for equality and a chance. It also came with our family knowing that education was the passport to a better life—an opportunity to maximize your potential and realize your dreams, as well as make your community and world a better place.

The road not taken for Patricia was medicine. Patricia came home after her freshman year at Yale University, sat in the family room, and lamented, "I don't know what I want to be, but I know I do not want to be a doctor."

"Great!" we exclaimed through the tears that were flowing as she spoke.

I said, "Decide on something—newscaster, journalist, or lawyer— but leave Yale with something, some direction. College is a place to find out what you like. who you are, what your strengths are and if you are lucky what you are passionate about.

Patricia had a first-love experience at Yale with Andre, a bright young man whose mentor was Cornel West. By graduation, that romance was over, and Patricia chose to study the law. She was admitted to UCLA Law School, coming home to California. She had her apartment and car and commuted to school every day. Life was beautiful. Four years flew by, and she graduated and then passed the California bar on her first attempt, with ceremonies at the Dorothy Chandler Pavilion. She was hired by Haight Brown & Bonesteel, a Santa Monica law firm with an office facing the ocean. Life was good. She soon left there, however, as she was researching for the partners and found herself in the archives and research all day—not the challenge she wanted.

Here comes the second big story about Patricia that I have found so inspirational. I tear up every time I relate it to anyone. Patricia left the private practice of law. The Public Defender's Office hired her. She worked there, defending people who did not have legal representation. She walked from her car to the downtown building each day, finding the grounds filled with homeless people sleeping on the lawn. She would go up to them and tell them Jesus loved them. She encouraged them to get up and give life a chance. She would leave them a card to go to the West Angeles Church of God in Christ. (She had been invited to this great church and its many ministries by Lulu Balton, a fellow UCLA Law classmate). Reverend Charles Blake, the scholarly minister and bishop, possessed a great entrepreneurial mind. He built a forty-three-million-dollar cathedral in the Crenshaw district, nourished many ministries and businesses of members. Soon the whole family joined West Angeles,Church.

I was empathetic to the homeless, but as Patricia's mother, I was more worried about my daughter. I always admonished her to be careful because many of these persons were mentally ill and could harm her. She continued with caution.

On a random visit to Los Angeles from my retirement residence in Las Vegas, Patricia and I went to the Magic Johnson movie theater. A security guard walked up to us in the lobby right after we had purchased our popcorn.

He came toward us and spoke directly to Patricia. "Do you know who I am?"

Patricia very put off. "No, sir. What is it? Have we done something wrong?"

He said, "No, but please look at me closely. Do you know who I am?"

Patricia answered, "Sir, sorry. I do not know you. Please excuse us."

He then said, "I am here today because of you."

Patricia turned toward him

He said, "I was homeless on the ground, and you encouraged me to get up and go to West Angeles Church. It took me a long time, but I remembered, and I told them what you told me. The pastor there had a member who ran a security service, and Magic Johnson had given them the contract for the theater. I was trained and hired. I prayed one day I would find you and thank you, and here you are!"

By this point, I was crying, Patricia was crying, and the guard was hugging Patricia.

This is the way she lives. What a moment! I admire Patricia so much. I could see God using our children for good.

Being a soap opera devotee and movie buff all her young life and having gone to Buckley with so many show business people, it must have been inevitable that entertainment law would become Patricia's specialty. She began with Barry Diller at Universal as legal counsel. She examined television scripts for content that would be ethically acceptable—what could be said and what could not—and legal contracts with actors, according to the television code of ethics. After about ten years, this company merged with NBC. There are many layoffs when a merger occurs, as the two merging companies each have employees for the same jobs.

One of Patricia's associates was slated for a layoff in the downsizing. This coworker's mother had cancer, and she was her mother's sole support.

This story is unbelievable even to me, but you will see how exceptional Patricia is.

Patricia went to the top brass and said to them, "Please do not lay off this woman. If you find her performance satisfactory, and it is just downsizing, please give her half of my job. She has to work; her mother is ill. I am married. My husband is a paramedic. We have two children, and we can get by."

They were so stunned that they agreed! They did this for a year and ultimately restored the employee and Patricia to full-time status. Obviously, that kind of empathy and leadership was noticed and praised.

Another Merger occurred between Comcast and NBC Universal a few years later. Patricia sustained her position and was promoted to Senior Vice President of Legal Affairs. She loves her job and is living her dream. She has a beautiful home with roses up an S-shaped sidewalk. She has a supportive mate in Robert and two beautiful children— Christopher is a sophomore in college, and Courtney is a senior in high school.

Their children have had the privilege of private school education and will be prepared for whatever their course of higher study will be. As parents, driving the children to football practice, games, soccer practice, and soccer games is all a part of being supportive parents. It takes encouraging their activities and sports as well as academics. This has been the formula for success and achievement. As parents they have tried their best, hopefully the children will catch the vision and light their torches.

Are there challenges at home and work? Yes, indeed! Is there stress and exhausted days? Oh yes, has there been a personal crisis that would cause many to stumble and give up? Yes indeed and counting.

All the difficulties of life have shown up, but Patricia has said if you want to see the rainbow, you must embrace the rain. Her Christian faith is strong; her love of God is constant and pure. Her devotion to people, known and unknown, is remarkable.

I see blue skies and clear sailing for Patricia's journey. What about you? I love you, Patricia. Your family and pet dachund Barney adore you. Like the song lyrics, "Ain't no sunshine when she's gone," you light up our lives and the lives of those around you. The party starts when you arrive. Glory to God for you and your life.

## Henry Dan Bailey ll, August 5, 1967

Danny was born in the eighth month on the fifth day and weighed eight pounds five ounces. The Boy, after three beautiful girls, at last had arrived—the prince, the namesake, that something greater than himself, a son. There were cigars, balloons, and candy. I had finally succeeded in producing a son for Dr. Dan. He looked precisely like Dan, and Dan was happy beyond words.

After becoming a mother to three unplanned pregnancies (by me at least, not Dan), this one had been a big decision—whether to try for a boy. John Anderson, Dan's best friend, and Emily had decided to stop at three girls. Two astrologers had told me that this time, it would be a boy. (That's where I was in those days not thirty yet).

Dr. Harry Martin, the most popular and handsome ob-gyn at Freedman's Hospital, delivered all four of our children. He was as happy as Dan when he delivered Dan Jr. Dan was called to National Guard duty before our release from the hospital, and my brother, Limuary Jr., brought me and baby Danny home from the Washington Hospital Center. Joy unspeakable was the only spirit that would closely resemble Dan's happiness. He loved all the children, but Dan Jr. was something special. Of course, he wanted a dozen kids, if I would have cooperated. I used to tell friends he wanted children so badly that he would have had them himself if he could have figured out a way. He had morning sickness when I did. That always made me feel better and made me smile.

Dr. Dan had gone to Riggs Bank for a loan, but was rejected. I was working at Group Health Dental Clinic with an excellent salary of $12,400 per year. I suppose I should be grateful to Riggs Bank, if they had said yes, and we had remained in DC, our lives might have taken a different course. Instead, we moved to California in Dan's first year, 1967. Baby Danny just months old when we moved.

The poverty programs and mechanisms of the Great Society program of my favorite president, Lyndon Baines Johnson, were in full bloom. Better opportunities loomed out west, with more possibilities for our young family at that time. Although skeptical and pessimistic about just about everything, Dan flew out to California, borrowed my Dad's Cadillac, drove back to get us, and drove us out to California. We both got Interns and Residents moving-and-settlement loans.

I then looked for a building to buy for my dental practice. I walked up to a lovely one-story duplex building with a vacant lot in the back that was occupied by Dr. Michael Epstein, MD, and Dr. Jeffrey Widen, a podiatrist.

I asked them if they would consider selling the building, that I was a recent graduate and only had five thousand dollars for a down payment would she take a note. Mrs. Epstein said, "Yes, $45,000 for ten years at four hundred a month."

This was wonderful; this was God.

Dr. Epstein moved to Westchester, where he rented for about a year or two before retiring and succumbing. Mrs. Epstein moved to Canada.

I had a tenant paying me $165 per month; this helped, and I got a job with the school district, fulfilling a lifetime dream of being a school dentist. I ran a mobile dental unit with preventive care emphasis— fluoridation programs and restoration of first molars. In the sixties, dental decay was the most prevalent disease in America.

I was finished by two o'clock every day and rushed to build my private dentistry practice. This worked well. Dan did the same and opened his private office on Santa Rosalia Drive in the professional building there. Both of us now had two incomes and stability in finances and family life.

Maria was our live-in housekeeper, taking care of Danny as a baby; she was loving and had sewed since she was nine years old in a factory in Morelia, Mexico. I planned the menus and she cooked the meals; she was like an extended family member.

At age two, Danny and Patricia integrated the Pilgrim School nursery. This was quite a big thing, but I made all the accommodations, and it worked. In the seventies, the church was taken over by Dr. Bradshaw, a John Birch Society conservative, and the school was impacted severely. The hot lunch program was eliminated. As a member of the parents commission, I could not believe what was happening. Money was diverted to private limousines, golf club memberships, and ideas that weren't Christian or educational.

Heated meetings occurred. It took some time, but Dr. Bradshaw was finally out. Many lost amenities were never replaced, but the survival of the school was stabilized. The Seaver family, who also were benefactors of Pepperdine University, had built the Pilgrim School but were not hands-on in these matters.

The sixties was a great decade, regardless. After John Kennedy's proclamation of putting a man on the moon, there was hope in every heart in America. *The Sound of Music* was a blockbuster musical, with Julie Andrews, Christopher Plummer, and children singing in the hills that were alive. The Beatles hit America in 1964 with a sound that put everyone into orbit.

The sixties were tumultuous as well, with assassinations like no other period in history. The killing of Malcomb X on February 1, 1965; the murder of Martin Luther King Jr. on April 4, 1968, and the assassination of Robert Kennedy at the Ambassador Hotel in Los Angeles on June 5, 1968. This was after the assassination of a president of this nation, John F. Kennedy, in 1963.

The sixties—I was married in June 1961; I completed dental school in 1964; Dan completed medical school in 1962. I became a mother of four children, all in the sixties—1962, 1963, 1965, 1967. We bought our first home in 1967 and moved to California.

The world was changing fast and furiously. Having Dan Jr. completed the cycle for us. We had new beginnings on every front. How did we handle all of this? We had more money than we had ever seen. Dan called his Mom and Dad and said, "We are rich." It was not true, of course, but our dreams were being realized and it was more money than Dan had ever seen. At last he felt his life was good.

Our home had a movie screen in the family room. I can't forget to mention our great custom-made green shag rug in the family room. Mr. Gladstone, of Gladstone Interiors, came to our home to help design our living room. He asked me to make him a cup of coffee, and when I did, he said, "Blue. You are a warm and generous person. I think your home should use blues."

We had a blue velvet sofa, an off-white crewel sofa, and crewel drape panels. The blue shag wall-to-wall carpet went down the halls and into the bedrooms; it was our season of blue. We had two off-white, down, wood-carved side chairs that still go with me everywhere, even today, over fifty years later. Our home was beautiful and comfortable, and we entertained a lot.

Danny got his first haircut at home by Mr. Latimore, my dad's friend. Danny did not like it and cried. As Danny grew, he seemed like an older soul—very pragmatic. Things needed to make sense to him—scouting, for example. He came home from a camping trip, quite angry and upset, and said that we, "as his parents, should have known better than to send him out in the woods with insects and animals when he had a perfectly good bed at home.". That ended scouting.

At Buckley, the Prince of Homecoming nominations were in process. Not hearing his name, Danny raised his hand and said, "I nominate Dan Bailey." He won, of course, and reigned supreme as Prince of Homecoming. He was a star football player.

As the fourth sibling, even as the only boy, it was tough for him, being last and waiting his turn for the spotlight, it seemed. The girls had debutante balls and graduations. Being the youngest did not suit Danny very well. He wanted to work, so,his first job was delivering telephone books to homes. These books used to be thick, five-pound mega-books that were updated annually. kids today do not know what this is.

I asked Paula to drive Danny on his route. He loaded the car carefully with hundreds of books. After a few hours of climbing stairs, strange people staring at him, dogs chasing him, and exhaustion, he and Paula returned to the loading dock, where he carefully offloaded the remaining hundreds of books and resigned the job.

Not to be deterred, I got him a job at Delta Air Lines as a baggage handler. He enjoyed this but could not believe the freakish things that were loaded into airplanes with luggage and all the mishaps that occurred daily. He earned enough that summer to buy himself an Apple computer and was proud of his achievement. I was proud of him too, as I knew the value of work is noble. His dad wanted him to have a life of privilege and not have to work hard like he did. We worked it out, and Dan Sr. was proud of him too.

By this time all the girls had left for college, Dan had adopted a new philosophy that was out of left field. He declared that our family placed too much emphasis on achievement. He believed that we were afraid of failure, but he wasn't—and it seemed he set out to prove it. This was shocking to Dan and me. All the girls had gotten the message

(Education is the key to a good life) and were taking advantage of every opportunity. My Lord, what was happening with our son? comfort and priviledge, a courageous drive to be different?. We were perplexed.

He was not excited by college, so we had to fill out his applications. Even so, he was accepted to Notre Dame in South Bend, Indiana, on a football scholarship. Jerry Faust was the coach; it was not the best time for Notre Dame. coaching. The campus is a sacred beauty. The football field is like a holy grail. What a wonderful place.

Dan had carpeting in his room, an elevator to his floor, and housekeeping services that cleaned the room. There were grand dining halls and a physical plant extraordinaire. When I went to visit him, he said: "I can take it, Mom." That brought tears to my eyes, and I cried on the way to the airport. He said that after football games, the way to celebrate there was drinking beer until they puked and peeing on the walls. He could not relate to this, week after week. That is what he meant by his comment that made me so sad.

It was also cold there and as different from California beaches as you could imagine. He was willing to tough it out but I said no son college should be fun as well as prepare you for a career.

He applied to Xavier University of Louisiana in New Orleans, transferred there, and had a good experience. After graduation, he was admitted to Howard University Law School. After his graduation from law school, he left immediately for South Africa to join Pamela and Allen in their business ventures. Dan was there for over two years, we were longing to see him come home. When he returned, it seemed he had more interest in business than the law. He discovered that South Africa did not want Americans in the market; they only wanted American investment. Allen and Pamela left there as well, but those were exciting years in South Africa. I was happy to have visited there for over a month with my mother, with Allen as our host.

Dan has lived the life of a bachelor extraordinaire. He spent quite a few years at Marina del Rey as a boat owner and loved to paint his boat and work on it, as boat owners do. Dan was gifted a Porsche 928, when he went to law school,(I am never late in my 928) license tag. He bought a Mercedes red convertible when he was at the marina and recently was gifted my Jaguar mom's gift to me, A Jaguar twelve-cylinder Cabriolet, only six hundred were made, which he still has. The prince has had a few toys.

Dan returned to the U. S. and took a position at Sony Studios, There he met and he fell in love with Marcela, a Hispanic woman with three children, and they were married. He was in love, and nothing else mattered to Dan. They had an elaborate wedding in a historic downtown hotel, with excitement, tall men, and entertainment into the night—a kind of Arabian nights affair, with sheiks and arabian dancing entertainment. They even dressed up the dogs that attended the wedding. It was another memorable event.

Dan and Marcela traveled a lot; he proposed to her at the Eiffel Tower in Paris. They were a loving couple, who adored animals. They had challenges, as one might reasonably expect; Marcela's children now had to share their mom, which caused issues, and there were other growing pains, even after moving to their own home. Marcella was a gifted head of IT at Sony and was a top executive.

All their shared love and happiness ended after eight years. Marcela is a brilliant and wonderful woman, whom our family embraced and loved. We continue to wish her happiness and blessings. Marcella has remarried and left the US to reside in Mexico.

Dan resides in New Jersey and is engaged to be married again. His fiancée's name is Juana, a brilliant woman loving and kind. They seem to be a strong team. I hope that they will be healthy and happy for many years.

Dan is happiest when working on hobbies with his hands and loves to build things, like porch decks and patios. He is very good at it. He also loves dogs and has several around him all the time. Being outdoors is a great joy to him.

Dan is a great son with a terrific sense of humor. He was a faithful caregiver to his father for some years. God has always protected him and stayed nearby to him, as well as his three sisters, and I adore him.

Dan, a brilliant free spirit and nonconformist, owns a company that allows him to work from home and do research, academic writing, tutoring, and consulting. He continues to travel the world and works from wherever he is. Dan has no biological children but always has had mates who have children, and he has been a wonderful father figure and friend to them.

He is happy, which makes me happy. Dan looks so much like his father that it is uncanny. He is loved by his sisters and family and will be there for them, if needed. He is the little brother who is the big brother, and our family is so blessed to have him.

Uncle Danny, Sonny (my pet name for him), Dan, HDB—he will answer to all of those names. No one ever called Dr. Dan or Dan Jr. by their first name, Henry, which is his paternal grandfather's name as well— Henry Cam Bailey, born on August 4, one day before Dan Jr.'s birthday. Danny is the son, brother, partner, and friend we will always admire and call. He has lived his life on his terms, and that keeps him happy.

He has created the freedom to do so. He has discovered that he enjoys creature comforts and a comfortable lifestyle as much as anyone, and he has always managed to obtain it. (That failure talk was only posturing.) Dan is brilliant and creative. He loves his hobbies. He's savvy and talented in computer skills, writing, and finance. He understands Bit coins and cryptocurrency investing and risks. Dan loves sports and his family and is a natural helper to those in need. Has everything been ice cream and cake? By no means.

He is completely selfless. When he and Marcela divorced, Dan took his beautiful memories only. He left her with all the material assets they had developed together, never looking back. Both independently have dealt with the pain and heartache of the ending of their marriage and have moved on.

Our family embraced Marcela and Dan with love during the good times, and we continue to cherish her and her children—Alex, Nicki, and Robert—and their eight years of a loving marriage as a part of our family.

I continue to feel blessed by the gift of Dan Jr., our young prince. Dan has brought me and his family love and joy and is as precious a gift today as he was on August 5, 1967. He is fun, dependable, brilliant, and loving, and he helps anyone in need. He is one of the most selfless persons you will ever know. I am sure that is why God always is standing near to Dan and gives him everything he needs.

Yes, God smiled on Dan Sr. and me with this gift of joy, the boy.

*"The Girls with Pearls" with Mom*

*Dan Jr. and Mom*

*Our Children Growing Up*

*Children Family Portrait: (From Left to Right)*
*Paula, Dan Jr. Patricia, Pamela*

*Hasten, Jason, get the basin; oops, slop, get the mop.*

*—Alzenia "Big Mama" Jordan*

*From Left to Right: Cary Booker Jr., Dan Bailey Jr., Pamela Herbert, Patricia Cannon, Cory Booker, Paula Bailey-Walton, Kimberly Jordan*

*The First Cousins*

# CHAPTER 20

# Home Is Where the Heart Is

The crystal chandelier in the dining room, which illuminated so many memorable family dinners at my parents' home when I was growing up, was passed to me, as the oldest child, when I married and we had our first home. Our new family also had many unforgettable family blessings, prayers, and dinners under the glow of this family keepsake. There were special announcements of honors, awards, and recognitions that called for a special dinner; there were birthdays or other celebrations. The memories mostly seem to be good ones, except when Dad announced he had cancer.

He had a lot on his heart that he shared with the family at the dinner table after dessert. I will never forget that talk. It was sobering and sad because our circle of life as a family rarely had been broken. We were proud of Dad as he recounted his life, from his roots to the heights to which he had risen and the blessings in his life. He also announced a handsome stock distribution to every child and grandchild and instilled his values about wealth and consumption and admonished us, "To whom much is given, much is expected." My mom stood by his side, as this was the most difficult talk Dad had ever delivered. He had great pride in his children and grandchildren. Dad knew he had been a great patriarch and family figurehead. He always had such a sense of humor, except on this day. This family talk will always be remembered.

The more common gathering were to share feasts of food, prepared by mom and many hands sometimes. Often, these after-dinner talks might be filled with messages of consternation as to some failing or shortcoming of one of us, and we dealt with it as a family. Once when I was the "keeper of the light"; I had great pride in cleaning the chandelier. I would spread plastic on the table and spray the prisms with a cleaning solution, and the prisms would drip onto the plastic and begin to glisten and sparkle. I always felt pride in a good cleaning job. I was good at sinks too. Even though we had household help, I enjoyed these kind of projects. Memories, memories.

Many years later, when we were about to move from our residence, my first thought was the chandelier. It had to stay in the family. It marked the beginning of decisions that, for many, were extremely difficult. I was no different. How do you let go of things that have become a part of you—traditions, comfort, enjoyment, and emotional satisfaction of collectibles, art, clothing, furniture, books, papers, pictures, crystal, china, lamps, clocks, straw baskets, old cameras, belts and hats that haven't been worn for years but have seemed too valuable to part with? The person with whom you shared that item brings a smile or a frown or even a laugh out loud. I have my carousels, my butterflies, and teacups, a few books I have not given away, and a few plaques and remembrances of honors from my peers. But my bowling trophies all had to go; my golf clubs, tennis racquets, softball gear was passed on. Why do I keep slips, girdles, and lingerie that are just pretty but not very useful? I regularly give away my purses, shoes, and clothing by the bagful to Safe Nest or Goodwill, but those contributions do not seem to make a dent.

I have so much office stuff—staplers, paperweights, pens, files, and notebooks of projects that it overruns my office. What is the fear of letting go or the attraction of holding on? I am not sure. I just can't seem to let go of papers. Some are treasures—old film from the Kodak projector, VHS tapes, 78 and 45 and 33 1/3 records and my old record player. Is this stuff a part of what provides the comfort of home sweet home? Is it the long association with the familiar? At last, I have stopped needing to own things. I can admire them, enjoy something, but I have lost that yearning inside that I must have it. I was downsizing and sending everything to the California kids.

Without regret, I called Miguel, my wonderful handyman, who is capable of doing everything, and he said he would handle the move. The holidays were approaching, so we shrink-wrapped all items; labeled them with a number for each household; put red bows on the sofas, dining room furniture, chairs, lamps, rugs, and so forth; and rented a twenty-four–foot U-Haul truck, and it was off to California and the homes for delivery. What was left went into storage, and over the months, slowly, more and more has been filtered out. For me, it has been a process more than a singular event; after all; we are looking at over fifty years of collections. There is the satisfaction, however, in knowing that my children are enjoying things that I enjoyed, and my letting go of things is progressing.

The chandelier is at the home of Patricia and Robert. It had been sitting in their garage for a year, so last year I took Miguel to Los Angeles to transfer the existing chandelier in Patricia's dining room to the breakfast room, and the family chandelier was hung, to the delight of all. Robert watched in amazement as Miguel carefully achieved the chore of hanging the chandelier, connecting the wires and prisms, and cleaning the dusty parts. Patricia placed cranberry-colored shades on the chandelier bulbs for holiday color. At last, it has been passed on and is still in the family. Christopher and Courtney will hear their family talks under the family light, and all the family will gather under it at their home.

A rather majestic heirloom chair in my bedroom used to be the cornerstone piece of furniture in my parents' living room, part of the Herndon collection of furniture. This collection has been in our family for seventy-five years. The chair has a pecan frame with a wide seat, cushion, and high back. The chair holds many memories, especially at Christmas, as our Christmas clothing and personal items would be put on a chair, and toys and other items were placed under the tree. My sister and brother each have a chair as well.

Passing furniture through the family has been an almost unconscious movement, no matter how far away we may live. It is actively practiced by my children today and almost taken for granted, which is a natural thing to occur. I am sure it will continue to occur for generations to come, as in our family, our homes are a place of gatherings of family and friends and cooking and entertaining. Having attractive, comfortable, and inviting furnishings has always been continuous and evolving; there is a bit of designing in each of us.

My mother said that my father's mother moved furniture so much while she held me that I inherited the need to move furniture, and each of my children move furniture continually as well. When you move it around, it inspires change as well.

There are humorous stories, as we have said, "If only that couch could talk." My brother-in-law, my sister's husband, was a very eligible bachelor who lived in the apartment below me when I was in dental school. He maintained a very fashionable place with an extraordinary black leather sofa that was about nine feet long. Many parties occurred in that apartment, and when he married, the couch ended up with my brother, who took the couch to New Jersey. After some years, Dan moved to California, where he enjoyed the couch until he moved to New York, and the couch came to my home. We enjoyed it for a number of years until my brother claimed it again. The couch clocked many miles in a Mayflower moving van.

Every time I visit my children's homes, I find it fascinating to see what has been changed around, removed, or exchanged. It's an adventure. When I downsized in moving to Las Ventanas, I sent two truckloads of furniture over, and it's like being at home when I visit them. It's a real thrill to see my selections getting new life in my children's lives.

I guess we will call them family heirlooms.

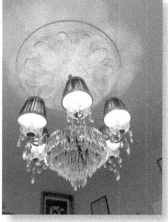

*Items that have been in our family for over one hundred years*

*When it rains, look for rainbows. When it's dark, look for stars.*

—unknown

# CHAPTER 21

## A Memorable Christmas

*Home on Le Petit Chalet, Queensridge*

The summer of 1999 not only was the final year of the millennium, but, in our moving to Las Vegas, it was the ending of thirty-two years of life in Southern California. It was the closing chapter of an extraordinary professional career in dentistry, as well as the closing chapter for home, husband, four children, earth mother, social and charitable maven, realtor, investor, and entrepreneur. I was sure that moving to this smaller city—the serenity of the Las Vegas community of Summerlin—would finally bring the retirement I had envisioned—quiet, peaceful, relaxed.

199

At Queensridge, a master-planned neighborhood, on a corner of the cul-de-sac sat s two-story five-bedroom home that was a beauty. It had a motor court fronting three full garages, Pebble Tec swimming pool, Jacuzzi spa, and built-in barbecue. Double entry doors opened onto a two-story foyer with a spiral staircase. This graciously invited you to glide up to the second level. It was beautiful, perfect, gated, secure, and I knew it was everything I was looking for—formal living room, formal dining room, casual dining room, walk-in pantry, a kitchen to die for, family room, large wet bar. It was a charming part of the Christopher Homes collection.

Within weeks, I was moving in and planning for the family to visit for Christmas. It had five bedrooms with loft areas, and the closets were custom-made and more substantial than many bedrooms. There were fireplaces in the master bedroom, family room, and living room. This was exciting—my first Christmas in Las Vegas was about to become an event. All the family was coming.

The foyer required a very tall tree. I had to get the bedrooms furnished, and I wanted to purchase a rosewood dining room set. There were not many furniture stores in Las Vegas, but I found a dining room set I liked in Chinatown. It had to be ordered, but I was assured we had the time; it was only September. A slow boat from China was my choice.

I began to stock wines, foods, towels, and paper goods. I prepared my table linens, crystal, china, and silverware, as I was expecting twenty for dinner. The children would have their table in the casual dining area, and I needed one highchair. Each family member was asked to bring their favorite dish. The dish was then named after the family member. Roasted Hen Turkey Limuary, Macaroni and Cheese Adeline, Rutabagas Marilyn, Roasted Candied Sweet Potatoes Paula, and so on. I would then print the menu and place it in a beautiful frame in the dining room—"Christmas Day 1999 Menu." Mother said she came across one of my holiday menus the other day.

Daddy would always carve the turkey. He made an art form out of it. First, he halved the bird and sliced the white meat and then the dark meat. He placed it on the platter, decorated with cranberries and pears or other fruits. We regularly served at least three entrée meats—roast pork, ham, salmon. Dad would always ask my mother's approval and called out, "Adeline, come here. Is this okay?" He would taste a piece too and always loved to get some of the stuffing that was inside the bird.

It took me a full day to set the tables. I had many beautiful table linens from our world travels, and I loved choosing my colors and new table appointments that were fun and interesting. I loved to decorate and have all the trimmings in place. There was a joy having all the babies and grandchildren, but sadness in our spirits, as my dad was battling prostate cancer, and my brother recently had been told he needed a heart transplant. While there was this cloud, there was just cause to rejoice, and we did.

Our family had grown rapidly, as my three daughters had married— two in 1994 and one in 1995. And now there were four grandchildren, and three more would be born in 2000. Obviously, our family had traditional dishes and recipes that were altered from year to year, as more and more ideas were available. But the meals were always the same. We loved good food and were blessed to have many good cooks; all learned from Grandmother Adeline, one way or another, with individual twists and additions to the traditional and plenty of good stuff.

Everyone was excited about coming; Cory was bringing his girlfriend, Shonda, to meet the family. Everything looked beautiful in the house. I had a cleaning company wash the windows so they were sparkling; the windows were huge, from floor to ceiling, up two stories. We could enjoy the serenity of the snow-capped mountains. They also cleaned the giant chandelier that was suspended high in the ceiling from a ten-foot chain beside the spiral staircase; only professionals could reach it to clean it.

The house was beautiful, with a garland ascending the stairs and a grand piano at the foot of the stairs. Everything sparkled and glistened with Christmas lights and presents. I used themed gifts for the kids. This year was pajamas for everyone who helped so much. At that time, we were still drawing names in the family for gifts. Mother always pulled the names and had the sizes to accompany the name you got.

It was time to check the delivery date for the dining room suite. I went down to the store and learned from the sales lady that there was some degree of uncertainty about my shipment arrival. After a discussion and review of my needs, I was assured that if it did not arrive that week, I could select a set to use as a lender until my collection came. As it turned out, that is what I had to do. I chose one that was close to the dark cherry finish of my set, but the cushions were not as soft or comfortable as mine, and after sitting for a while, we could notice it. I explained to all what had happened, and nothing was lost, although I did have a little anxiety over my set not arriving.

Everything was so beautiful, just perfect, and the family arrived safely. We shared many prayers of thanks that our family had so much to be thankful for. Our family scripture is the Psalm 121, and every child in our family learns it. We say it before travel and upon arrival and in times of needing the presence of God.

Arrival of the family brought on hugs, tears, and laughter. On Christmas Day, Daddy offered the blessing for the food and the occasion. We dined and enjoyed our festive dinner. We followed our cherished tradition of sharing, and each person around the table spoke about what Christmas meant to him or her. It didn't matter how long it took; there was reverence and the expectation of lasting words of love. This also was a time of affirmation, of belonging, of having a place within the family. It was intimate togetherness and cherished family time for all—cherubic babies, the young and the old, and the celebration of Jesus.

We remembered our grandparents and from whence we had come; we remembered our parents and the sacrifices made for us to have the type of lives we were so blessed to live—the education, abundance, health, and fruitfulness with which we were blessed. Those moments made the memories that we cherished. The words spoken were branded into our hearts. The young sat still, the old shed tears, and all were grateful to be a part of a special family.

My father instilled in each of us that if someone in our family had lost their way, If he was a scoundrel; He was our scoundrel. It was our family, and we should love one another and learn to forgive. We were always encouraged to have our reach exceed our grasps, to live by faith, and to serve God and our fellow humans. We were to marry off and not carry on and to remember who we were. He also told us "A man is known by the company he keeps."

After the sharing and tears and sniffles came the opening of gifts, if not already done; kids' gifts were early in the morning. Then we would find our favorite things to do—jokes, laughter, card games, and board games, after the food was put away, and we each did some part of clearing and stacking dishes. Everyone was full, happy, and blessed. What joy! One of the children would play "Joy to the World" on the piano, and we would sing Christmas carols. Our babies were hugged tightly and kissed as they giggled and clutched a toy.

John 3:16 said, "God so loved the world that he gave his only begotten Son." Theologians like to pause at the word *gave*. God was a giver. One thing is sure: you can give without loving, but you cannot love without giving.

Daddy passed away three years later. The Christmas 1999 is one of my fondest memories, as Daddy and Mother were so happy at the sight of prayers answered and the goodness and promises of God before them—children, grandchildren, and great-grandchildren.

Fifty years prior to that Christmas, our family had arrived in California in a car with a U-Haul trailer. We moved into a house, and my dad had worked night and day to obtain a better life for his family. I thought about Mr. Henry Carroll, who told my father when he left Louisiana back in the fifties, "A rolling stone gathers no moss."

Christmas, a religious holiday celebrating the birth of Jesus Christ, has come to mean so many different things to people over the last decades. The commercial emphasis on sales has had a dominant grip on our culture for many years. Christmas trimmings and trees begin to appear in stores in August, before Halloween and Thanksgiving. There is also the call for the equality and inclusion of all cultures. If you place a Christmas tree, you must also place a menorah.

This change has the country taking the name of Christ out of Christmas, using "holiday season" instead. This change is to honor other cultures. Christmas tree lots, Santa Claus and reindeer, wreaths, and eggnog are other cardinal signs of the season and the traditional music that begins earlier each year. The songs and music start on the airways the day after Thanksgiving on every radio and TV station, after Santa Claus has come to town during Macy's annual parade. From then on, the season is on! Pull out the decorations, pull out the party clothes, make the beauty shop appointments, get the tablecloths ready, polish the silver, and get ready.

Even with all the changes, from the time I was a little girl, it has been the most magical time of year. Traditions within families are born and practiced each year. They are always special times; we make every effort to make people we know feel special, loved, and appreciated. Hallmark does an excellent service every year, making greeting cards relevant to changing lives; they create and maintain an American sensitivity to not just the birthday of Christ but the meaning of his teaching's. We reach out and send peace and goodwill through words and pictures that touch lives, spreading the gospel.

For me, it has always been apparent that this is not a time that just happens; there is careful preparation, planning, list-making, trips to the post office, standing in lines, supermarkets bustling with people, smells of baked goods, and good things in the markets. The outside temperatures make for fresh, crisp air and bundling up to keep warm. The days are short, and the evenings have candlelight at home and Christmas lights that are enjoyed all month. We come home daily, enjoying our homes and cozy, warm, beautiful evenings by the fireplace, wrapping gifts, hiding gifts, and drinking hot chocolate and eating cookies after dinner, talking to friends, planning parties, and deciding what to wear.

With our large family, there was always a calendar listing everyone's parties and school plays, musicals, and church programs so that we could support everyone by being there. That meant Dr. Dan and Dr. Shirley gave their office staff notice of the times they needed to complete appointments so they could get to the school or church. Time was needed to see one or all of the children, dressed as wise men or as angels. Cookies and punch, hugs and congratulations—you could expect a lot of those. This continues now with the grandchildren, while the tradition grows. Those special moments in the sanctuary with the red ribbons and wreaths in the church and the voices of the children singing Christmas songs go to the heart of the season.

As the big day fast approaches, there are so many interests in our family—music, sports (football and basketball games), board games and card games. We have lots of big readers, but the food is a traditional memory of tastes of years gone by.

We grew up with excellent cooking. My mother made a beautiful home with all the formalities of dining at dinners, with all the particular china and appointments. Our tables and centerpieces were as elaborate as the food. Even the small children were trained to use good manners so they could appreciate the fine china and crystal used on this special holiday. While dressed up for dinner, they comfortably enjoyed all the individual appointments. Today, the traditions continue with my children and grandchildren. Breakfast is salmon cakes, fried apples, grits, egg frittata, hot biscuits, coffee, cranberry juice, and hot chocolate with peppermint candy canes. Breakfast is served at about 10:00 a.m.' dinner is at 4:00 or 5:00 p.m.

We usually have three types of meat: turkey with cornbread dressing and giblet gravy; boneless pork roast filled with garlic cloves; and duck or Christmas goose. In the old days, it was coon and possum, as well as sweet potatoes or yams candied with pecans; macaroni and cheese, made with Cracker Barrel extra-sharp cheese; string beans almandine; greens with ham hocks; rutabaga; jellied cranberries and a cranberry relish; hot rolls and butter; sparkling cider and cranberry juice; and sometimes a Jell-O mold salad. There also were sweet potato and pecan pies; chocolate and yellow cakes; ice cream; and bread pudding. The Christmas tree glistened, and red poinsettias brought color and excitement to the house. We all used them in our homes; they are so beautiful.

When everyone was full and happy with their gifts, we then talked to the ones who were not present. The telephone rang on the other side of the country, and we talked about the day and the gifts. "Did the pajamas fit? Did you like the color? I love you. I miss you. Thank you, thank you so much. Merry Christmas. Merry Christmas."

Amid the hustle and bustle of the season and the madness of planning and preparation, you add more—endless trips to the market, all the smells of spices and brews. You think about all the people you have greeted, the church musicals and tributes to Christmas you've seen. You finally come to the end of the day and sit in a comfortable chair, put up your tired feet, and feel a sense of fulfillment that only comes with giving. You smile that you have touched others in any small way, and you say, "Thank you, Lord." You take a sip of Christmas wine, close your eyes, and to all a good night.

*Progress is impossible without change, and those who cannot change their minds cannot change anything.*

*—George Bernard Shaw*

# CHAPTER 22

## Love Letters to my Grandchildren

Dear Shelby,

How are you?

I remember the day you were born and those dazzling little eyes, like a gem of light. You are still the embodiment of light and enlightenment. You have a unique ability to cut through the rhetoric and get to the point; in other words, tell it like it is. I remember when Oompa first was ill. No one was telling me exactly what was going on, and I asked you, and you said, "Grandma, I saw him, and he is sick," and sick, he was. That is the way it is: if Shelby is to give an answer, it's straight to the point.

I really enjoyed my time with you last month when you and Courtney and Christopher and I went to the movies to see *The Lorax*, the 3-D animated film. You are entirely a leader in conversation; you know what you want, and you know what you enjoy. You are happy when you can have it—pretty typical of an eleven-year-old.

You will be twelve this year—unbelievable! Noah was just twelve this week, and Chris will be twelve in August. The dozen cousins soon. (Three turning 12 this year). We had chocolate, In-N-Out, yogurt, Panda Express for dinner, and then a "poker game," all after the movie, and you guys had been to church while I was driving there from Las Vegas. I had not seen a 3-D movie since *Journey to the Center of the Earth*, when all the Herberts were here, and I was screaming, and you said to me, "Grandma, it is only a movie. This is not real." As the picture zoomed right in to my nose.

You are growing up so fast. It is always fun spending time with you and listening to you talk. You seem to have a viewpoint on most subjects and are eager to share it. I know you are spending some time working through last summer and all the changes that happened in your life and family, your home, and school. Young people sometimes are faced with crises in their lives. They don't always understand or like it, but they must accept that this is life and believe there will be a better day soon.

You are Paula's baby girl, much loved, born one day after her birthday, filled with her DNA, and filled with her teachings—her values on life, character, citizenship, and what is right and wrong. Your mother faced the biggest challenge of her life last summer. Neither she nor anyone knew what to expect or how to plan. Your mother managed those times with all the dignity and faith and grace that one could ever admire in getting out of the home on Victoria and getting moved and repositioned and adjusting her home, work, and health. You will come to understand, like each of us, the urgency of many necessary decisions in time, as more was unknown than known. You should be so proud of her accomplishments and her love for you, all of these days, especially when there were times you could not be with her.

She was planning for you. I am not minimizing your pain or disappointments in any of this. Just know there are many sides to a story, and there is the truth standing silently.

I am giving a voice to the love for you, a voice for my truth.

The important thing for you to always remember is that you are loved; you are unique. You are very important to our family; you are very precious as a daughter and a granddaughter, as a great-granddaughter, and you are thought about, cared about, prayed for, and planned for, and you are the gift of God that we are all grateful for. You need to remember that in difficult times.

I think of you as my granddaughter who sparkles like a precious diamond. Diamonds are made under conditions of tremendous heat and pressure, far beneath the earth's surface. A diamond is one of the hardest minerals in the world, and it is a single element of carbon. A diamond is formed 90 to 120 miles beneath the surface of the earth and at temperatures of 900–1300 degrees Celsius.

Just an update in 2020—you are now nineteen and a beauty, a college freshman at Spelman in Atlanta and searching for your passion. God has smiled on you, and I know he will continue to do so. You have grown into a kind,caring, giving and beautiful young woman. Follow your dreams; never give up! Keep God by your side always.

Why do I liken you to a diamond?

They are beautiful to look at and to be with, like you.

They are universally sought after as adornment for royalty, kings and queens.

They are a "girl's best friend."

Everyone desires to have one or more.

They have many uses besides as jewelry: dentist drills, saws, sharp instruments.

Diamonds are a symbol of everlasting love. Bride usually wear one.

Diamonds can never be destroyed; diamonds last forever.

Even if they lose their luster, they can be polished to gleaming beauty.

An instrument of Peace. Peace.

Bodhisattva (a new word for you)

Bodhisattvas are those who aspire to achieve enlightenment and, at the same time, are equally determined to enable all other beings to do the same.

They are conscious of the bonds that link them to all others. In this state, they realize that any happiness they alone enjoy is incomplete. They devote themselves to alleviating others' suffering. Those in this state find their highest satisfaction in altruistic behavior.

Altruism: the principle or practice of unselfish concern for or devotion to the welfare of others, as opposed to ego or self

When you read this aloud, it will make more sense to you.

You are loved. Write when you can.

Love,
Grandmother Shirleywhirl

Dear Sofia,

How are you? Sending a shout-out to say I love you and to remind you of how beautiful, unique, and special you are.

I witnessed the tornado last week that touched down in middle America, blasting its fury through the town of Woodward and causing loss and destruction in just minutes.

You may have seen it on television. They seem to come every year to some areas, and afterward, there is the rebuilding, cleanup, and people coming together to help and make things right again. The dark clouds are gone, blue skies are back, and the storm has passed.

Looking back at last summer, our family faced a similar storm—your mom's illness, hospitalization, and treatment going forward. Amid that storm, as a family, by telephone and limited communication that we had, we worked to survive and move the family residence, schools, and life as you knew it. It had lots of changes, pain, and resistance, which sometimes goes with that all around. No one knew exactly what was happening from day to day, including your mom and me. I will always remember your leadership, your faith, your obedience, and your cooperation at that difficult time. If it was overwhelming, you managed to control yourself and try and help. No one was untouched by that storm—not your mom, me, each of you children, or countless others.

I liken you to the element of gold because gold can never be duplicated by man. It is created by the fusion of smaller items during a star's supernova explosion. They condense and eventually are found as ore. It is known as a precious metal with many uses. The beauty of gold is unmistakable, like your beauty, inside and out. Its value is known worldwide, as yours will be. Coincidently, you come from pure gold. Your mom is a rare and precious gem who has shown enormous faith and resolve in taking herself to new levels of being and has met the most significant challenges of her personal life with grace, dignity, spirituality, and love. She has made changes that are enhancing her health and well-being. This is like the blue sky at the end of the storm. It's like building a skyscraper, which can never be stronger than the steel holding it up.

I know your personal rebuilding is progressing, and you are loved all the more. I see you like a quiet internal spirit that kept moving and kept working, even when you could not completely process what was going on. This ability should serve you well as a young woman, with many important decisions ahead in your life and career. You have leaned upon your learned values and your faith, and you are an esteemed member of this family. I am confident that you will rely upon your inner faith in setting your goals and meeting them forthrightly, knowing you are the best of the best; that is easy to see in you. I hope you recognize your gifts and abilities.

There are opportunities in the worse adversities, if we look for them. The message here is that the storm is over, the rebuilding is continuing, and the people are united in this family to make things better. Annie sang it: "The sun will come out tomorrow." Robert Schuller said that tough times never last; tough people do. Remember that light removes darkness, and remember the words to this song. Please keep in your heart:

> Row, row, row your boat
> Gently down the stream
> Merrily, merrily, merrily
> Life is but a dream

And the ideas you make will be the life you will have.

A 2020 update: You're Now a college graduate from Spelman and looking at neuro sciences research, your passion and to medical school. You are beautiful, determined, passionate, and brilliant. Keep God as your road buddy, and the journey will be unbelievable.

Saint Francis Prayer

> Lord, make me an instrument of thy peace.
> Where there is hatred, let me sow love.
> Where there is an injury, pardon.
> Where there is doubt, faith.

Where there is darkness, light.
Where there is sadness, joy.
O divine Master, grant that I may not so much seek to
be consoled as to console,
To be understood as to understand,
To be loved as to love.
For it is by giving that we receive.
It is by pardoning that we are pardoned.
It is by dying that we are born to eternal life.

We have much to be thankful for, mainly that God has brought us, as a family, through the storm. I love you, Sofia, as a beautiful granddaughter who demonstrated enormous poise, strength, and intelligence during a severe trial of life.

Like gold, born through a supernova, you remain a rare gem.

Love,
Grandma Shirleywhirl
Peace!


Dear Sydney,

Spring is here; I have flowers on my patio, and the little fountain your mom gave me last Mother's Day in a basket arrangement is pumping gently, flowing waters over the flat black rocks layered on the three tiers of the black slate fountain. I also have roses and annuals that emit an explosion of colors, as well as one tomato plant. I must admit I only have two small baby tomato buds, about the size of a marble, but I am nurturing them proudly with pruning, water, and food.

I want to take this moment to remind you of how much you are loved as my beautiful granddaughter, and what a blessing it is to have you as my granddaughter. I consider myself very blessed to have you and four more granddaughters—wow! You are growing so fast that it does not seem possible that you will be fourteen next month. I must say

I enjoyed seeing you enroll and being with you in Rancho Pico Junior High last year, getting your gym clothes, getting the right fit, and going to all your classes with you and meeting your teachers. Some things work out, some don't, but the fact that we tried is what is essential. I often wonder if you have picked up the flute anymore and unlocked the music within that beautiful instrument. I thought the music teacher was very understanding, as was the wonderful homeroom and science teacher, who talked about shooting rockets off the roof and having so many explosive chemicals that she was on the FBI watch list. I loved the algebra teacher too, who brought the most enormous tarp I believe I had ever seen—Mrs. Kim, I think her name was, a born teacher.

It had been a while since I sat at a pupil's desk, and it was really cool, seeing what they teach in junior high. I still laugh about the first day of school, when the police stopped me for backing up to get in the line. What wide eyes you had, but my explanation made it all okay, as he told me to stop talking over and over. I still think he thought I was going to hit the police car. Last summer had its challenges; the main thing is we tried, and it was difficult for everyone, but a life lesson can make us all better individuals, if we try to learn from it.

There was a family crisis, and many of the comforts that you had come to enjoy and rely upon were not available, such as your own private room. That can be upsetting; loss generally is. Having needs, talks, missing your mom, and all the pain of the time—your mom was not able to be there with you and didn't know how long I would be your substitute parent. It took a toll on you; you acted like a typical teenager. a few verbal outbursts and pouting looks typical of your age and level of maturity. But know this: you are still loved by me, and I look at the time as growing pains at the most challenging time in your life. Thirteen is when it is hard enough to figure out yourself, your thoughts, your friends, and relationships, much less a family crisis and all the changes that were about. That is honestly understandable and hopefully behind you. I know you are working through processing everything as well. We know one thing: we all did the best we could with what we knew and when we knew it. Being the scientist that you are, I thought you would appreciate the rare jewel that I have selected as you: the pearl.

Typically, when a parasite burrows through a mollusk's shell into the mantle tissue, the defense of the mollusk surrounds the intruder with a "pearl sac." The interior of this sac is lined with epithelial cells that deposit nacre (aragonite and calcite) around the intruder. This process continues until a beautiful pearl grows—quite a process. Attack! Defend! But something precious and beautiful results—a pearl. So many think it is from the sand irritation of the oyster that causes the pearl, but it is not.

Pearls are worn by queens and kings and most women in high places in the world—presidents' wives (Jackie Kennedy and Barbara Bush) and prime ministers (Golda Meir and Margaret Thatcher).

The most famous and the most expensive are Marimekko Japanese pearls, and there are freshwater pearls. The result is a rare and precious adornment that is treasured the world over. Mother-of-pearl has many uses; it is fragile, unique, and expensive.

Sydney, you are my pearl!

I am extremely empathetic and sensitive to last summer. The unknown was more significant than each of us knew. I see you as a strong—powerfully strong—young woman with the DNA of a powerful mother sending you forth. Your mother faced the biggest challenge of her adult life. She did so with the grace and beauty of the pearl. You are described as a pearl in the mode of your mother. She had no control, but she was obedient to the task. She was powerless, but she kept the faith. Paula continued to love you, even though she was not there. Life throws us a curveball sometimes; how you respond to that curveball is telling of what you are made of. I am grateful that I got to know you better with our time together.

You have an eager mind and a good heart. You have always had an attitude of excellence. You also have a sense of knowing what is essential and when it is necessary. You have a great sense of accountability and responsibility. These are characteristics I much admire. The times I was able to look at your homework and see your desire to get it right and understand the principles being taught demonstrated to me that you will be all right because you want to be okay! You are diligent, a self-starter, and confident.

The important thing now for you to know is that you are loved, prayed for, admired, thought about all the time, and cared about, and you are a unique and special person in this family and elsewhere. Knowing your self-worth can be very reassuring. How you feel about yourself is very important. As your grandmother, please count me as one of your many admirers.

2020 update: You are now a Spelman graduate. Wow! Covid 19 deprived you of the pomp and circumstance at your school but as a family we celebrated you and you know you are loved. At Spelman, you arrived there a girl with hope but uncertainty and now you have returned a woman, full of confidence, poise,purpose, determination and faith. You know what you want to do and when covid subsides and the universe reopens you are ready. Walk, run, pray, work, laugh, play, never let your dreams stray.

You are gorgeous and beautiful. Keep God as your close friend. Where there is injury, pardon.

> He who forgives ends the quarrel.
> —African Proverb

> Forgiveness is the fragrance that the violet sheds on the heel that has crushed it.
> —Mark Twain

> Outside ideas of right-doing and wrongdoing, there is a field. I'll meet you there.
> —Rumi

St. Francis Prayer

> Lord, make me an instrument of thy peace.
> Where there is hatred, let me sow love.
> Where there is an injury, pardon.
> Where there is doubt, faith.
> Where there is despair, hope.

Where there is darkness, light.
Where there is sadness, joy.
Oh divine Master, grant that I may not so much seek to
     be consoled as to console,
To be understood as to understand,
To be loved as to love.
For it is by giving that we receive.
It is by pardoning that we are pardoned.
It is by dying that we are born to eternal life.

Love,
Grandmother Shirleywhirl


Dear Noah,

This is a love letter from Grandma Shirleywhirl. It was wonderful speaking to you on the occasion of your twelfth birthday. It just does not seem possible that you have whizzed through eleven years and have grown into such a wonderful young man.

Any time we get to be together, it is unusual for me because you are so unique, honest, and trusting. One of the reasons we have Camp Shirleywhirl has been to come together, spending quality time together and talking about our lives, playing games like poker and water play, bowling, and watching movies, eating, and sharing with each other. You are a millennium birth, born in 2000, just like Christopher and Shelby. I have dubbed you three the Dozen Cousins, in that all three of you will be twelve this year. You are the oldest of the three.

The pictures I have of you show your personality clearly, as there is straight-up honesty!

You can express in words what you are feeling. When you are tired, you want to rest. When you are hungry you want food.

You know what your strengths are and what you may procrastinate at. You have boundless energy, and you like a little drama in your life, just to keep things interesting. You observe others keenly and respect a sense of fairness. You have all the character and integrity it takes to be the dreamer and dream-maker. You have the potential and personality to be anything you determine is your path in life. You also have a wonderful, caring, and sensitive side that reaches out to others as to their well-being. That will ultimately be one of your most powerful gifts.

If I were to pick an element to describe you, it would be steel. I am happy to tell you why. In Iowa, while you were yet a baby, Granddaddy Limuary and I were babysitting you in the hotel during a family reunion of Grandmother Adeline's side of the family. You ran into the leg of the desk head-on, and we were sure we would have to call the paramedics and that your head was gashed open. To our amazement, you bounced back; you were momentarily stunned, rolled over, laughed, and started to run again. Granddaddy and I looked at each other, let out the breath that we had been holding, and took a sigh of relief. You have kept that get-back-up resolve as you continued to grow up. Finding your passion at Purdue University in engineering was amazing. You wanted nothing else, and no other university or program, and you risked putting everything into your dream. Your had hundreds of scriptures in your cell phone of affirmations and dreams to ask God to grant you that opportunity, and he did! How can I not applaud that faith you have? On the ship to Hong Kong, we spoke privately, and you shared your resolve with me. Those are moments I shall never forget. I love you, Noah, and God is at your side because you have called him to be there.

Ancient steel production, excavated from archaeological sites in Anatolia Kaman Karahoyuk, is about four thousand years old. Other antique steel comes from East Africa, dating back to 1400 BC. Steel is an alloy of iron, usually containing carbon. The content of carbon is from .2 percent to 2.1 percent by weight. Other elements used are manganese, chromium, nickel, vanadium, and tungsten. Some are hardening agents, some add ductility, and some add tensile strength. Efficient production methods have made steel one of the most versatile and useful products in the world—rebar and mesh in concrete, railroad tracks, structures of modern skyscrapers, significant appliances, magnetic cores, automobiles, trains, ships, cutlery, rulers, surgical equipment, and wristwatches. There are literally thousands of applications, and I liken you to this beautiful, versatile elemental alloy—precious, rare, necessary, versatile, durable, flexible, relevant, vital, and beautiful! I challenge you to read about steel and steel mills. There are hundreds of references in Wikipedia. Now that you know I love such a strong boy who has now become a strong man, 2020 update, What a blessing for me that you are spending some time with me this summer. The summer of Covid19. You will be a Junior at Purdue next year, you are brilliant !, Athletic and a have a passion for skateboarding. You tell me it is a great way to expend energy and center yourself. We have to be cognizant of health advisories so we walk around the house with our masks on when within six foot of each other. You have the whole upstairs to study your summer school online learning a course in Linnear Algebra and Differential equations.

I am so impressed by how hard you work to learn your studies, when the help and aid of a professor could maybe help. You say "Grandma I would rather not email a professor wait for a reply that may take days, I just get more inspired by figuring it out myself. WOW!. That is determination. You are excelling in the class as well by your grades so this is good. I have enjoyed your vegan cooking this summer and us making a grocery list on line ordering your seaweed, lentil pasta, wild rice, okra, crushed tomatoes or puree, cucumber, kale, lettuce, and rice, rice, rice, smiles I could go on. You are fit spiritualy as well with an abiding faith in God and your abilities. Getting this sacred time alone with you has been such a special blessing for me.

I hope you understand what beautiful abilities you have that are known to others and seen through your exciting persona. This is translated to mean you are strong enough to accomplish anything you can dream of. From ancient history to outer space, you can create your plan for your life. You have what it takes to do it. You come from significant DNA. You have love and encouragement from a family that adores you and holds you in high esteem. You have a good heart and a beautiful spirit, and I always love to spend time with you. Lastly, you care about people from small kindnesses to sweet and powerful aspirations of how you want to help make the world a better place.

This is another chance to say happy birthday, grandson! I want to share a poem that I hope you will enjoy and also do some research on Saint Francis. Write when you can.

### Saint Francis Prayer

Lord, make me an instrument of thy peace.
Where there is hatred, let me sow love.
Where there is an injury, pardon.
Where there is doubt, faith.
Where there is despair, hope.
Where there is darkness, light.
Where there is sadness, joy.
Oh, divine Master, grant that I may not so much seek to
    be consoled as
to console,
To be understood as to understand,
To be loved as to love.
For it is by giving that we receive.
It is by pardoning that we are pardoned.
It is by dying that we are born to eternal life.

Remember a very wise song:

Row, row, row your boat
Gently down the stream
Merrily, merrily, merrily, merrily
Life is but a dream

The dreams you make are the life you will live

Love,
Grandma Shirleywhirl

Dear Christopher,

Your arrival to our family was a special blessing of God's grace. You see, your parents had been wanting a child for some years before the gift of you was granted. You are a celebrated son for reasons we rejoice about and also for reasons none of us may ever fully know. Your arrival was met with celebration and thanksgiving. You have enjoyed a privileged, prestigious education at Sunshine, Legacy, and Sierra Canyon. As a pensive, quiet type of guy, you are wildly handsome,mysterious from the eye, and playful and deep as a character.

I am delighted to write to you and tell you how much you mean to me as my grandson. You are now twelve years old! The years have flown by. From the day you were born, I have loved you and admired you. As a very young boy, you had a knowing smile, looking cute in your sailor suit or just relaxing, maybe eating one of your favorite foods. You have always been a happy, loving boy, grateful for your family, secure, and assured that you knew God had surrounded you. Everything was good. You have thrived in academics and sports.

You love having a sister, and you are protective of her. You love knowing that your mom understands you and is there for you when you need her. You cherish the fact that your dad is so supportive of all your endeavors as your coach and cheerleader, as you have excelled in academics and football, basketball, and baseball. You love all your family and your cousins with whom you revel. You have always been able to express your needs verbally with articulation and purpose. Knowing what you want and need is an excellent attribute because you can obtain what you need to be content and happy. I have always been impressed by your intelligence, self-control, and the ability to think when those around you may be stirring chaos. You try to figure things out and offer options. Those traits are also described as the characteristics of leadership. You work hard, you play hard, and you love video games and television, and I won't hold against you the fact that you prefer the Celtics to the Lakers. I am holding out hope.

You have been blessed with parents who support and love you. You and your mom used to read the same books to connect. Your dad is your biggest cheerleader at your football games, where you excelled as defensive end. You were mentioned in the newspapers often and won a state conference championship and a four-year scholarship to Amherst to play football, which you declined for a more academic, cultural experience at Morehouse College in Atlanta. You have had opportunities laid before you, and you have been able to choose, and that is a good thing. Keep God in your plans, find out his plan, to find your true north.

I lenjoy comparing my grandchildren to something in nature, and for you, I have chosen granite. What is granite? It is a common, widely occurring type of intrusive, felsic, igneous rock, which is granular and crystalline in texture. It consists mainly of quartz, mica, and feldspar. Granite is nearly always massive, hard, and sturdy.

It has density, compressive strength, viscosity, and high melting temperatures. The word comes from Latin, meaning "grain." You can only find it on earth, where it forms a significant part of the continental crust. (Otherwise said, you are the crust of the planet earth to me.) Granite is a natural source of radiation, as are most stones. Some granites have uranium as well as thorium in all of them. The red pyramid of Egypt, twenty-sixth century BC, was named as such for the light crimson hue of its exposed granite surfaces.

In that it is such a hard stone, practical uses did not come until the invention of a steam-powered cutting tool by Alexander MacDonald. Today, modern methods using computers cut the granite. Granite is the rock most prized by climbers for its steepness, soundness, crack systems, and friction; this includes venues such as Yosemite, Mont Blanc, the Alps, Corsica, Patagonia, and countless others. Practical applications are building materials, counters, floors, commercial buildings, and more. One last note: it is a beautiful stone with colors and patterns unique to nature and the conditions of temperature, wind, and the elements that impact it.

I found in my study that many of the characteristics of this magnificent natural compound are within you, Christopher. You are my granite grandson. I hope you will read more about this superb rock that is so prized and sought after.

In speaking to your mother, I know you have to leave for school very early now, but you had your ice cream and cake, for your birthday and I know Hunan's is on the calendar for some very good slippery shrimp very soon. Please know how much you are loved and admired. Many eyes are upon you as you navigate challenging times, as well as fun times, and those eyes find that you are wise beyond your years. You have a caring and grateful heart; you are considerate of others, and when you have to be severe, you can do that too. Everything I have ever observed about you adds up to your being one terrific young man with a perfect life ahead because you have reverence for your God, your home, your family, your community, and yourself. I love you and hope this is the best year of your life, as well as ahead and beyond.

2020 Update, Christopher matriculating at Morehouse college in Atlanta, your cousins Sydney and Shelby at neighboring Spelman College, this too has been a blessing in your life. Family support close by. Your future is in your hands, you love the financial monetary system of the world, crypocurrencies and bit coins, the stock market and beyond. We have had some great conversations on those subjects. Remember Education still, is the key to a good life. I pray you will embrace that always and walk with God, you will need him and he is willing to walk with you.

Love,
Grandma Shirleywhirl

Poem for you (please read aloud): Rudyard Kipling's "If"

If you can keep your head when all about you
Are losing theirs and blaming it on you,
If you can trust yourself when all men doubt you,
But make allowance for their doubting too;
If you can wait and not be tired by waiting,
Or being lied about, don't deal in lies,
Or being hated, don't give way to hating,

And yet don't look too good or talk too wise;
If you can dream—and not make dreams your Master;
If you can think and not make thoughts your aim;
If you can meet with triumph and disaster
And treat those two imposters just the same;
If you can bear to hear the truth you've spoken
Twisted by knaves to make a trap for fools,
Or watch the things you gave your life to broken,
And stoop and build them up with worn-out tools;
If you can make one heap of all your winnings
And risk it on one turn of pitch and toss,
And lose and start again at your beginnings
And never breathe a word about your loss;
If you can force your heart and nerve and sinew
To serve your turn long after they are gone,
And so hold on when there is nothing in you
Except for the will which says to them: "hold on."
If you can talk with crowds and keep your virtue,
Or walk with kings—nor lose the common touch,
If neither foes nor loving friends can hurt you,
If all men count with you but not too much;
If you can fill the unforgiving minute
With sixty seconds worth of distance run,
Yours is the earth and everything that's in it
And—which is more—You'll be a Man, my [grandson]!


Dear Courtney,

My youngest grandchild. The "baby," and what a beautiful baby you were. Everyone said you looked exactly like your mother, Patricia, then and now, at seventeen, as well. Fair of face, long locks of black hair, big eyes of wonder, and a brilliant mind, strong as a steel trap. What a blessing for me to have returned here to California in time to see you grow from middle school to high school, picking you up at the bus stop, grabbing a snack, and now seeing you pull up to my home and park your own car. It is an overwhelming experience to see a beautiful girl transform into a pensive, graceful, elegant young woman in the course of four years, and if that young lady is your granddaughter, That young lady is sweet as sugar, it is just awesome.

You, the baby girl, baby grandchild, the youngest of the eight we are blessed to love. What a joy you have been from birth to the present. I have watched you keeping up with your older cousins. With trusting eyes and courageous vigor, holding tight when necessary to Sofia or becoming best buddies with Shelby after everyone left for college. You used to say to me, "I'm smart, Grandma."

I would answer, "How do you know?"

You would say, "My mom told me so."

Well, your mom was right. You excelled at Legacy Christian Academy and now in high school. You are a brilliant writer, with many academic skills. Your teacher's comment—"I can hardly wait to see how you handle this subject"—is remarkable. You have so quickly grown up. Now, at seventeen, you are driving a car, playing soccer, surfing and snorkeling, snowboarding, and even taking voice lessons. What an experience, having you travel to Spelman College to launch Shelby, and the trip to New York last year to see Broadway shows and have you discover Central Park with your mom via bicycle was joyful. You are active in Jack and Jill of America, and you love to hang out with your cousins and family. You have a love for words, carrying a dictionary to learn new words and use them in conversation. This erudite gesture of new words makes eyebrows rise and ears perk up. You are exploring your passions beautifully. Voted most likely to be a writer by your Legacy graduating class, you are blessed with many gifts and work hard to refine your skills. I admire and love you very much. You have indeed been the student whose vessel is not only filled but one whose torch has been lit.

The inert substance I have likened you to is the stone of sapphire because of the properties I liken to you.

Sapphire is the most precious and most valuable blue gemstone. It is highly desirable due to its excellent color, hardness, durability, and luster. Throughout history, it has been known as the stone of wisdom and wealth. Going back to the Bible, it has been a symbol of power, strength, and wise judgement. Sapphire is a symbol in Hebrew lore of true royalty and sincerity. In the book of Exodus, sapphire represents the Lord's holy character and divine nature. Sapphires were placed under the Lord's feet to signify the foundation of holy character and divine nature.

Your strength and wisdom in tough times, good days, and great moments portray your character and personality. Wear the mantle well. Keep God ever so close.

2020 Update. You are a senior in high school, I loved having you come over and study at my home during last semester due to the Covid 19 virus which we are still in the midst of. Driving your car parking in the garage and proceeding to your study area with purpose and dedication. You never failed to ask Grandma, can I get you something a cup of coffee?, juice.? you also shopped for me and just have the sweetest ways. Those things made life safer for me and less isolated having you in the house. I would love you anyway but wow you make it easy for me and everyone to love you.

Love,
Grandma Shirleywhirl

> Though I speak with the tongues of men and angels and have not charity, I am become as sounding brass or a tinkling cymbal. And though I have the gift of prophecy, and understand all mysteries, and all knowledge; and though I have all faith, so that I have all faith, so that I could remove mountains, and have not charity, I am nothing. And though I bestow all my goods to feed the poor, and though I give my body to be burned, and have not charity, it profiteth me nothing. Charity suffereth long, and is kind; charity envieth not; charity vaunteth, not itself, is not puffed up. ... When I was a child, I spake as a child, I understood as a child, I thought as a

child; but when I became a woman, I put away childish
things. (1 Corinthians 13:1–4, 11 KJV)

Dear Natalie,

The oldest grandchild. Firstborn! What a thrill for all of us when
you arrived. I was there and at the birth for each of our next seven
grandchildren. What a special moment when you were born. You were
special then as you are now, twenty-three years later. What a life you
have experienced already. You have traveled far and wide, from infancy
to adulthood.

For your first Christmas, you came to California. Dressed in red
and white, "baby Natalie" was passed around the table at the Ritz-
Carlton Hotel in Marina Del Rey, like a cherub in a basket, reflecting
a bundle of joy. You would soon leave for South Africa. We were able
to visit you via Skype, a new technology then for the public, and
exchanged many pictures.

Later, living in Virginia, you and the family came to Camp
Shirleywhirl in Las Vegas in 2004. The first of many to come. After
private elementary school in Virginia, you had home schooling in
Washington, DC. Later, you selected and were granted acceptance into
West Point Military Academy in New York. What a huge achievement!
I do not stand alone in admiration for your tenacity and perseverance
in mounting the obstacles of physical endurance and capacity during
training. As a tall, slim young woman, you were tested, mentally and
physically, to the maximum. After shin splints, surgery, crutches, mental
anguish and an inability to meet the physical standard, you never gave
up, and on the ninth try, you succeeded in carrying a man on your
back, plus your gear, in the field-training aspect of your military career.

After graduation, you had many options—an opportunity to teach
at West Point—but Paris called, and a master's degree, then London for
a second master's degree. This Christmas 2019 brought you back to the
United States for a California family reunion that was wonderful. Rain

or shine, you were up jogging and conditioning. I could not believe your discipline and endurance. Your sights are now to try out for the elite Ranger Corp. Amazing is all I can say! Your journey has been blessed, global, and nothing less than historic. You are a confident, mature, empathetic, and thoughtful woman who is setting an extraordinary example for young women everywhere.

How does one understand how you garnered the resolve to never give up? Sheer grit, I would say, and your faith in God that you can partner with him to achieve anything. The majestic grounds of West Point on the Hudson River in New York are unforgettable. Your education of nearly half a million dollars has prepared you in Chinese, Japanese, and French. You spent your summers in Taiwan and learned the language and lived the culture.

The inert substance I have chosen for you is the sun. Global woman that you are and have been, from birth to the present, you are always shining somewhere. Like the star that the sun is, you may not always see them, but you know they are there. The sun has been worshipped and feared. It provides the vital ingredient for most of life on earth. Without this energy, vegetation cannot grow, and animals would not have a source of nourishment. The vastness of its size of 870,000 miles in diameter is more than one hundred times the diameter of the earth. The sun is thought of, generally, as a unique celestial body. To me, you are unique, unlike millions of other human beings.

Natalie, I love you very much. As a daughter, sister to two younger brothers, cousin, and niece of your aunts and uncles, and as a granddaughter, you have had much success and made us all so proud of you. I know you will continue to soar and climb the heights before you. Pray unceasingly as you circumnavigate this planet and enjoy the journey.

2020 Update, I love your notes to me thanking me for any help or assistance, they are so sweet. Your thoughtfulnes of me with a beautiful Hotpad that says "God save the Queen" from Harrods in London.

Love,
Grandma Shirleywhirl

Now faith is the substance of things hoped for, the evidence of things not seen. For by it, the elders obtained a good report. Through faith, we find that the worlds were framed by the word of God so that things that are seen are not made of items which do appear. By faith Abel offered unto God a more excellent sacrifice than Cain, by which he obtained witness that he was righteous, God testifying of his gifts; and by it, he being dead yet speaketh. By Faith Enoch was translated that he should not see death; and was not found, because God had translated him: For before his translation he had this testimony that he pleased God. But without faith it is impossible to please him; for he that cometh to God must believe that he is and that he is a rewarder of them that diligently seek him. (Hebrews 11:1–6)

Dear Nathan,

Oldest grandson of three grandsons in our family. A great day! Proud family and parents. On the day you were born, we were all there. You were quite a beautifully endowed, bouncing baby boy. Our first grandson. You kind of entered the world with a *wow* from the nurses and family. Your eyes were big and focused, and you had command of the moment.

Today, you could easily be a clothes model, as a button-down shirt and suit looks very stylish on you. You love smart fashion, including hoodies. You have a neat moustache, attractive beard, and short-cut curly black hair, and you make a dashing appearance.

You grew to be a very handsome six-foot-five-inch man, now at age twenty. A sought-after prom escort, smooth dancer, everything Hollywood and West Coast. We are always happy to see you. You are about finding your passions, and there are many. High fashion, acting, video production, plays, writing, music, movies, and even a small business, Capliments.

You chose Belmont University, a school embracing your skills, in Nashville, Tennessee. You have excelled there as a dean's list student. Last year, you learned Chinese to participate in a foreign exchange program that allowed you to live with a Chinese family in Shanghai, China. It was a special joy to have you as a house guest for the summer before your trip. I saw so much growth in your confidence as you worked as an intern. You battled through your fears and growing pains with relationships, and you emerged wiser and stronger. You know the competition in your industry is fierce. Being capable and talented, even excellent, is not always enough. Your material must be what someone needs. You need a match, a connection, and a strong spiritual base. You are a giver by nature. You will say yes when others would not. You worked with special-needs children at summer camp. You wrote skits and plays for them.

You had a meaningful experience in China, even visited friends in Japan.

You are creating a meaningful and selfless life experience. God is surely directing your path and leading your journey. I love you, Nathan, and I am very proud you are my grandson. I have likened you to the natural phenomenon of the mighty redwood tree. Redwood trees, at 250 feet average, are the tallest trees on earth. They live up to two thousand years. The leaves are green, flat, and sharp-pointed. They are one of the greatest wonders of the world. They live so long because they are ancient and perfectly adapted to the foggy, temperate climate where they flourish. They have been on the planet for more than 240 million years. About three hundred miles north of San Francisco and fifty miles south of the Oregon border is the Redwood National Park. The best time to visit is autumn. These are the sunniest and warmest days.

I hope you will be able to visit there one day soon. Keep your faith and always pray.

2020 Update, You are a senior in college next year at Belmont, Wow! You have worked all summer in Washington, DC and are gathering your esxperiences and forcus for the finish line. Your sheer enthusiasm and gifts of optimism, skills and kindness will take you where you need to go. Keep God by your side I love and admire you so much.

Love,
Grandma Shirleywhirl

> The proverbs of Solomon. A wise son maketh a glad father: but a foolish son is the heaviness of his mother. Treasures of the wickedness profit nothing; but righteousness delivereth from death. The Lord will not suffer the soul of the righteous to famish: but he casteth away the substance of the wicked. He becometh poor that dealeth with a slack hand: but the hand of the diligent maketh rich. He that gathereth in summer is a wise son: But he that sleepeth in harvest is a son that causeth shame. Blessings are upon the head of the just: but violence covereth the mouth of the wicked. The memory of the just is blessed: but the name of the wicked shall rot. The wise in heart shall receive commandments: but a prating fool shall fall. He that walketh uprightly walketh surely: But he that perverteth his ways shall be known. He that winketh with the eye causes sorrow: but a prating fool shall fail. The mouth of a righteous man is a well of life. (Proverbs 10:1–11)

*2004. From left to right: Shelby, Noah, Natalie,*
*Courtney, Sydney, Sofia, Nathan, Christopher*

*2019. From left to right: Sydney, Shelby, Noah,*
*Natalie, Nathan, Courtney, Christopher, Sofia*

*Grandsons, from left to right: Noah, Nathan, Christopher*

*Granddaughters, from left to right: Natalie,*
*Sydney, Shelby, Sofia, Courtney*

*Good people are like candles; they burn themselves up to give others light.*

*—Turkish proverb*

# CHAPTER 23

## With the Wind at My Back: Jobs That Kept My Hands Busy

I observed my eight grandchildren, aged ten to eighteen, growing up and examining their own life decisions as they looked at colleges and asked a lot of questions about family. I came to the realization that they did not know much about me as a young person, and they were fascinated when we talked about those times.

I was born on a Saturday, a workday, and it seems I have worked for as long as I can remember. To this day, I am reluctant to give up working, having retired from my primary occupation as a dentist three times.

As the oldest child in my family and physically sturdy, durable, and healthy while growing up, I helped my father with chores and projects. He would call me to hold this or hand him that. Working with Dad had many advantages, even though it was not easy. I learned how to do a lot of things, and he had confidence in my abilities. I learned to drive a car at ten years old, and by eleven, I had a learner's permit. I drove the truck to pick up slop for our beautiful reddish poland china hogs in Louisiana. It was a distasteful job, cleaning the troughs and hog pens, but it had to be done, and I was promised one of the pigs. Grandmother had about thirty head, as well as chickens, ducks, and dogs that had to be fed daily. At home with Mom, house chores were dishes, setting and clearing the table, washing pots and pans, cleaning the sink, sweeping the floor, and vacuuming the carpets. I even vacuumed the elderly neighbor's home and stairs on Saturday mornings.

I could handle a water hose pretty well for a girl, as my dad was a big proponent of washing things down—the lawn and flowers, sidewalks, side of the house, driveways, and curbs. This was before there water conservation thoughts. Dad had whitewashed rocks that adorned our yard. Our family values were Saturday work and recreation on Saturday night, but church on Sunday.

I took the streetcar at ten years old to the Edison Company to exchange old light bulbs for new ones. By age fourteen, in Los Angeles, I was working at a chemical lab downtown, upstairs in an old building, washing glassware. I learned the names of beakers, petri dishes, distillation tubes, and all the glass from tests done all week. I was almost alone, except for other cleaning going on, as the lab was closed on Saturdays, and the pile-up was significant, waiting for me to clean it all for Monday morning. I gleaned a specialized knowledge of chemicals, from ammonia to sulfuric acid. I wore goggles and gloves and was keenly aware of the safety precautions needed in doing this job. I felt lucky to have this position, as my interest in the sciences accelerated.

My next post in Los Angeles was at Bullock's department store at Seventh and Hill, downtown. I caught the bus there. I was fifteen and landed a job doing inventory for four weeks. My job was to inventory in the fine gloves department. I had to arrive there early, go to the employee entrance, take the elevator down to the basement to place my time card in the clock in the slot, and report to my department. I was standing on my feet all day, taking specific instructions from an exacting manager, and got only a fifteen-minute break and thirty-minute lunch. I never dreamed there were so many types of gloves—elegant over-the-elbow, under-the-elbow white-felt gloves, three-quarter-length gloves, short gloves, knit gloves, leather gloves—all colors, all lengths, all kinds of materials. I saw gloves, morning, noon, and night. I stuck it out but saw gloves in my sleep for weeks; my feet were tired. It was the most monotonous, mindless activity I had ever done. It was personally demeaning to go to the basement to time in and then to have someone looking over my shoulder every minute to determine my work ethic. It was the worst and most important job I ever had.

My next post was in Beverly Hills as a shampoo assistant at Charles of the Ritz. My aunt Lelah arranged for me to work for her two-week vacation. It was mainly washing combs and brushes, my affair with Barbasol, and getting lunch for the well-heeled patrons who spent the day there for salon treatments. They sent me to get lunch at a nearby sandwich shop. The tips were great. I got the orders correct, had fun, and the thrill of a lifetime was when Doris Day, the reigning songstress and actress of the day, came in one day. I was starstruck anyway, but she was an idol. I only smiled at her—no other contact, as she was whisked into a private area. My impression of this job was that work can be fun if you find something you love to do.

My uncle John owned a restaurant, Ivy's Chicken Shack, where all the black celebrities came after hours to eat. I got a recommendation from him, saying I had kitchen experience, and took a job at the county general hospital. Now sixteen, I worked the vacation of an employee temporarily. This was big. I had to there at 4:00 a.m. for breakfast and lunch meals and went home about one or two o'clock.

I arrived there, got my white uniform and hairnet on, clocked in, and was directed to the kitchen, where two large vats for oatmeal were awaiting me. The hot water was already running in. I asked the directions and was directed to the dry cereal bin and scoops. I was told to put six scoops in each vat and to keep stirring as the temperature rose and began to cook the cereal. Everyone was busy doing their own jobs, and no one seemed to wonder if I knew what I was doing. They seemed unbothered by my youth or low level of knowledge.

Breakfast went fast, as the food was quick, and the trays were filled, according to dietary plans—"little salt," "diabetic," etc. Time passed like a blur. Shortly, I was told to prepare one thousand salmon cakes. I was led to a walk-in cold-room freezer that had a prep table and stool. I was exasperated. One thousand salmon croquettes. It took me an hour and a half to finish. I was cold, exhausted, and bored.

I played tennis in the afternoon, saw my friends, and got to bed early. I knew the hospital was a fascinating place, but I also learned the kitchen was not where I wanted to ever be again. I stuck it out but eagerly left.

I graduated high school at sixteen and knew I wanted to become a doctor and major in pre-med. After going to Washington, DC, on a grant from the NIH, I entered dental school and worked as a research fellow. When my roommate, Ethel, got married, I could not pay the rent alone, so I found a job as a counselor for free room and board. This was my job at Hillcrest, which also provided maid service and a monthly stipend. I had to be there by ten o'clock nightly and work some weekends. This place was beautiful—green lawns and gardens in upper northwest Washington. I kept this position until I was married. It was a dream job.

The staff at Hillcrest consisted of Grover Dye, psychologist; Dr. Yacoubian, psychiatrist; Mrs. Bluestein, case manager; and the counselors—Joe Maxey, Dan Graves, Fred Stone, and me. We counselors became fast friends.

After a pedodontic internship at DC General Hospital and a Guggenheim fellowship in New York, I went to work at Group Health on Pennsylvania Avenue. I worked on White House staff. I was earning $12,400 a year, more than the $3,600 internship stipend, and more than my professors at Howard, who were making $7,500 a year. After my husband finished his residency in general surgery, we headed to Los Angeles and into private practice, and I also became a Los Angeles public school dentist. I directed a mobile dental unit to underserved areas of Los Angeles with a fluoridation program and caries prevention program and practiced in my own office after work at the schools. I was living my dream. I married at twenty-four and had four children by age thirty.

We were blessed with purchasing a beautiful home and raised our four children there. I bought a medical building and practiced for thirty years before selling and retiring from clinical care. I served as dental director for Delta Dental PMI, Century Dental, and Continental Dental Plans.

During the early years, thinking ahead to retirement, I became a real estate broker in the course of investing in real estate. I invested in a franchise for selling condos at sea and sold those in 2005

In 2011, I took a memoir-writing class and finally embraced a desire to write. My purpose in writing my memoirs is to share our family history and values with my children and grandchildren. It has come to my attention that journals are a great book selection by the reading public.

My hands have found much to do all of my life. I learned something valuable from each experience. I have felt the wind continually at my back, which, to me, is God directing my path.

*Know when to hold 'em and know when to fold 'em.*

*—"The Gambler" by Don Schlitz*

# CHAPTER 24

## Favorite Things

My thoughts are memorialized in print because I want my children's grandchildren and great-grandchildren to know what I have held dear—my favorite things, my strong value systems taught to me by my parents and grandparents, the importance of family and extended family as principles that have guided my life.

These values are God first, family next, and myself third, respect for others always as our brothers keeper. Learning about Christianity, the Bible, the reassurance of hymns, the comfort of knowing a loving Savior, learning basic respect for others, learning, and trying to live the commandments of the Bible—these were family values from early childhood that became my values as I became a wife, mother, and grandmother. Our family is a God-serving, church-going family. My uncle David was a Baptist minister in Williamsburg, Virginia, and a Rockefeller restored the church. We had many discussions centering around the love of God versus the fear of the wrath of God. I have a robust belief system. Faith in that value system helps to identify who I am.

I have heard several phrases on that topic. I once heard Maria Shriver say that the two most important dates in your life are the date when you were born and the date you found out why. When leaving for college, I received some words of wisdom: "Remember who you are." This meant my family had given me all the tools I needed to survive.

This wisdom included values to make reasonable decision, lessons to keep me safe, the courage to take risks and to fail and try again. I remembered that I was not alone and had the security of a loving God and a loving family. You get back what you give; you reap what you sow.

Family—in this country, at least, we don't usually choose our family. We are born into a family and have the good fortune and blessing—or not—that it is a loving, nurturing family that wants a child to parent and make a home for. We have only the grace of God for this pairing but no choice.

We do choose our friends, our boyfriends and girlfriends, our husbands and wives, educated or not, tall or short, sick or well, inspired or uninspired, rich or poor, wise or foolish. We make choices on persons other than our families. It is somehow preordained how we arrive in this world and whose nurturing we will grow up under. When children are adopted or separated from a biological parent, there may be lifelong wondering about this lost connection. Laws have been written and rewritten; reunions have been special after years of searching for that giver of life. Family is important.

Even if you have an impaired parent, children long for that connection at some point, even if sustained by pain or an inability to forgive. Family is important. No matter the relationship with your parents, you will miss them when they are gone. I was blessed to have my mother until she was ninety-seven years old, and not a day goes by that I do not think of my father and his witticisms. "Don't forget the family," he would say. "Even if a family member is a bastard or a son of a bitch, he is our son of bitch."

You have to spend time with family members to know them, to ultimately love them and understand them. Every family has those oddballs who marry in, or sometimes the in-law is more desirable than the blood relative. Sometimes things can get so weird that you wonder if God has played some challenging tricks on families, bringing in such different personalities. Or you can think these are gifts to you, laid out generations before, when God selected your family and you in it. Daddy always said, "Bloom where you are planted."

Camp Shirleywhirl has been an ode to the family. Getting all eight grandchildren together for the last ten years for a couple of weeks or more in a vacation venue has been the fulfillment of a promise to family. The cousins all know and love one another. What joy to see our kids growing up, having the security of family. They have learned the fun of simple pleasures and the fruits of hard work and of service to others. They have discovered our family values of respect for each other.

As the first grandchild left for West Point last year and another is to go this year, the family values travel with them.

Now looking at blessing's, Shirleywhirl. What a wonderful world; what a beautiful life; what joyous blessings. Thanks to God, I was born into a loving family, one that believed in education. College life was a blast for me—sorority life, student life. The honor of getting into professional school, earning a doctorate degree, blessed with success, awards, honor and distinction in a pioneering career in dentistry. Finding love, dream husband, big wedding, friendship, eight bridesmaids, motherhood, four beautiful Christian children, eight magnificent grandchildren. God has smiled on me.

I am known by many names in our family. Number one and universally is the "Queen of Fun." I love planning events and great things to do with my family. Since the kids were little tykes, that name has stuck.

I come from a working family and hard work. I like to give equal time to pleasure. "Enjoy my best life" has always been my motto. I believe that no task before you should be too daunting to complete to the best of your ability. Difficult is not impossible. Mother said, "The Lord will provide." Daddy said, "Friendship is essential to the soul."

Big Mama said, "Push, pull, shove. If you give out, don't give up."

Grandmother Rosa said, "Can do, will do—no such thing as can't do." She also said, "Hasten, Jason, get the basin; oops, slop, get the mop."

I am also known as the fixer. When the kids have a problem, they generally ask, "Who is going to tell Mom?" They know once I get wind of it, there will be an answer. It may not always be yes, but it will get settled.

My response to my children is, "Always remember who you are. Generations before you have prayed for your success, your service and contributions to this world. Be the best you that you can be."

After achieving a trifecta of personal and professional success, security, and personal growth in eighty-two years, what's next? Oh! That word retirement sounds like giving in or giving up. I have not done well with that. I am indulging in my passions of the piano, though I will always be an amateur player; it keeps reminding me of many of the intricate mysteries of artistry. The keyboard is the pinnacle musical instrument for me.

Words that spring to mind for a great time, the first invited guest must be music. Some from ages as wine, cheese, fruit, crackers lavish, good friends, good conversation, knowing smiles, dazzling eyes, warm embraces, sweet kisses, holding hugs, and no thoughts of hurrying, shoes off.

Favorite vacation: cruising. The beautiful part of my more than twenty-five cruises is the confinement on the ship and the expanse of miles of ocean at the same time. I enjoy flying less and less.

Friendships also define who we are, as we learn to trust, love, admire, and grow from relationships like no other experiences.

Keep and make good, strong friendships where possible. Some come for a season, some for a lifetime, and some are toxic, and you must be strong enough to say goodbye. Hang on or let go—you will know. Sometimes you let go of the good to make room for the great.

Know and count your blessings day by day. Count your many benefits; name them one by one. Count your many blessings. See what the Lord has done.

Good God, good friends, good life, good love—that's what Shirleywhirl has won. These are my favorite things.

*He is digging his grave with his teeth.*

*—Morroccan proverb*

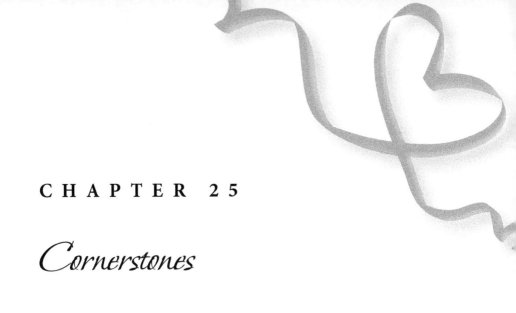

# CHAPTER 25

## *Cornerstones*

### Favorites

Plans and goals are important. Imagery and visualization also are great to do. If you want to do anything, you must see it and believe it! Get a picture in your mind. Then, the thought evolves into a picture. Take the picture, and put it on paper. The picture will be a real image on a real piece of paper, and a thought has become a thing. Take the thing and develop it into a project or a goal—some kind of reality. You now have a beginning. The middle and end is up to you.

### Community Service

Community service makes you a better person, as it allows you to get outside of yourself. The appreciation and recognition plaques in my office remind me of the I've work done and its significance. It has promoted leadership; it has made a difference in my community and in my family. My mother led the way as a role model in community service. I simple followed, and it has been great.

## Friendships

I think friendships are a major part of life and totally worth the effort and time needed to nurture relationships. The relationships forged of trust and loyalty in the course of spending time with friends. Unless you have serious pathology, therapists may not be needed friends will listen without judging, offer advise from the heart. Tell you the truth as they know it and know you when necessary.

Friends can be onversationalists personified, laughter on tap, companionship, and fun. Friendship is two-sided—to have a friend, you must be one. Being there sometimes is all we can do, silence sometimes is the most we can give, a shoulder to lean on, a companion to cry with, one to while away hours of our lives in hobbies and travel, Having a friend is essential to the soul. This saying and blessing in my life is directly from my dad. He knew the special joys of companions and the sharing. He believed it essential to the soul—brotherhood and sisterhood. He was right again.

## Travel

The world is amazing. People are different, yet the same in many ways. Oceans are similar, but the beaches are not. I recommend travel as often as possible. I have been blessed to have seen most of the world, almost every continent, and many more than once. Languages, accents, foods, customs, transportation, scooters, bikes, trains, planes, ships, autos, and buses are all unique, depending on where you are. Travel is renewing to the spirit and can be motivating when you return home. Though people look and speak differently, the human experience is universal. We're all looking for the same things—love and acceptance. We learn to appreciate beauty in many forms, from mountains and rivers to plains and valleys, from skyscrapers to villages and high-rises to huts. You see the smiles of thousands of faces and the eyes of thousands of souls.

## Food

I always have been a foodie. Born in the South, it's part of my culture to place a high priority on enjoying food. From sweet potatoes and greens to watermelons from the fields, my favorites also include any kind of corn, biscuits, cornbread, Southern-fried chicken, catfish, salmon, oysters, crab, shrimp, gumbo, coffee, fried apples, grits, and eggs. I enjoy *Southern Living* magazine that features, for example, thirty-four ways to prepare sweet potatoes. Other food favorites are cabbage and beans (almost any kind), soups, sorbets, and anything sweet. I love nuts—pecans, walnuts, cashews.

My favorite candies are peanut brittle and pralines, followed by chocolate. In fact, there are hardly any foods I don't like. Mom, a home economics major, was a fantastic cook and homemaker. Fine dining was always important in our family. We made a lot of sacrifices in our lives, but I don't recall a time when I ever was hungry or longed for a full tummy. We talked about good food and made grunting sounds, like, "Ummm good." This only inspired my mother to cook even greater dishes. Pineapple upside-down cake was a Sunday favorite; chicken any way you name it, greens, yams, mac and cheese—ummm, ummm.

## Music

I think the world would not turn without music. The rhythmic, mathematical syntax of music is compelling. The timing, energy, movement, and beauty of music is a ministry to the soul. No matter what type of music, the impact of sound is enormous. I have been an amateur pianist since I was ten years old, when I had my first music lesson. My grandmother had a player piano with a paper roll. It was amazing, rocking to the likes of Scott Joplin and other sounds I heard as a child.

I have never become an accomplished pianist, although I've had many teachers. I have continued to play for my own pleasure and absolutely love the time spent on the piano, playing all my favorites. I love classical music and popular music; I adore waltzes; I love country music and ragtime. I love Christian hymns and marches, as I used to play the French horn in the band. Beautiful ballads and vocals are my favorites—Dinah Washington, Ella Fitzgerald, Shirley Bassey, Sarah Vaughn, as well as male vocalists like Nat King Cole, Louis Armstrong, Dean Martin, and Frank Sinatra. Certainly, seasonal Christmas music brings joy and the peace of the season. Now, with Amazon's Alexa and streaming, I start music in the morning for background energy in the house—Chopin, Strauss, Wagner, Souza, Satchmo, Scott Joplin, John Williams, and all the artists of the day that I love, like Sarah Vaughn, Etta James, Chita Rivera, Renée Fleming. What a blessing to hear the gifts of these artists.

## Libations

I learned to enjoy beer while at Fisk University, at Collier's in Nashville. Beer was sold by the quart, and after exams, the pitchers and quarts of beer would fill the table. I developed a taste for it. I prefer beer to most wines.

I also enjoy iced tea and hot tea, and I have experienced high teas in England at the Dorchester; in Australia, at Queen Victoria's Palace; in China; and in Paris. Everywhere I travel, I enjoy a high-tea service. This includes scones, sandwiches, petit fours, sweets, and a good passion tea for me. As for whiskey, Jack Daniel's is my guy, mixed with ginger ale or 7-Up. It has been a favorite since college, where I began enjoying bourbons such as Old Fitzgerald, Old Grand-Dad, Southern Comfort, and Wild Turkey. Bourbon is made from corn, so it fits my roots. I do not fancy scotch, which is made from barley. There is a saying that people on the way up drink bourbon, and that scotch drinkers have arrived. I'm still on my way up, for sure.

## Games

Our family always has enjoyed board games. This has provided the socialization that is so important in family dynamics. It has the competition, the gaming, and the winning. It's no fun to lose. No matter

LOVE A LA CARTE

what kind of face you put on it, winning is better. It's fantastic to do things with other people, like cards, as well as to enjoy things together that you do alone. There are many types of card games. I think it's very important to learn some of these games—bridge, pinochle, Tunk, bid whist, canasta, and many board games. There are hours of enjoyment and socialization to be had if you know how to play board games.

## Cooking

My daughter Paula says cooking is chemistry; baking is science. Paula is a great baker. She makes her own breads. My friend says if you can read you can cook. Just follow the recipe, and soon you may have the recipe mastered. So many people say they can't cook, or they only cook to eat and not starve. I say, if you enjoy food, you probably would enjoy cooking. There are so many shows on television that teach virtually everything about cooking. I think they can make a gourmet cook out of anyone.

I love to cook. I love to hear the sizzle of onions and celery and peppers lightly caramelizing in a skillet. I think about what I want to eat every day and what I want to cook. I love vegetables and tried a plant-based diet for a year, but I could not get enough protein, so I have added lean meats again. Cooking is so easy now that anyone can learn. Just watch all the great chefs on television, or read recipes in magazines. Oh, the spices are exciting!

## Children and Pets

I think children and pets are our blessings and gifts, entrusted in our care to look after, develop, and love. People today often opt out of marriage and children and, instead, choose a pet. It's all good; we all need love to survive. I have evolved on this subject, learning that many couples today choose pets over having children. I think it's amazing— pets have no college tuitions, are always happy to see you, and offer unconditional love.

My chapters on my children relate my personal experience in being blessed with four amazing children, and I will reiterate how awesome they are as human beings. I would admire them, even if they were not my children.

## Aging

At eighty-two years of age, I feel the same mentally as always; it's just that my body does not. It's stiff in the morning; it demands food and drink all day; add a few medicines, quirks, cracks, pains, and itches—something new daily and weekly, but you won't hear complaints from me. I have a chronic back condition that I live with. It sometimes puts me down for a week or more, but I'm alive and feeling blessed. Things wear out, like tooth fillings and implants, like knees and feet, but we press on. These are the golden years, and we know they are not made for the faint of heart.

## Laughter

Laughter is powerful! I love a good joke, story, a comedic play, stand-up comedy. I love ordinary people who are just funny. In my exercise class at Las Ventanas, we began the day with a joke. I was a joke researcher. I had to find a clean joke that was funny. There are thousands, and you must look for the sunny side of a situation to get people to laugh. I must admit that I cuss. I was raised on it by Big Mama, even though I never heard my dad or mother say a single cuss word. For me, it's cathartic; it's also funny.

After my first semester of college, I announced to my parents that I wanted to use the words s***, damn, and hell. Also like many questions I put to them, awkward ones in particular they did not answer me. However, when profanity is used, there is no mistake about your feelings. I know my vocabulary is not limited; I'm not word-lazy. I just feel the right word for some actions is a cuss word, and that is my bad habit—one of them anyway. years later as a more evolved scripture reading christian, my use is limited. I am still a work in progress.

## Spiritual Life

The sustaining force and presence in my life is my relationship with God. The joy and peace I have of being aligned with such a loving power is magnificent. When telling others of the good news, I recount my journey of searching for this wonderful peace. My life has been so blessed, and I have found a deeper relationship with God through study, small groups at church, reading, and my thirst for a closer walk with God. I have recounted my evolution as a Christian, from psychics and astrologers, to Religious Science practitioners, to my current state of joy. This is not to say that I do not panic; have thoughts of fear, distress, or calamity; or worry about my children and myself. But as soon as I can center myself, talk to a friend, or get quiet, I remember the scriptures that I rely upon—God's Word, God's promises, God's grace, God's mercy, God's love. Amen.

*When a person shows you who they are, believe them.*

*—Maya Angelou*

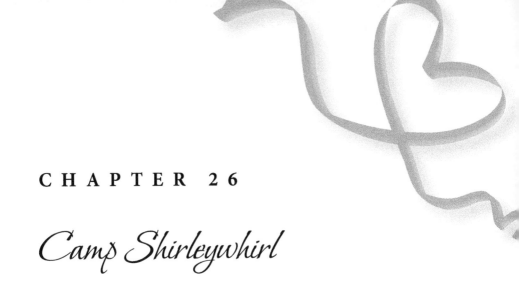

# CHAPTER 26

# Camp Shirleywhirl

The first Camp Shirleywhirl began innocently enough in 2004 and with mostly excitement at just seeing and spending time with the grandchildren. There were eight—five girls and three boys. There is a joy—unlike other gifts to the human spirit—that is deeply evident when you see yourself and your parents and family manifested into the tiny body of a grandchild—the eyes, the determination, the smile, the nose, the ever-constant genes and chromosomes that mark our characteristics.

These times also brought our children together. I was eager to plan our time together into meaningful and memorable moments and hours every day. The daunting reality was that with eight children, from ages two to eight, there would be many logistical challenges. Three meals a day, laundry, and changes of clothing once or twice daily; constant stimulation and entertainment; swimming; mobility; first aid; hair combing; snacks, etc. Paula, who coined the term *Camp Shirleywhirl*, sent along Bere, her live-in housekeeper, who could manage things, much as she did at home.

Each of my three daughters took turns staying a few days as well. I solicited information from other grandmother friends who had entertained their grandkids and got leads on the most exciting age-appropriate venues. The Stirling Club at the Turnberry was a fixed asset, with its hotel-type pools and recreation facilities. Also, the restaurant's swim-up bars were great for salads and burgers after swimming. It is amazing what appetites you can work up after swimming.

I chose to divide the day with two weeks of Bible study at First Presbyterian Church's morning program. It was called "Fun in the Son." That would get them up and into different classes. They did painting and art projects, saw films, had programs, wore special T-shirts, and made new friends. They went with the housekeeper in the limousine daily, Monday through Friday. That gave me time to organize our afternoon, plan lunch, and have it ready when they returned and shared what had happened from nine o'clock to noon. Then they'd get ready for the afternoon.

One venue I chose was the children's museum—truly awesome, as each age group had challenging things for the children. We divided into three groups for supervision, and they loved it. They dressed up as broadcasters, firemen, doctors, and storekeepers, with real sets and pretend roles. They didn't want to leave; they loved it. They could act out roles of adults, and we had pictures galore of them getting into the roles.

Circus Circus Adventuredome was a big request item—the cars, the rides, the merry-go-round, the school bus ride, the airplane rides, the log rides, the screams and thrills of good times were so gratifying. The joy of being with their cousins was amazing; they just loved being together. That first year, the three born in 2000 were four years old. What a group that was. Courtney, at two-going-on-three, kept up with the best of them.

Bonnie Springs, the western ghost town, was a huge hit—a train ride, western clothes, hats, belt buckles, gun fights, and pictures in western clothing. It was so much fun. They also had horseback riding, cows, ducks, and lakes. We had a wonderful meal there, and the animals were a big hit. On the ride up, we viewed wild burros near red rock canyon, and the kids snapped pictures and said, "Look at that, Grandma!"

Once home in the evening, it was more swimming. It was ideal, as the day wasn't as hot, and water games of volleyball and beach ball were really enjoyable. The adults could lounge on the recliners with cool water and books, keeping a watchful eye on the eight children. The rules of water play were carefully repeated—no running, no jumping, and safety first!

"Look out for your brother or sister or cousin"—each child had a partner for the day, and we switched up. Of course, there were timeouts, when one had to sit with me because he or she forgot the rules. But all in all, they were very good.

After swimming, like their mothers and dads before them, there was a daily reminder, after the shower and pajamas, that your towel and swimsuit must be hung to dry and not left on the floor; that your dirty clothes went into the hamper; and that socks and shoes were to be put into the closet in the assigned places. Some liked to tell on someone else who did not live up to the standard expectations, and we had our nightly meetings and discussions of what was really great about their day and what was not. Oh my, we had funny times, laughter, and some tears. Bedtime and root beer floats as a snack was always eventful. We had chores assigned as well, to help Bere and me in the kitchen and with laundry, folding clothes and putting them into assigned places. This all went well, except for the occasionally lost toothbrush, comb, or someone's special ointment for a miniscule pimple or scratch. Swim goggles, fins, and floaties all had color IDs, as did sunglasses. Everyone had a bag with their necessities for motor trips. We had the support of friends and family, and my brother planned a swim party and barbecue one weekend; other family did the same at other times, so we had so much entertainment that they slept well every night.

After all the swim parties and shows we were worn out, sunburned, chlorine eyes, sleep, tours, ice show, movies, shopping—there was no end to the activities or smiles. They fell in love with limousine travel. Nick, the limo driver would serve soft drinks occasionally, and they would be thrilled. Barney, the purple dinosaur, was big at that time. I loved him too. We sang and danced along and had great fun. The success of this venture led us to make scrapbooks for each family, and that was fun in itself. But the next question was, "What are we going to do next, Grandma?"

## 2006—Cory Booker Elected Mayor of Newark

This was a triumphant achievement for a family member. Cory is the son of my sister Carolyn Jordan Booker, my nephew. (2020 update, He is now the U. S. Senator from New Jersey)

We decided we would all go to New Jersey for his inauguration celebration, combining it with Camp Shirleywhirl in New York, staying at the Marriott across from the Statue of Liberty embarkation point at Battery Park. I looked for a hotel with a swimming pool, knowing that after a humid day, the best thing for the kids before bed would be a swim.

I also knew I had to plan how to get around in New York. I remembered their love of limousines, so I contracted for limos to pick up and drop off each at the airport, and then we would have a daily party bus, complete with juices, water, movies, and music to go to each of our venues. The bus took the twenty-two of us everywhere; we even had a stretch Hummer for the World Trade Center, Chinatown, Saint Patrick's Cathedral, and Rockefeller Center. We went to all of the inauguration events, to the nine-acre estate of one of my best friends in South Hampton, and had a family softball game, where everyone had to hit the ball off a tee. The youngest and smallest kid could run the fastest. As Courtney rounded the bases, we could see she was going to be a runner. Two years later, she was a star soccer player on the Pink Cheetahs and now is on a team called Avalanche. Danny and Marcela brought the balls, bats, gloves, and tees from Los Angeles, and the event was amazing. The Museum of Natural History was a day; the Statue of Liberty was a half day. *The Lion King* was awesome, and FAQ Schwartz was a sensational trip—what a store.

We did all the major New York landmarks—Central Park, Times Square (night and day), as well as breakfast and dinner events in New Jersey.

In 2011, we planned a visit to the Grand Canyon, Our family arrived in Las Vegas staying in a deluxe suite at the Sun Coast—bars, bedrooms, game tables, TVs, and fun. Mandalay Bay Hotel cabana rental for the day was the scene for relaxing and picnicing swimming up the lazy river at the hotel; motor trip to Williams, Arizona overnight there and then we boarded the train to the Grand Canyon the next morning.

El Tovar Hotel was awesome at the south rim of the Grand Canyon. The kids dressed for dinner and ordered such dishes as veal chop and apricot chutney. They saw moose, elk, and deer; hiked into the canyon; enjoyed a luxury breakfast overlooking the canyon at El Tovar; shopped; and explored all the tours we had planned. In the hotel at night, we told stories, admired the hotel, and enjoyed the moms and dads who had come along. The train ride back had a western hold-up staged, and the kids enjoyed the entertainment, there and back.

Camp Shirleywhirl is synonymous with family togetherness and fun times.

Since 2004, when the youngest of my eight grandchildren was two years old and the oldest was eight, they have come together for grand adventure trips—Las Vegas, New York City, Grand Canyon, eastern Caribbean cruise aboard Royal Caribbean Cruise Line's largest ship in the world, the *Allure*.

In 2015, we flew from Los Angeles to Paris via Air France and then to Barcelona, Spain. We toured Barcelona for four days and then boarded the *Allure of the Seas* again, two years later, for the western Mediterranean ports of Mallorca, Spain; Provence, France; Florence, Rome (Vatican City), and Naples, Italy; and visiting the islands of Capri, Sorrento, and Pompei. After that, we cruised back to Barcelona, Spain, to disembark and fly to Paris and back home to Los Angeles.

Eight travelers were in this party with me—two daughters (Paula and Patricia) and five of the eight grandchildren: Sofia, Sydney, Shelby, Courtney, and Christopher. My oldest granddaughter, Natalie, was in Paris as a junior cadet at West Point Military Academy on an exchange program. Noah was at Purdue for an internship, exploring his passion for fast motor cars. Nathan was doing summer academic study in Washington, DC.

Barcelona! Arriving in the afternoon after the one-hour flight from Paris, I took a deep breath and exhaled as all the months of planning, schedules, tours, passports, and anticipation was now a reality. We were in Barcelona, our first destination. We quickly checked into our hotel, the Marriott Renaissance Fira Hotel. The kids quickly explored the environment and were immediately scampering to get into swimsuits for a swim on the rooftop pool to relax before dinner. The adults opted for a pitcher of refreshing fruity, fresh sangria and happy-hour chips and salsa on the roof, overlooking the city. The temperature mid-seventies. Barcelona was beautiful.

From the ancient history days of Hannibal in 218 BC and Caesar's Roman conquests around 19 BC to modern-day Barcelona, we found a histoic and fascinating city by day and by night. The template of history was evident everytwhere. Democracy returned to this country in the 1970s, with the Catalan social and cultural institutions building the city we see today. The 1992 Olympics recognized the city as a world capital and a welcoming city that has conserved its historic roots while assimilating the changes brought by modern times.

We first visited the Gothic Quarter building and then to medieval Barcelona, the Picasso Museum, and the Church of Santa Maria Del Mar. We strolled the Rambla, enjoyed the fountains and trees of Placa Reial, the monument to Christopher Columbus, Fisherman's Dock, Gaudi architecture, the La Pedrera balconies, and the Park Guell by Gaudi, which is a mix of architecture and nature. We used three types of transportation to see Barcelona—taxis to main squares, double-decker buses with narrated rides describing everything around us via earphones in English, and the subway, which was a fun, efficient, and safe experience.

After four days of dining at recommended restaurants, enjoying fresh fish to iconic cultural dishes, and being thrilled by the sights, day and night, it was time to leave Barcelona and board our ship, the *Allure*.

The *Allure* was ranked number one out of the fleet of twenty-two Royal Caribbean ships and deemed number one by news reports. You might magine how extraordinary this ship was. This was our second Camp Shirleywhirl voyage on this ship, and we knew it well. We reserved balcony cabins again in the Boardwalk neighborhood so we could sit on the balconies at night and view the aqua shows and zip lines, and clearly the ocean off the back of the ship.

Fascinated with our maiden voyage to the Caribbean, we began following this ship. It was the world's largest ship, holding 6,318 passengers. (2020 update larger ships have been built) The Allure has a ton of activities for the whole family, seven unique neighborhoods that house a variety of events, shows and dining options, surf simulators, a free version of Central Park with twelve thousand trees, jazz concerts in the park, and fine-dining restaurants all around the park. There is a portrait studio, art gallery, and wine cellar. There is an abundance of youth-focused programs, designed by age, with kids and teens-only areas. There are arts and crafts, twenty-five dining options nightly, interactive scientific scavenger hunts, and the world's first Starbucks at sea. The staffing was amazing—a three-to-one guest-to-crew ratio, and the ship seemed so quiet and pristine. We did not see thousands of people. The ship was so well designed. Nonstop entertainment enriched our local port experiences.

The ship was our entertainment at night and our hotel in every port. We saw a show every night after daytime touring. *Mamma Mia!*, stand-up comedy, an ice show, an aqua show, specialty-dinner night, nightclubs, dancing salsa, jazz in the park, the spa, massage, casinos— what a magnificent ship and trip.

On most mornings, the adults loved our tradition of room service; the kids did so sometimes or went to the Wind Jammer deck or dining room. At 6:30 a.m., we had coffee or tea, fruit plates, assorted pastries, and all the trimmings on the balcony while reading the morning newsletter of the day's activities. Then we showered and dressed for the day. Our kids were troupers; they were great—well behaved, appreciative, and helpful.

Mallorca, Spain, was our first port—the beautiful home of Majorica pearls. We toured a factory and passed house in Manacor, owned by the number-one tennis player on clay in the world, Rafael Nadal. In Mallorca, the kids chose to see the Drach Caves. The caves are a subterranean paradise of strange sceneries of silences and petrifactions of limestone. The limestone carbonates have created incredible wonders, which are thousands of stalagmites and stalactites. Why the interest? Because of its unique beauty, the caves have attracted notables, royalty, musicians, politicians, and aristocracy, such as the grand duchess of Austria, and the Paris publication of twelve magnificent lithographs of the best views, making the caves a historical and cultural attraction that did not disappoint.

La Provence in Marseille is a gorgeous French city on the Mediterranean Sea and is breathtaking. We chose to see Marseille by a motorized train on wheels, not tracks, which had about twelve cars holding about sixteen people in each vehicle. The train meanders around the marinas and cafes and up and through the sometimes-narrow city streets. It's necessary to climb steep hills to ultimately arrive at the Basilique Notre-Dame de la Garde built in Romanesque Byzantine architecture. The basilica sits on the highest peak in the city, and the sphere is a statue of the Virgin Mary and child in gold. One look at this centuries-old completed work of art and labor, and I stood in awe and wonder of what man has created to the glory of God! The basilica complements the blue Mediterranean Sea and the blue sky, an image that I will never forget.

The hundreds of steps to ascend to the cathedral are formidable and seem impossible at first, but we soon found ourselves meeting the challenge, as hundreds of tourists climbed and stopped and climbed some more until they reached the top. We felt triumphant at the top. The view was more than spectacular, and the cathedral was magnificent. The city is surrounded by marinas, and the sea. The city awakens late mornings to shopkeepers getting the sidewalk cafes ready for lunch and coffee and people walking everywhere.

We traveled via motor coach from the port through the hills of Tuscany, en route to Florence, to see Italy in its most beautiful natural beauty. We passed the white-marble quarries of Carrara and soon saw the facade of the famed Basilica di Santa Croce. Here lie the tombs of the likes of Michelangelo, Machiavelli, and countless nobility. We experienced a wonderful reserved luncheon of pasta, pizza and caprese salad, sangria, and bottled water in Florence. We enjoyed lots of gelatos and did a lot of shopping for leather goods here.

We walked the squares, where thousands of tourists surrounded us. Everyone was taking selfies as we listened to our tour guide from our earbuds. I had never seen a selfie stick, but here, they were everywhere for sale.

We found the people to be warm and friendly in Italy. Most were patient and helpful, and the architecture was amazingly ornate, with baroque and Romanesque detail; it was evident on most structures.

So much to see, so much to do—the most exhausting day of touring Rome but worth it. We had excellent tour guides throughout this trip; they were well educated and proud of the culture. We had another exotic "The Best of Rome" tour that included lunch at a five-star hotel that was awesome and relaxing. We started the day early, at seven o'clock. The first venue was the Colosseum. Climbing to the top was another challenge, as each step was more than fifteen inches deep. But once on top, we could see it all. It was surreal—we could imagine the chariot races and lion fights of the day. We saw where the animals were kept below the floor of the Colosseum in stalls. There were the elegant porcelain bathrooms for the nobility of the day. Because of its unique design, it could empty all spectators in eighteen minutes.

It was on to the Vatican Museums after lunch, which was typical Italian fare—baked ziti pasta, chicken, broccoli, bottled water, sparkling champagne, and a fruit tart for dessert. Oh, so good—fabulous hotel.

After the Vatican Museums, much improved since my last visit there, with very modern escalators, substantial and bright windows for natural light, there is constant construction and refurbishing, We continued from the museum into the Sistine Chapel and heard some prayers; there were hundreds of tourists there. We viewed the tapestries on the walls and the famed ceiling of Michaelagelo, of course. Then we were on to Saint Peter's Basilica, with all the art, gold, ceiling frescos, incredible architecture, history, and traditions for us to embrace.

We saw the changing of the guard at the Vatican and sculptures and tapestries too many to recount. European history came alive for the grandchildren; some would be studying that subject that fall.

Motor coaches took us back to the port and our ship, and everyone took a little siesta on the ride back from such an awe-inspiring and warm day in Rome. We were back to the ship by six in the evening and took showers. Dinner and a show awaited.

Everything was reserved and preplanned months before. When there is so much to see, you must plan what and when you are going to do it. Time is precious; you get more and miss fewer trip highlights. Our planning was superb; everyone was happy, excited, and overwhelmed. It was the grandchildren's first trip to Europe, but their parents and I had been more than once. We knew what we wanted our kids to see.

Naples was beautiful! We docked here and took a smaller craft that held about four hundred people to the Isle of Capri—one of the most beautiful places in the world, untouched by man, left to its natural beauty. The city is atop the mountain, and access was by *funicular*, a vertical railcar on tracks that ascended to the top. Moments later, we are in a square of exotic designer shops, sweet shops with lemon everything, gardens, and boutique hotels with views of the sea. Everyone drank lemonade while walking the paved, winding paths of this charming city. exotic lifestyles for the very wealthy. The parks, gardens, and flowers manicured and natural were of unusual beauty. Beautiful leather goods and designer clothing filled the shops. Totally tourist or honeymooners attractions. Mariah Carey and her billionaire boyfriend had just left there. The Town was still buzzing with the excitement of her beauty and their visit.

After a few hours, we went back on the boat and took a half-hour cruise to Sorrento, where we had another exceptional tour that included a VIP lunch. The restaurant was waiting for us, and our tables were ready. After bathroom breaks, we enjoyed a sumptuous luncheon that included live violin music, singing, and all kinds of musicians. This was so very special, as the family saw the culture come alive, with music and feasting. The food was outstanding, and e the waiters were gracious, making for a grand time.

Sorrento is a very modern city, with beautiful buildings with flags and elegant architecture. They also make excellent lacquered and hand-painted wooden boxes, as well as all kinds of furniture, game tables, and so on. We toured one of these facilities after lunch. The plates were costly, starting at about one hundred US dollars for a tiny box. The labor of this specialty craft is the reason for the cost. We boarded motor coaches at this point.

We motored to Pompei, the site of the AD 79 eruption of Mount Vesuvius. This volcano erupted so suddenly and unexpectedly that more than thirty thousand people were killed. The city was left buried beneath nearly twenty feet of volcanic lava. The ruins visible today have been stripped of all value—some say by churches, for preservation—and stand as an emblem of a great city that once stood. It was sobering.

The last night on the ship was excellent. After packing and dinner and dancing, we said goodbye to waiters, cabin stewards, and friends we met and realize how fast the time went.

Why can't vacations last longer? We celebrated Patricia's fiftieth birthday, and waiters brought out nine types of meat in a feast to remember at Samba Grill, a specialty restaurant on the *Allure*. Nothing topped that feast—not dinners, the desserts, salad bar, or exotic drinks. It was another Camp Shirleywhirl to remember. We returned safely to Barcelona, to the airport, and back to Paris, to Charles de Gaulle Airport. It is an adventure in itself to navigate through this vast, unique airport, as we were to fly to Los Angeles from there. Air France was the right choice; the service was great, the in-flight entertainment package was excellent, and the food was tasty—nice hot meals and plenty of food, drinks, and snacks. We were all together, four in a row in two rows, one behind the other. It was nothing less than beautiful memories forever, and lots of "Thank you, Grandma," and hugs.

This was far more than just a family vacation. My grandchildren did not see families that looked like them on Air France or on the *Allure*. These excursions are really about the saying, "To whom much is given, much is expected."

> I say thank you, Lord, for safety and protection over
> land and sea
> For sights to behold that our eyes did see
> For hearts of thanksgiving and spirits of glee
> All due to your love and blessing of thee

*Voyager of the Seas, Singapore, 2017*

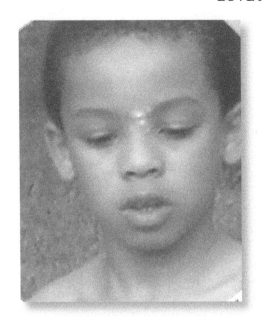

*All work is noble.*

*—Maria Montessori*

# CHAPTER 27

## *5831 Overhill Drive*

*Dental office from 1967 to 1994*

On the southwest corner, at 5831 Overhill Drive, a one-story brick building stood on a large hole with a vacant lot in the rear. The area was mostly residential, except for this building, and directly across the street was a pediatric medical facility, headed by Dr. Burack, and Overhill Pharmacy, owned by Sam Baskin.

My husband, Dan, and I were both newly licensed doctors in California. Before we moved, I just had completed a one-year hospital internship at DC General Hospital and a Guggenheim fellowship in pediatric dentistry in New York. I had a posh job at Group Health on Pennsylvania Avenue. I treated White House patients and made $ 12,400 a year. Dan had just completed his surgery residency and a year at Sloan Kettering Medical Center in New York. Patricia, our baby girl, was only a month old. We had very little money. Fortunately, we had no student loans, like the students today have started out.

To move, we each borrowed five thousand dollars from the Interns and Residents Association. Our four children were aged two months to five years in 1967, so we decided to leave our Mustang in Washington, to be shipped out later. Instead, Dan flew out to California to borrow my dad's Cadillac; then he returned to bring our family west.

We both quickly took jobs to have the income to qualify for a home. I took one paying $16,500 a year, and Dan found one as chief of surgery at the Watts Health Center for $26,000. This income was more than enough for us to qualify and afford the beautiful home in the hills that I had dreamed of. My husband had thought it was all a fantasy that we could even get to California or that we would be able to immediately buy a home within weeks of arriving, get the children settled, and get help. Thanks to my parents, we were introduced to the Bank of Finance, a bank for blacks with area businessmen on the board, including Tom Bradley, who became the mayor of Los Angeles.

We called a realtor, and it looked as if there were no obstacles, only possibilities. Eventually, I found the house. It had a beautiful backyard and a fire pit, swimming pool, diving board, and an extended covered patio. The floors were terrazzo, and all of the built-ins reduced the immediate need for furniture, except beds and seating.

The kitchen was a dream with cove base flooring, multiple built-ins, and even a milk door that opened into the kitchen. The home had maid's quarters, a central vacuum, a sunken living room, and lovely, large bedrooms. After closing, we settled in within a few months. After getting an excellent live-in housekeeper for the children and enrolling them in private school, Dan and I set our sights on transitioning into work. I knew I wanted to get into private practice, as did Dan.

Dan found an office space in a high-rise building on Santa Rosalia Drive, which was the mecca of professionals practitioners. Dan never quite left what was supposed to be a temporary job at the Watts Health Center. Instead, he stayed there for the next thirty-two years, doing surgery in the hospital in addition to his private practice. He kept that office as well for the next thirty years.

I had a different plan. I went looking for a building to buy but could not see one close to our home for sale. We lived high in the hills; the area was often referred to as Pill Hill, as so many doctors lived there. Dan's office was down in the valley, on the east side of the hill.

I saw the one-story brick building on 5831 Overhill Drive and was drawn to the potential of the building. As I've mentioned, Dr. Epstein's medical office was on one side, and Dr. Jeffrey Widen's podiatry office was on the other side. I went into the medical office and told the receptionist that I was looking for an office to open my practice. I asked if they had ever thought about selling. This lovely woman, Dr. Epstein's wife, asked me to have a seat in the waiting room and shortly called me into the office. That's when she explained that Dr. Epstein was not well—he had emphysema—and they had talked about renting until he was ready to retire, but they would consider selling.

We negotiated a note for the purchase—five thousand dollars down and four hundred dollars a month on a ten-year note. This was a blessing! I purchased the building, which already had a paying tenant in the rental unit—the podiatrist Dr. Jeff Widen paid me $165 a month.

I accepted a job as a school dentist until my practice built up to ensure cash flow, but my practice built quickly and became very successful. After a year or so, I had to quit the school board job. Before I left, I was offered the top dental job of director when the director and his wife were killed in the Tenerife airport disaster. This was tragic, but I still felt it was time to say goodbye to the school-dentist experience at that point. I had secured a lifetime teaching credential with a specialization in health to qualify for the position.

There were several experiences that I knew I did not want, and one was having a lot of debt. I furnished my dental office with used equipment, which cost a fraction of the cost of new furniture. Vic Clark was a dental supply salesman down on Pico Boulevard. He helped me furnish my entire office. I watched as he installed my equipment, and I learned how to repair my tubings and water lines, run my compressors, and manage all aspects of the maintenance of my machines.

After a year or so, I did buy a new large panorex, or panoramic dental x-ray machine. That was great for my pediatric practice because no intraoral film was needed. It was the latest and greatest thing in dentistry. It helped with the diagnosis of everything from fractures of the jaw to orthodontic and eruption studies. It was not intended to detect dental caries or decay. It was also quite a profit center for the office.

Our children were enrolled in the Pilgrim School, affiliated with the First Congregational Church of Los Angeles, which today still has the largest pipe organ in the city. The Christmas programs there are legendary; we always attend if we're in town. The issues of integration, the John Birch Society, and other stories of high drama at the church make for another story. Nevertheless, our children were served a hot lunch daily, studied a core curriculum, and got an excellent education. As I've mentioned, Dan Jr. and Patricia integrated the nursery school. Evalina Clark was the headmistress, who later left and assist Robert Schuller in building the Crystal Cathedral in Orange County.

Daily chapel was a part of the school regime. I desired for my children to learn the Bible, as well as how to treat other people, while being educated. The public school in our area was not an option because our children, who began school at age two in Washington, DC, had read everything in the public-school curriculum for their grade level. They would not have been challenged. I knew we had to continue with private schooling. It took a rigorous search and three full weeks for me to locate a school. My history of Congregational Church attendance was the key to finding the Pilgrim School. A teacher at the Pride School in Hollywood had asked what religion was I, which led to a recommendation.

Thirty years later, Pilgrim is still producing top students, and three of my grandchildren attended the same school. When I was in town and picked them up, I opened the same gates that were there when my children attended—déjà vu.

Our housekeeper, Maria, would be with us for the next nine years. Maria had become a member of our family. She flew home when her mother was ill. We helped with repairs to her mother's roof in Morelia, Mexico. We dealt with border guards to help her get back into the States after all efforts she had tried failed. That is another story as well.

The overall result was a bustling dental office, only about eight minutes from home. It was such a blessing to be so close. Ultimately, the success I enjoyed led to hiring five dentists to work with three hygienists and me, at my peak. I enlarged the office, of course, and took over the rental office suite. Dr. Widen moved to Oregon.

As I was appointed by the governor to the State Board of Dental Examiners, the Northeast Regional Board of Examiners for over fifteen states, and as a commissioner of the American Dental Association in Chicago. I was always coming back home to Overhill Drive. We held meetings there with our state representatives, other dentists, and community leaders. I founded the Association of Black Women Dentists there on Overhill Drive.

We raised money and scholarships and mentored young women in how to build a profession, a family, and a business. Upon retirement from clinical practice, I sold the building for over six times what I'd paid for it and, and the goodwill of thirty years.

The buyer, a Black Woman dentist named Dr. Joni Forge, has been there for twenty five years now and is also very successful. Overhill afforded me the ability to help a lot of children and families, as well as providing me extra family time, a good income, the flexibility to accept a governor's appointment, the proximity to home and children, and an extraordinary career. Dr. Epstein passed away three years after selling me the building, and Mrs. Epstein returned to Canada.

They were paid off earlier than ten years and remain one of the many blessings to our family and me. Overhill Drive will always be so very special to me.

Dr. Pop Walton at Howard University College of Dentistry, Prosthodontics Department invited me over to his private office one day in Washington, DC, along with some of my classmates, to see his vintage office, pump chair, and antique cabinets. He had a name for this sacred place where he spent so much of his life, a name I have never forgotten. He called it the "Glory Hole". Well, Overhill was indeed glorious.

*There is no fool like an old fool.*

*—unknown*

# CHAPTER 28

## *Letter to My Younger Self*

Dear Shirley 48,

Upon reflection, with all humility to my parents, teachers, friends, and, not the least, God, I find myself with my hands up in the air, applauding most of the decisions and accomplishments you have made in your life to this point:

- wife
- mother
- dentist
- appointment by governor of California Jerry Brown to the State Board of Dental Examiners
- honored by your peers when elected as president of the board
- first black woman dentist in the United States,
- appointed to a dental licensure board
- elected by your peers as a five-year commissioner to the American Dental Association in Chicago (national board exams)
- consultant to the Northeast Regional Board of Dental Examiners
- owner of a successful dental practice, employing five dentists, three hygienists, and five dental assistants,
- founder of the Association of Black Women Dentists
- publisher of a dental newsletter

- mentor for young dentists
- serving on volunteer dental teams to Jamaica
- delivering health care services to the underserved in summer

Good on you, Shirley. With this busy life, the number-one priority was family; quality time to nurture and care for four intelligent children, now all college students—Paula at Harvard, Pam at Yale, Patricia at Yale, and Danny, the last off, to Notre Dame. Remember the exhilaration? The feeling of *he's off*! Not a feeling of an empty nest at all. Husband, Dan, felt it a lot more; he missed the activity at home. You? You did all your crying at Harvard Square, New Haven Commons, and South Bend, Indiana, when you said goodbye at the universities.

Your philosophy with your four children had always been to give them roots, and give them wings, and watch them soar.

Dan Sr. went on his annual hunting trip to shoot deer in Oregon. He went every year with the guys for the last ten years, so you thought, *Why don't I take off for Europe with friends?* You've been blessed with high energy and good health, and you loved adventure and achievement, and this was a milestone you wanted to celebrate—the last child off to college.

You sent your live-in housekeeper, Maria, to Mexico for a month and put your staff on rotating vacations. You left your office manager in charge, and your dear friend Marilyn was "all in" to go with you. You kissed Dan goodbye as he left for his hunting trip, and then "Birdie" (Marilyn's nickname) and you were off.

There used to be an airline called TWA (Trans World Airlines). They featured TWA get-away vacations. This looked good—Amsterdam, Germany, Switzerland, Vienna, Budapest, Venice, Genoa, Nice, Monte Carlo, and a Rhine River cruise. Foods and wines and tours—this was awesome. You could climb stairs, dance in Vienna, walk forever in Budapest and Italy, and enjoy pasta and desserts to your heart's content. You had been twice before with the family, and it was enjoyable, but you had been much more guarded with the children while showing them points of interest and keeping up with them. Their safety and your being Mom were most important. This was *freedom*, with no one to look after and a great friend with whom to share the tours and fun. You had a month.

It was a triumphant point of fact that the last child was off to college, and motherhood, as you once knew it, was done. You'd had twenty-three years of total responsibility for your four. Now, it would never be the same. That was a milestone for you and one that was to be remembered, Shirley 48.

I am so grateful you had the wisdom to know that you must see the roses as well as smell the roses along the journey and drink the wine. It energizes you with even bigger dreams. Going forward, cruising became your favorite mode of travel, and Dan enjoyed those vacations. Although he had many responsibilities as chief of surgery, you managed to get him aboard at least once a year. Travel has added so much enrichment, enlightenment, and joy to your lives. It also was beneficial to your patients and staff, as you always were so inspired upon returning.

Shirley 78, at fifteen months shy of age eighty, has this note to express why she is so thankful to Shirley 48:

Today, many things have changed. Red-eye flights are over. A wheelchair is usually waiting for me curbside, as my back prevents me from standing at length in lines or lifting anything that weighs more than ten or twelve pounds. Security lines are too long and painful to call these "pleasure trips." A cruise or other vacation now requires me, Shirley 78, to arrive in the departure city two to three days, minimum, before sailing to recover from the flight to the port city. A good hotel with a firm mattress and a spa is a fundamental desire, and words such as *rest*, *decompress*, and *assess* are the first to come to mind. After refreshing myself and resting, a high tea or a comfortable city tour might work or just a nice dinner and a good night's sleep. I may then be ready to set sail for destinations planned in a day or two. Doing the same self-care on board the ship, I can usually enjoy all activities and tours and still fly from the port city directly home without a problem. I must allow a week to recover before the resumption of normal activities—exercise, appointments, etc.

Shirley 48 never thought about these adjustments that might be needed in thirty years so that she could enjoy travel and vacations in her senior years. So thank you, Shirley 48, for packing as much life into every day and year, from those times until now. I have seen a lot of this world—about thirty cruises—since you started your magic travel jaunts, from jazz-themed cruises to historical points or island retreats. I have many memories that allow me to continue to enjoy those experiences over and over again. The pictures that are so easy to take now are like a miracle when compared to all the cameras we used to lug around.

Sincerely,
Shirley 78


Shirley 82,

You can see how long it is taking me to write this book. Each day is a gift and a blessing indeed. Complaints—I have a few but too few to mention. Thankful is my mantra to God for all that I see and experience every day.

Sincerely,
Shirley 82

*Some people dream of worthy accomplishments while others stay awake and do them.*

*—Dr. Alan Zimmerman*

# CHAPTER 29

## *Just a Mouthful*

I have learned a few things about the pearly whites and their supreme importance to the health and wellness of each of us. Let's look at a few fascinating facts and some theories. For an expectant mother-to-be, it's an exciting, vibrant, life-affirming moment in her life, as well as the baby on board. Just six weeks into gestation begins the complex process by which the primary dentition is formed, and permanent teeth start to form in the twentieth week. Teeth are formed from embryonic cells, grow, and erupt into the mouth. At the cellular level, it is a fascinating process. Hundreds of thousands of pages of research have been written on the stages of development of teeth, called *odontogenesis.* From the bud, cap, bell, apposition, and eruption stages, beginning to end, if the teeth do not form at near precise time frames, they will not develop at all.

If the mother has some difficulty at any stage of the pregnancy before the twentieth week, the difficulty in her health may cause defects in the teeth, malformation, or no formation. The process is mostly the same for nonhumans. By the time the baby is born, all twenty teeth are formed. The stage of initial calcification is done by fourteen weeks in utero, the crown at one and a half months after birth, and the roots at one and a half years after birth.

Each tooth type—incisors, cuspids, molars—has a separate developmental stage. Teething starts at about two to four months.

Just a little anatomy review tells us that enamel, the hardest substance in the body, covers the crown; cementum covers the root. We have dentin inside the crown, which is usually impacted by decay, and the pulp, where the nutrients are supplied to the tooth. We have the gingivae surrounding the tooth at the level of the crown. The space between the gingivae and the tooth is the periodontal space, which can become infected, harbor microbes, and is the leading cause for loss of teeth in adult patients, while dental decay (caries) is the prominent cause of loss of teeth in young people.

In the United States dental caries has become a totally preventable disease. More than 60 percent of children are free of this disease, due to fluoridation of public drinking water, fluoride toothpaste and rinses, topical application of fluoride as public health initiatives, sealants of fissures in the crowns of teeth, regular check-ups, and brushing and flossing at home.

Electric toothbrushes, water sprays, Waterpik, sonic care, dental tape, mint floss, every size and shape of dental aids are available for preventive care. Our drugstores today have a plethora of manufacturers with preventive aids. We have come a long way in the last fifty years. Most children find it exciting to see their dentists. There are colorful offices, high-tech equipment, headphones, toys, information, hygienists, x-ray techs, and so many beautiful people. They love going, plus they get a new toothbrush and no cavities.

In many other countries, this is not the case. Education and prevention have been hallmarks of the dental profession. Loss of teeth in the deciduous dentition is a natural process, as the permanent teeth normally follow into the dentition. Loss of teeth is unnatural when attacked by dental caries. Teeth are treated in a variety of ways, but the infected dentine must be removed from the tooth, conventionally done by a drill.

The evolution of the dental drill alone is a fascinating story. We have water spray to cool the drill, high-speed drills and lasers, diamonds, carbide—all things that can cut through the hardest substance in the body, enamel. We can fill the cavity preparation with a variety of dental materials. Amalgam used to be used universally, but it mostly has been replaced by resins that are tooth-colored and esthetically and cosmetically attractive. We can do onlays, inlays, precision attachments, and crowns, full and three-quarters. We used to use gold foil, gold crowns, but now mostly use porcelain fused to precious metal for crowns and implants.

If you have a healthy underlying bone, the best way today to replace a tooth is the use of a precious-metal implant. If you do not have good bone, most of the time, cadaver bone can be inserted into the area surgically, or we can use some synthetic material to create stability around the implant. A significant benefit is that you do not have to cut down two perfectly good teeth to make a bridge in the loss of a single tooth. Titanium is very tissue-compatible, and the success of these procedures has a more than thirty-year record of proven success. The cost may seem prohibitive at the outset to the average patient, until it is compared to a fixed bridge or the damage that a drifting tooth can do to the dentition.

We are living in a significant period of many options for dental tooth replacement. Cost is still a difficult hurdle for many people, and only a percentage of the population has dental insurance. Dentistry can be a postponed service unless there are pain and infection, and many go without replacement far too long. This leads inevitably to more dental problems and more cost.

Payment plans should be requested, and care purchased as soon as possible. Dental clinics of dental schools, if you have the time wait, is another portal of access to care. Public health and free clinics usually focus on emergency care and the alleviation of disease and pain. Follow-up summary—digestion begins in the oral cavity with the mastication of food and the mixture of salivary gland secretions with our food and enzymes, such as ptyalin, that start the process. Our incisors tear the food, our premolars press and manage the food, and our molars grind the food before swallowing.

Your teeth are the beginning of the alimentary canal that provides nutrients to the entire body. If you do not have a healthy oral cavity, you are not a healthy person. So many people do not recognize the importance of proper dental care and treatment until it is cost-prohibitive, or they have periodontal disease, and dentures become a final option. Implants can be used here, especially in the mandible for retention, and the prosthesis snapped in. We have not discussed relevant specialties of dentistry such as endodontics, prosthodontics, oral surgery, and orthodontics, but all are tremendously evolved and high-tech advantaged today.

Today, people are living well past one hundred years old. The quality of life, enjoyment of food, and esthetics are directly related to a sound dentition. My ninety-four-year-old mother has all of her own teeth and has never had periodontal disease. She had orthodontic treatment, full braces, at sixty-four years old and has generally enjoyed excellent health. This history is multiplied thousands of times over today in healthy seniors. From babies to centenarians, taking your teeth seriously is a wise consideration. They are saying today, "Save the baby teeth of your children. They may one day save their lives." Research is doing so much.

All other cells of our bodies are replaced through mitosis, cell division, and new batteries. This is not the case in odontogenesis or the morphology of teeth. There is only one window of opportunity for development. Nature only gives one chance to form teeth—once and no more. Research is working on tooth regeneration, but it is not here yet. For health, wellness, and a great smile, attractive, healthy teeth are absolutely necessary. Whether yours or Artificial replacements, no smile is complete without them.

Just a word on dental implants: they're a good thing. Years of success now provide quality care and treatment for anyone and everyone. Access will get better as costs decline. It's very expensive for the low-income population, but technology has been phenomenal—and that is a mouthful.

*The cave you fear to enter holds the treasure that you seek.*

*—Joseph C. Campbell*

# CHAPTER 30

## Las Vegas and Beyond

Factual data compiled from the Greater Las Vegas Association of Realtors and State Demographer—Population Facts:

    1850: 0
    1860: 6,857
    1990: 1,201,833
    2000: 1,998257
    2012: 2,690,531
    2020: 3,452,283
    2030: 4,282,102
    People per square mile: 10.9 in 1990; 18.2 in 2000

I want to take you on a trip to the year 2275. None of us will be here, but would you look into the future of our world for a few moments? I promise you some new and exciting data and a world we have only seen in the movies. At the very least, we can imagine life in the future as, I think, a little better than our ancestors, say, two hundred years ago. Would they believe air conditioning, supersonic jets, cell phones, the internet, or thousands of people living to one hundred years old? No, I do not think so.

But we can see and believe life in two hundred years from now because of the infancy of many technological projects we are already using. For example, most of us now live in some kind of housing on land—single-family, clusters, apartment buildings, mobile homes, high-rises, farms, huts, trailers, mansions, estates, retirement homes, ships, boats, caves, whatever.

In 262 years, almost one-third of the entire population will be living in homes that float in the sky or on the sea, rather than permanently fixed on a plot of land. They will be tethered on dry land for lengthy periods or sea barges. They will be lightweight, with air vacuum lift, alongside advanced propulsion and maneuvering systems, relatively as hard-shelled balloons with living spaces hanging at the bottom. Should I repeat that? Living above the land and on and above the water.

Sixty percent of the high middle class or average elite will live in an environment of 100 percent automation of home, office, vehicles, and aircraft, which they will completely fly and operate themselves. This life requires minimal levels of human intelligence because programmed robots will be doing everything. Appliances will not be needed to cook food or wash clothes, and individual possessions that do not maintain themselves will be rendered obsolete. (The poor will be land-based, with only partial automation.)

Many light-speed transport vehicles are already available and acceptable for human transport within the solar system and beyond. Wealthy individuals now use much of this technology for security measures, making doorways, for example, obsolete. There will just be portals of entry and exit in the future. This is a simple progression of existing technology, expanding as much as has occurred over the last fifty years. Are you even just a little bit interested yet?

This is not a science fiction; this is the reality of science and technology that has evolved in our lifetimes, and this is beyond known forms of automation, robots, transport, lifestyle, life expectancy, energy, entertainment, health care, movement, and life to new innovative plateaus that keep changing.

Okay, let's look closer to home. Let's move to the next decade—ten years, not two hundred.

According to state demographer Jeff Hardcastle, Nevada will have a sizzling population growth by 2024. With 1.1 million more people living in Nevada, the population will swell by 59 percent in twenty years, with southern Nevada growing by 69 percent. Nevada will grow to 3.6 million people in 2024, from the current 2.3 million.

Nevada's growth will continue to outpace the nation as a whole. National growth is at 19 percent and Nevada at 69 percent. These new projections, while substantial, are actually a slow-down when compared to the boom of the last twenty years, when Nevada's population soared by 150 percent. But southern Nevada climbed to 197 percent. People are coming; they are on the highway right now.

By 2030, Nevada will be the nation's fastest-growing state, with an aging population that should double by 2030. Of the 2.3 million people we will add over the next twenty-five years, one in four will be older than sixty-five years. That is a 264 percent change in the elderly population.

*Ten thousand people a day are turning sixty-five, and this will continue for another fifteen years.*

I was saving that data for the end of this book but could not resist slipping that in right here. That is such powerful information for investors and creative people who look to make life convenient and easier for people. They know that the senior population will have many needs, and they will be there to supply them and create them.

I know what you are thinking: how long will it be before Nevada has the clogged freeways like California and all the inevitable challenges associated with population explosions—the fears, the dreaded change? That word *progress*—I don't like it. But let's take a closer look. Why is Nevada such a sizzling center of growth? You must be wondering how this desert state, with a history of boxing and mining, is now so popular.

It takes the following parameters to attract high-tech companies and working people—and Nevada has them all:

- Major air and rail system
- Major military installations—we have two: Nellis Air Force base and Area 51 at Creech. Ninety-seven percent of the land at these installations is owned by the federal government. Nellis Air Force Base was built to protect a major source of energy power at the time, Hoover Dam. Creech Air Force Base is the nation's primary launch pad of drones.

- University-level engineering school to facilitate high tech—UNLV. In the last decade, Nevada has added the Boyd Law School, a dental school, and enhanced medical school. UNLV continues to grow.

In addition, consider that Las Vegas has the following:

- a desirable climate
- Lake Mead and Mount Charleston
- desirable retirement living
- largest internet hub in the United States

Of note: Because of the Dakotas natural gas deposit discovery and fracking processing was rendered relatively inexpensive to earlier methods of oil extraction, it is projected that within the United States, we have a four-thousand-year supply of energy. This is huge. We do not need Middle Eastern oil. Sh! We have reserves.

Let's look at water. The Colorado River and Lake Mead are not the only sources. Under the town of Pahrump is the second-largest water reserve in the United States. The technology problem of utilization is a challenge that science is now working on, and, like fracking and other challenges, it is just a matter of time. Removing the water without the sinking of the land is the issue. Where we live, Summerlin was the largest master-planned community in the United States for fifteen years. Lake Las Vegas was the best luxury condominium community in the United States for two years.

What will the growth look like, ethnically and culturally? By 2020 in the United States, there will be the following:

- 255 million whites, an addition of 40 million
- 45 million blacks, an addition of 13 million
- 23 million Asians, Pacific Islanders, an addition of 8 million
- 3 million American Indian, Eskimos, and Aleutians, an addition of 1 million
- 51 million Hispanics, an addition of 24 million

Hispanics will account for one-third of all population growth. Large growth areas will be 150,000 to Parumph, 180,000 to Mesquite, and 150,00 to Coyote Springs.

New business models for growth management are in process in every area of our society. No longer do people just sit and watch television. Television must go where people are to hold their attention. No longer can content stories and data be produced and televised, because a sponsor or producer desires it. if a program is loved by the audience the audience loves back via twitter and other interactive media outlets as to their satisfaction of the programming in addition to ratings and numbers.

We live in a world of scanners, lasers, robots, internet, faxes, and phones not in use.

Five years ago, items were deemed smart. Printers were not repaired; they were replaced. There are new knees, legs, organs, eyes, ears, and a world changing so fast you have to constantly read and watch *60 Minutes* and Bill Maher on HBO to get a glimpse.

The Brookings Institution think tank moved to Las Vegas in 2018. I thought then that it was huge. Now, I know it is.

Within five years, there will be no more paper in real estate transactions; you will get a CD for papers of ownership. Paper is leaving the business world for transactions as rapidly as they can transform systems. "Go paperless" is all you see online in banking. We are nudged gently until—kaboom—it will be gone.

Ten thousand people a day are turning age sixty-five and will continue at this rate for another fifteen years, by 2028. City and county housing planning target dates.

In the immortal words of Limuary Jordan, my father, "There are three kinds of people in the world: those who make things happen, those who watch things happen, and those who never knew what happened."

He would turn to me and say, "Which one will you be?" There is the challenge today: which one will you be? Hang on; the ride ahead may be bumpy. If you can manage the day-to-day technology, you will enjoy the ride.

Use the automatic scanner at the supermarket. Use the ATM occasionally. Get a smartphone. Stay connected as long as you comfortably can. We are moving very rapidly to the cessation of many strongholds, such as mail and telephone service, as we traditionally know them.

Seventy percent and upwards of young people no longer maintain home phones, for example. Mobile phones are the only contact, with texting, tweeting, and email.

And they are living the mantra of "Be the change you want to see."

*God must have loved the common man; he made so many of them.*

—Abraham Lincoln

# CHAPTER 31

## *November 2012*

Here are some words: one billion dollars in ads. A definite choice for women! Real consequences for families with a radical difference in the two candidates.

As Americans, every four years we are bombarded with, "This message was paid for by citizens for the president of the United States." I'm Yankee Doodle Dandy, and I approved this message. Or a political PAC or Super PACs from "voters in America," or Crossroads, or Who Counts. We must preserve our freedoms. These are the words and phrases and sounds on the nation's airways and social media outlets we have heard.

Here are a few: Medicare, tax cuts, national deficit, national debt, China, election fraud, Affordable Health Care Act, Obamacare, repeal, the middle class has been buried, the 47 percent who pay no taxes, the 1 percent, cultural warfare, jobs, jobs, jobs, unemployment numbers, 8.3, 7.8, polls, those who have stopped looking for work.

Who is leading in what? Polls, polls, the Gallup, Marist, CNN, ABC, *USA Today* poll, exit polls. The truth is, there is so much polling today that the statistical reliability of yesteryear is unreliable. It is very expensive to do good polling. There are bad polls and good polls, state polls and national polls, liberal polls and conservative polls. Biases are invisible, and reliability and probability are not as certain.

We have swing states, battleground states, toss-up states, red states, blues states, and the United States. We have ground game, campaign workers, challengers, registering to vote, early voting, absentee voting, Latino vote, African American vote, Jewish vote, union vote, white male vote, women's vote, young people's vote, independent vote, right-wing conservative vote, liberal vote, gay and lesbian community vote, gay rights. We have failure. Expiration of the Bush tax cuts—how we got into this mess in the first place? The Bush administration.

Worst recession since the Depression of the 1930s. Thirty consecutive months of jobs gains, TARP, education opportunities for all, fair share, same-sex marriage, turning back the clock on women, Planned Parenthood, anti-abortion legislation, Roe v. Wade's repeal, women's health center for reproductive rights, preexisting conditions, Muslim, Mormon, illegal immigrants, dream act, Florida, Ohio, Virginia, $452 million spent. single-payer plan, voucher system, cuts in programs, fiscal issues, seniors, disabled, getting out the vote, veterans' vote, congressional races, rising gas prices, value of the dollar, control of the House, control of the Senate, balanced budget, debt ceiling, teleprompter, debates, performance, winner, *Meet the Press*, *Face the Nation*, *This Week*, Fox news, Bill Maher, Stephen Colbert, talk radio, NPR, pundits, spin, campaign, race to the top, contest, numbers, margin of error, loser, spiral, leading from behind, Chicago, press release, next debate, on the trail, disaster, strategy, campaign speech, stump speech, tradition, rally, ideas, game on, surge, momentum, stalled, US military, defense, foreign policy, dodges, spins, Libya, eliminate, deductions, credits, tax cuts, distribution, fair share, $5 trillion, wrong, incorrect, facts, fact check, waste, savings, interview, centerpiece, a plan, press secretary, 2012, November, stronger, middle class, Al-Qaeda, Taliban, Afghanistan, Syria, Iran ambassador, terror, terrorist, consult US embassy, Washington, DC, State Department, United Nations, security adviser, Bibi Netanyahu, General Petraeus, wounded, Pakistan, rules of engagement, gravitas, credibility, Secretary Hillary Clinton, President Bill Clinton, Navy SEAL team.

Bin Laden is dead, drones, dangerous, economic collapse, 911, Tunisia, assassin, protect ourselves, peaceful, freedom, human rights, women, children, young girls, 2008, agreement, democracy, Arab Spring, commander, anti-American, truth, dominating, conditions on the ground, money needed, money spent, record, election, Big Bird, Sesame Street, question, Democrats, Republicans, Tea Party, Benghazi, offshore drilling, Keystone pipeline, television ads, telephone surveys, reckless path, EPA, clean energy, American coal, biodiesels and fuels, Wall Street, Main Street, patriotism, business, protests, unrest, Susan Rice, security, politics, committee, hearing, warning, scandal, allegations, politicized, intelligence, community, story, breaking news, the facts, status quo.

Emergency room, Buckeye State, equal pay, the *Daily Beast*, the *New York Times*, *Newsweek*, *Time* magazine, the *Huffington Post*, CNN, MSNBC, moderators, Jim Lehrer, Candy Crowley, skepticism, flip-flop, tax cut for the wealthy, capital gains, reduction, federal government, bankrupt, bipartisan, across the aisle, moderate, tax reform, Grover Norquist, fiscal policy, religious right, foreign policy, severe conservative, economist, science, arithmetic, tax bracket, class warfare, arctic drilling, small businesses, reporters, violent crime, inner cities, preview, backlash, rating, off camera, college graduates, rising incomes, 100 percent, American people, fight, loopholes, gains, struggles, reelection, poor, God, flag, Lilly Ledbetter, public subsidies, Social Security, war, opposition, pro-choice, pro-life, auto industry, uninsured, gun laws, NRA, seat belt, tight race, electoral votes, hard sell, serious issues.

Joe Biden, Paul Ryan, tone focus, course correction, leadership, platform, choice, advantage, into the fold, disenfranchisement, engaging, a stake, drugs, incarcerated, loyalty, important, legitimate, authentic, contraceptives, crime, map, election reform, voter ID, gender gap, women in binders, Bain Capital, my team, offensive, independents, undecideds, ads buy, sketchy plan, out schools, Rose Garden speech, terrorist attack, buried, tempers, rudeness, contentious, presidential decorum, the country is safe, reverse, closure, Clinton and Springsteen, rock-star power, investigation, panel, electoral tie, popular vote, wrong note, blunders, walk it back, stepped into it, nineteen days to go, one more debate.

Ohio. No Republican has won the presidency without winning Ohio, ads, money, ground game, forward, under the policies of the president, putting people to work, "Hail to the Chief," fired up, attack, 538 electoral college votes, 269 each, senior political editor, happening, delegation, Thomas Jefferson vs. Aaron Burr, seventy-three each.

Health, dynamic, Federal Reserve, US Treasury, Americans, in charge of their own future. The heart in each of us. Pocketbook, banks, housing, family. Does the math add up? Prompts, results, coalition, together, resume vetting, collaboration, process, years, trends, correcting the record, charity, the world.

Israel, five-point plan, twelve million new jobs, House Republicans decree of obstructionism to the president, the rebuke of bipartisan efforts, pulse, sensibility, listening to people, New York City, Ann Romney, Michelle Obama, Governor Romney, President Obama. God bless you, and God bless the United States of America.

*No matter how you feel, get up, dress up, show up, and never give up.*

*—Regina Brett*

# CHAPTER 32

# *The Drive-Through*

My fascination with the drive-in restaurant began when I was a teenager in Los Angeles. My city was the mecca of drive-through food service. The drive-ins were attractive to look at and were part of many a date night after a volleyball or basketball game, movie, or just coming home from the beach. The architecture was similar to all of them—a round one-story structure that had parking stalls. They radiated out like the spokes in a bicycle wheel. There were sparkling lights and spheres into the sky, beckoning customers to stop by for a moment of pleasure. This was in the 1950s. The names were Stan's and Stucky's. One in Beverly Hills that stood as a landmark, until recently, was Dolores Drive-In.

A metal tray was attached to the window with the food. Young women and men came to your car —they were called carhops—and they took your order and then returned with the chocolate milkshake and hamburger. The activity was generally with a car full of friends.

The fascination with automobiles also was big. The '57 Chevy was the hottest car of the day and became a classic. I did not have one then; we had what was referred to as a jalopy, a '37 Chrysler with a gear on the floor, but the guys drove Mercurys and Impalas. There was nothing cooler than driving up in one of those shiny cars. Looking good, eating right, feeling good. The guys would polish those cars and work on them in their spare time. They worked nights at the post office or wherever to pay for the gas and upkeep.

Well, the seed was planted way back there in the fifties for that kind of service and fun food delivery. Public demand began to grow for food in a hurry. Companies such as McDonald's and Wendy's saw and met the need for producing food quickly. They soon abandoned barbecue because it took too long and concentrated on burgers and fries and later fish. But the drive-in as we knew it began to fade out of style, as we spent hours there, and people wanted fast food. After streamlining the production of food and menus, they still needed to deliver food fast, and that fascination with the American automobile still had an intimate connection, so then we had the first drive-through, started by Wendy's in 1971. That was twenty years after the first drive-ins. McDonald's, following Wendy's, did not have one until 1975 in Sierra Vista, Arizona, near a military base, to serve soldiers. We went from driving up to the drive-through.

We are still attached to our automobiles, but we grab and go, and the experience produces little more than convenience, a receipt, your food, and have a beautiful day. We look for the golden arches, the In-N-Out arrow, Wendy's girl, and the Jack in the Box corporate symbols of welcome; come on in here. The marketing has improved mightily, as has the creativity of new twists on the old, until you want to try the new chalupa or the 12,000-calorie Baconator. I never have tried these things. But the marketing can make you salivate by just looking at the picture, and voila! You are in Starbucks; they know what you want in that morning strike of energy, that jolt in the form of such beautiful names as a chocolate mocha latte, Frappuccino, cappuccino, macchiato, espresso, skinny vanilla latte, caramel mocha, an iced beverage, or Tazo beverage

Whatever you design, they will make. You do not even have to add your own sugar or cream; they do that and stir it with a wooden spoon. And cars are lined up, waiting for that opportunity to spend more than five dollars for a cup of coffee and a muffin or banana bread, in the car, listening to sports talk, talking on the phone, getting breakfast, coming from exercise, going to work or home. It is one of the best moments of the day. If you are hooked, you know it and make it a treat once or twice a week.

McDonald's, next door, does the same for you. McDonald's has added a fancy name, Cafe McDonald. The coffee costs one-third the price of Starbucks, but it tastes like it too, at sixty cents for a senior cup. Sometimes they will *even* put in the cream and sugar, but mostly it is in the bag with a stirrer. For me to realize the special brew of Starbucks, I have it once or twice a week. I use gift cards or just *savor* the depth of flavor. I buy it and grind the beans at home but cannot get the exact character they have at the store.

Starbucks almost has its own language, an extra-large coffee is a venti, a small is a tall, etc. People have downloaded apps to their phones and pass by the window while holding up a phone, which is clicked and subtracted from their gift cards, all to make things faster, quicker, and save time while multitasking. In Southern California, with long commutes on the freeways, it is a daily ritual. You feel you have to have something to help you over the hills. My daughter drinks coffee while managing a conference call from New York almost daily on her commute from Valencia to her office at Universal Studios. The drive-throughs in California are as much a ritual as going to work. Yes, they have Keurig, the one-cup coffeemaker, which is the get-up coffee. They shower and dress. The kids make their own breakfast and lunch. They drop the children at school and then go to Starbucks for the commute coffee.

We are a drive-through culture, and it is expensive, anywhere from $2.50 to $8.00. And don't let the kids order—oh, my goodness. That is another language yet. For the last year, I've bought a pound of Starbucks at $7.99, beans or ground, returned the bag, and got a tall coffee, free. Oh, I loved that promotion. I had the bags in my car, and it smelled, so right now, they have stopped the promotion. What is it? A habit, a pleasure, an addiction? Is it lazy to want a drive-through, justifying convenience? In the hot weather of summer, I love the tea at McDonald's. If I have a lot of driving to do, I will get a tea—one dollar, no matter the size. The automobile and the drive-through are connected, and while driving, let's drink up.

My fascination with eating in the car has not waned one bit. I have many warm memories of my childhood, the conveniences during motherhood and commutes, and the sheer extravagance of my golden years in enjoying such a simple but inexpensive pleasure—available any time I want and just loving it. Hm, life was so good. I can smell the french fries, taste the burger, and recall chats with the carhops we got to know.

I think that having lived through the drive-in, drive-up, and drive-through, the future might be picking it up on your porch, delivered by a drone.

*Sweet and bitter water never flow from the same well.*

—James 3:11

# CHAPTER 33

## *September*

Oh, how I love this month, with so much that is special to me. There is something unique in the air, a sort of buzz when September comes. It kind of slips up on you quickly, as it marks the end of summer, the period of carefree days, parties, vacations, and late summer nights. Everyone seems to have a need to get ready for September in some small way, whether it's merely servicing the car or shopping as school starts for little ones. Children, grandchildren, teachers, adults in continuing education classes, colleges, and universities all over the Northern Hemisphere, they will begin new academic years. This all means *get ready; be ready.* New things to learn, new beginnings, new plans. Cooler weather, rain, making plans for the biggest holidays of the year, so close you begin to visualize the faces and smell the foods. Thanksgiving, Christmas, New Year's Day.

It's lovely to reminisce at the right times for a few moments. My enjoyment of those warm, fuzzy memories and laughter crescendo into a quiet panic that kind of grips me as I think about how much still has to be done and the time left to do it.

Looking around as I walk in the park, admiring the foliage of Summerlin, I remember Rock Creek Park in Washington. I remember the drives I made so many times in the fall up to Yale and Harvard when the girls were students and the breathtaking colors of the trees and leaves as we went up to parents' weekends or just taking the kids back to school.

The English lyrics by Johnny Mercer and uniquely sung by Nat King Cole say it all for the most beautiful of seasons, autumn, with "Autumn Leaves":

The falling leaves drift by my window
The autumn leaves of red and gold
I see your lips, the summer kisses
The sunburned hands I used to hold

Since you went away the days grow long
And soon I'll hear old winter's song
But I miss you most of all, my darling
When autumn leaves start to fall

September is also the month of my birth, always a time of reflection and thanksgiving for my life and blessings. It means hearing from old friends, with birthday cards and gifts; hearing from children and grandchildren and family, with reminders of love and thanks for my motherhood to them all.

Special dinners, cheers with friends, flowers, always beautiful flowers, and again thanksgiving for my life and blessings. I am reminded that I am unique to a few people and that I am remembered at this time with thoughts of love. It is a joyous time because it is a month of new beginnings, of preparation for things to come. There is anticipation and expectancy in September. Clubs reconvene with exciting plans for more prosperous new club years. The Christmas dance and parties are planned—the dates and themes are finalized. It is so exciting, so old, but so new. Nature reminds us, in a beautiful way, of the changes. Birds migrate. Animals hibernate. Our terrain begins to look different, as we move more indoors. Our homes become the center of our lives. Soon, the time will change.

September is the ninth month of the year in the Gregorian calendar and is one of four months with thirty days. September begins on the same day of the week as December every year because ninety-one days separate September and December, which is a multiple of seven, the number of days in a week. No other month ends on the same day of the week as September in any year. In Latin, *septem* means seven. It was, in fact, the seventh month on the Roman calendar until 46 BC—that was a long time ago.

"The Star-Spangled Banner" was written on September 14 by Francis Scott Key. California was admitted to the union on September 9. Charlemagne called September the harvest month. Principle ecclesiastical feasts occur in September. Jewish and many other religious observances take place.

September 11 is a day of infamy because of the 2001 attacks on the World Trade Center and the Pentagon. We remember those who lost their lives and their loved ones with commemorative observances of that horrific day. Television programs relive the South and North Tower explosions and honor New York's first responders and all the human stories of survival, man helping man in that time of need. It reminds us that life is precious and loved ones are even more cherished.

Celebrations abound in September, from Labor Day in the United States and Canada to Independence Day in Uzbekistan and National Day in Vietnam.

The sapphire, a precious gemstone, is associated with September, as are the astrological signs of Virgo and Libra. Sapphires are worn as jewelry and can be found naturally. Because of the remarkable hardness of this stone, it has many other applications: infrared optical components, scientific instruments, high durability windows, wristwatch crystals, movement bearings, integrated circuits, and electronic wafers.

Everything beautiful and significant has happened in September, from the signing of the Treaty of Paris in 1783 to Elvis's first appearance on *The Ed Sullivan Show* and becoming an international phenomenon. The Beatles recorded their first single "Love me Do," in September 1962. *Perry Mason* premiered on CBS in September 1957 and still airs today, fifty-five years later. *The Tonight Show* with Steve Allen premiered in September 1954. Why, even the US Army was established in September. Catherine Zeta-Jones and Barbara Walters were born in September.

Christmas decorations are available in Costco in September, before Halloween. If we dare mention sports, the fall classic, baseball pennant races get really good in September. The NFL begins its schedule. Tennis has the US Open. Golf is winding down its majors. Even Congress returns after the August recess in September.

All in all, Maxwell Anderson and Kurt Weill said it best in "September Song." I salute them again today, as September is majestic.

Oh, it's a long, long while
From May to December
But the days grow short
When you reach September

When the autumn weather
Turns leaves to flame
One hasn't got time
For the waiting game

Oh, the days dwindle down
To a precious few
September, November

And these few precious days
I'll spend with you.
These precious days
I'll spend with you

*He is great who can do what he wishes; he is wise who wishes to do what he can.*

—August Iffland

# CHAPTER 34

## Money

The world over, money is glorified. People who have a lot of money are viewed differently, even if we know nothing about their character, unless they are known criminals. They are often envied and admired for the things money can do—social position, opportunity, luxuries, even their posture of philanthropy. Great works are done by the rich for the environment, education, medical research, hospital libraries, and parks, etc. and they obviously have more advantages in our society than others.

However, the poor are condemned and blamed for their situation. Many people are pitied, such as the homeless, mentally deficient, and children on the streets. Some people think that recipients of charity or welfare are not trying hard enough. Society tends to blame them for being where they are and who they are. When the needy appy for assistance, the lines at these offices are long, It can take a full day, Our govenment does not allocate adequate funding for the administration of social service programs.

You see the handicapped, mentally compromised, abused and sick at these offices and we need to do a better job all around with the distribution of wealth.

Many born into such conditions find it hard to rise out. Those in communities that are riddled with drugs, crime, and blight and neighborhoods that offer little support for growth, development, or employment find themselves more in difficulties and challenges than others. Can you imagine trying to live on minimum wages? This is a sensitive subject; somewhere in the mix of things is money. How much is spent per pupil for education? Why allow our major cities to fall into despair and decay?

What is money? I always was taught it is a medium of exchange and becomes very important, mainly if you do not have any. If you have it, you use money for its function as everyone knows it to be—in exchange for goods and services, a tool backed by the faith and credit of our government; in God, we trust.

The word *money* has been around since the fourteenth century, from the Latin phrase *moneta*, meaning "mint." We have many slang words for money—cabbage, dough, moola, shekels, Benjamins, dead presidents, C-notes, legal tender, loot, currency, chips, bread, fortune, wealth, etc. Some like to use brokerage terms, such as shares or portfolio. Money! Success or failure can depend upon it; life or death can depend upon it. Justice or injustice can rely upon it—marriage, divorce, wills, trusts, lotteries, casinos, real estate, investments, purchases, and sales. There was a song—money, money, money makes the world go round. How true. It's a sensitive subject, but why?

One of my earliest memories of money was having a piggy bank, which was a glass pig with a slot in the top, where I saved my gift money. This placed importance on saving money, as I learned early that this was essential. Next I had a savings account at the bank, and I learned that by amassing cash in my account, I had something of value, and I could use it to get something else of value when I withdrew the money and used for that purpose.

The transformation of money in the last one hundred years has been astounding. Paper money used to represent real value locked away in a vault of gold bars. Today, we have technologically evolved with the use of debit cards and credit cards, digital banking, wire transfers, and online banking. But regulation, hacking, and security are still a struggle. Cell phone apps, Wall Street, and securitized money backed by mortgage-backed assets are out of control, globally and digitally speaking. Other currency models are active, such as Bitcoins and Kickstarter and many others that are not government-backed but backed by mathematical algorithms that allow anonymity and are elusive.

David Hume said in 1792 that it is not money that influences human behavior visa versa. What matters is what we make and do and feel and want. Money is just an imperfect tool to add it all up. (You can count it and store it.)

Other great economists, such as Adam Smith and John Maynard, said money gets at who we are and how we can live our best lives.

Our cycle of life is intertwined with money, whether we are conscious of it or not.

We educate our children by providing the best schools we can afford so that they can pursue their dreams and aspirations. They can then offer the best family life, education, homes, cars, vacations, medical care, and hobbies to their children. For them, it may be a 401(k) pension, retirement plans, savings or real estate, stocks and bonds.

Our government is allied with other countries. We offer money in the form of humanitarian aid, investment credits, or weapons. When we are at odds with these governments, we then limit the money or withhold it and call the penalty *sanctions*. Farmers are paid not to grow crops, while the poor are scorned for wanting a living wage—a sensitive subject. One percent of the population in the United States owns 99 percent of the wealth. Distribution of wealth and more equality is a distribution issue, and it is a political one as well. Money.

People commit crimes for money—robbery, fraud, murder, assault, and on and on. People save the money they earned throughout their lives and then donate it to a worthy cause. My dad's college roommate and his wife lived very modestly in Los Angeles for over fifty years. She's a teacher, and he worked for for the State Dept of Motor Vehicles. They had no children, yet they donated one million dollars to their college. Who knew? Money—charitable donations, something thousands of people do every day. Money—the good that it does.

Money means something different to everyone. Opportunity, dreams fulfilled, or deferred. For some, it's bus fare, lunch money, money for the power bill or to pay for gas, money for repairing the car, money for medicine copays, diapers, milk, babysitter, food, vacation.

I am always touched by seeing homeless persons, beggars in the streets, or women or veterans holding signs that ask for money for food in extreme weather. We know what the lack of funds do daily; we have to care. It's a sensitive subject.

Our local, national, and global business pages publish daily our performance in the stock market and bond market, as well as the Dow Jones averages, S&P index, Nasdaq, commodities, futures, and so on. We can get this info on our cell phones, as trades and commerce are the lifeblood of Wall Street.

The lifeblood of these firms is the eager beavers from our best colleges and universities as new graduates, who flock to these firms for the opportunity to learn the business and make their fortunes.

This is not even considering all the global markets and trillions of dollars traded daily.

Yet our jobs are sent overseas for cheaper labor and manufacturing, where there are no unions to contend with and low capital gain taxes. The infrastructure in our American cities is devoid of industries, jobs, employment, and vibrant life, due to improper taxation of these corporations and their lack of pride in providing American jobs.

So few things are manufactured in the United States today. Robots, drones, and high-tech innovations are leading indicators.

Yes, freedom of speech has brought unions and trade agreements, all labels for, yes, money. We know why, we know how, and we know when this happened.

Now, I can step down from my money soapbox and say that for many, entire lifetimes are spent trying to just get clean water, safe homes, medical care, and enough to eat. Thank God for not being one of them, but do what you can to help all of them.

We look at people born on the other side of the world or the other side of town, and maybe we pause, shake our heads, discuss with friends, and then move on with our lives. We examine civil protests and unrest and move on when the cameras have gone. For others, the essentials of life and the luxuries of class, affluence, wealth, and advantage have come more naturally. Even though it might take hard work, commitment, and determination to build wealth and achieve success, millions have done that.

Are we created equal, with inalienable rights to life, liberty, and the pursuit of happiness? Not quite. No! The civil rights movement proved that fifty years ago, and while we are not where we need to be as a nation, we are not as bad as we used to be.

The Civil Rights movement beginning in 1957 afforded us many tools to make life better. Some of those gains were in the legal arena. Laws passed such as The Civil Rights Act of 1964,The Voting Rights Act of 1965, The Fair Housing Act of 1968, Affirmative Action, and bans aganist emploment decrimination were laws only. Testing them and making them a reality has been a very different road. Descrimination is structural in our democracy. 2020 update, We are fighting the overturn of many of those very laws. We are fighting a disproportionate percentage of Blacks living in high risk enviroments in housing, access to heatlth care, rates of going to prison, inadequate education, low percentage of homes having wifi, laptops and ability to participate in remote an online learning. Now, at the forefront is the supression of the voter with a Presidental election coming up this year 2020. When many states have limited voting machines in minority areas, native american communities, rural communities, the southern states particularly, Voters have stood in the heat for four to twelve hours just to cast a vote. Mail in ballots (Vote by mail) are being supressed by the President while the virus is still rampant and the crowds could expose voters to the risk of infection. It is a direct threat to our democracy.

The subceptibiltiy to the Covid Virus Pandemic that finds them infected and dying at a higher rate than other populations, these conditions are also often related to money. The homeless populations, people living in closed spaces with large families, these conditions impact all minority communities Black, Hispanic, Asian, Native Americans and the immigrant population.

Big tax cuts for the wealthy, cuts in aids and services to the needy. This cycle of greed continues. While there are thousands of really good people of all cultures. There are those that want a different America that does not embrace the values of the constituion or our birthright of equality, justice and freedom for all.

Thomas Jefferson, who was among the proponents of espousing equality and inalienable rights to life, liberty and the pursuit of happiness, owned slaves and sired children with slave women; the Hemingses were one of his black families. One of whom attended my parents church (Church of Christian

While those words may be a good platitude of hope, they are far from being accurate or factual for our reality. We remain hopeful and working.

Money is always somewhere in the mix, and it's a sensitive subject.

*Don't you love judging other people? It makes all my fears disappear, and all the things I don't like about myself seem so much less important.*

—unknown

# CHAPTER 35

# A Week in the Life: October 2012

I awoke at 5:00 a.m., as I usually do, only today I had to arise, dress, and dispense with my usual morning routine. I gathered my things, packed the night before, and got ready to get going. Sunday morning, October 21, was an electric time of the year. The national elections were going to be the buzz of the Sunday talk shows, and the final presidential debate would be the next day Monday, October 22.

I was mildly excited about my trip, as I always am about seeing my children and grandchildren, but more so this time because I felt happy to do something nice for my daughter and spend time with two of my grandchildren at the same time.

Plants were watered, lights turned out, and as I turned to lock the door, I noticed that I had not placed my newspaper delivery on vacation hold. I made a mental note to call them from the car later. I rolled my suitcase down the long corridor to the elevator, and the stillness and darkness of the morning neither greeted me nor said goodbye as I made my way to the car. Once inside the car, I recited the traditional Psalm 121 scripture for safety. My mind then turned to coffee—Starbucks across the street—and banana bread, NPR 88.9 on the radio, and then to the 215 freeway.

Grandma was on her way, fortified with scripture, food, and the melodious voice of NPR radio streaming gently through the speakers as my wonderful companion. The highway was all mine, as few vehicles were there, and within an hour and a few minutes, I was at Baker, Ca and less than two hours, later I arrived in Santa Clarita Valley. It is a beautiful drive. I called Patricia and told her I was minutes away.

She said, "Mom, great, come lie down. I have to take the Christopher to the coach's house."

I said, "Please wait. I want to take you and drive so I know how to get there next week." And within minutes, we had begun the indoctrination for the week.

There was a considerable amount of driving, sports events, and school events to learn about for the next week. Patsy, as I call Patricia, was aware of the rather strenuous task ahead and wondered if she had been wise in asking me to do so much. I was trying to reassure her that I could manage it, and she should relax and only think about having a great time.

Patricia is an attorney for NBC Universal Studios, and her husband, Robert, is a paramedic with the fire department. They both work hard all the time. This was to be a getaway for them that I was delighted to help facilitate. NBC was sending Patricia to the Bahamas for the Black Entertainment Lawyers annual meeting, and Robert got the time off to go with her. I had a small green notebook that had an elastic loop on the side for a pen. All my info was carefully recorded in this book—alarm codes for the house, TV parental codes to unblock if I wanted to see a certain show, cell phone numbers, coaches' numbers, doctor, dentist, veterinarian for Barney (the lovable family dog, a pecan-colored dachshund with floppy ears), daily menus, times for soccer practice for Courtney and football for Christopher and guitar practice for Christopher. The gardener comes on Tuesday. The children have chores and days for certain things—feeding Barney, cleaning poop from the yard daily, emptying the trash, trash day, recycling bins. They would have lunch at school for this week to cut down on the number of things I needed to do.

I unpacked, got comfortable, had dinner and conversation with the kids, and talked to Barney.

We had one day, Monday, for a dry run to the practice sites and to go over the schedule. I found my way around Valencia very well, and we planned the menu for the week with foods the kids enjoy and menus easy for our schedule. I wanted to go food shopping, which I did and which kind of got me in the mood for cooking. I made dinner on Monday night, their last night home. There was no practice on Monday, and it was the night of the last presidential debate. We had a wonderful dinner, then the debate, review of the schedule, homework, sign off, and early to bed, as Pat and Robert were to leave very early the next morning.

Tuesday, October 23: The limo was in front of the house in the early morning darkness, parked, and waiting for Pat and Robert to come out of the house. The children were anxious, and Courtney began to form tears as they came downstairs with final carry-on bags in hand. There were lots of hugs, and "Mom, don't overdo it.""

"I'll call you. I'll text you. Kids, be good. Help Grandma. Bye."

We now had thirty minutes to finish getting ready for school; today was going to be a long day. Pick up at 3:30, home, change clothes, soccer and football practice—Courtney 5:00–6:30; Chris 5:30–7:30. I checked my schedule; we were set. After dropping them off at school, I returned home to let Barney into the house, as the gardener was coming. I planned dinner, picked up house, and cleared the breakfast dishes. About noon, the school called to say that Courtney was okay but had had an accident: someone on the slide had kicked her in the head; she had a slight headache. No cuts, no swelling, no broken skin, no bruises; she was fine, but it was a rule that the parents had to be called. The teacher and the nurse, knowing I was the surrogate parent, chuckled to me. "This is day one."

I arrived at the school early to see the teacher and be reassured that Courtney was okay, and she was. Courtney is a pretty girl, tall and rather thin but with well-developed muscles, and long black hair in a ponytail. In her Black Watch plaid uniform and white shirt, she seemed oblivious to the earlier incident. "Oh yes, Grandma, it was okay." She is razor-sharp smart and can do things herself—dressing, her hair, the computer, and more. She learned to tie her shoes at such an early age that I was amazed. She is an honor student and athlete and says with confidence, "I am smart, like my mother." And she looks exactly like her mother, who graduated from Yale University and UCLA Law School.

Christopher looks much like his dad; he is a stocky, 160-pound, muscular football star and straight-A scholar. He's known on the whole campus as Chris. He is sweet and helpful, a self-starter and a finisher.

They attend Legacy Academy, a Christian private school that is so warm, colorful, inviting, and exciting that anyone would be enticed to go to school. They feel blessed to have found such a nurturing school.

We got home and had a little more than an hour before practice. Dinner was ready. They loved the meal. Barney was fed. They changed clothes, and we talked about the day and got the gear to go. Courtney was in her pink shin guards and long soccer socks, shorts, and shirt. Chris wore practice whites with pads, backpacks, and carried another bag. They felt good.

Patsy had put a very comfortable fold-up chair in my trunk for me to sit on the sidelines during practice. For Chris, there were the bleachers. Chris, being older, was dropped off first; he was about two hundred yards north of the soccer field. We were picking him up at 7:30.

I sat on the sidelines with my cell phone and a book that I was never able to read, as other parents came up to me to talk. I watched the rigors of the practice in amazement. I thought, *My lord, those are hard sprints, toe taps, moving the ball down the field, more sprints, more drills for ninety minutes without stopping, except for water sips.* For Chris, it was the same—run, hit, tackle, run, sprints, plays, whistles, and yelling.

We had an hour after Courtney's practice before Chris was ready. It was getting dark. I was thirsty and had to go to the bathroom.

Courtney said, "Let's go to Starbucks. We can do both." We went; she had a strawberry Frappuccino, and she suggested we order Chris a vanilla bean Frappuccino. I found a nice chair at Starbucks and relaxed. Courtney said we should play a game, so we played tic-tac-toe. She won all the games. I was rusty, it seemed.

We headed back to the field to wait for Chris. He finally came off the field with all his bags, dragging more slowly than Courtney, and I could see he'd had a tough workout. He was happy to see the vanilla bean Frappuccino.

We headed home. I did not have to tell them to do their homework. They dug right in.

It was now after eight o'clock. I put away any remaining food, tidied the kitchen, and headed upstairs to make some calls. Pat and Robert had traveled for most of the day, and when they got into Miami, they were told there was a tropical storm headed for the Bahamas. They pondered returning home, as American Airlines had booked them on American Eagle for the last lap to Nassau, and Pat thought the plane might be a small one and heading into a storm. They were told it held seventy passengers, and they would be fine.

They had arrived and texted me pictures of their hotel suites and the Hotel Atlantis. I asked Chris to put the alarm on and put Barney in his room for the night. I made a few telephone calls, and then I was asleep.

Days two, three, and four were all routine.

"Grandma, could you get me some flowers for my teacher? It's her birthday."

"It's color-war day, Grandma. We need colors. I need orange, and Chris needs white." So we went shopping and got those items.

Saturday was the final examination and test. It was game day. After all those practices, now it was the big game—and big it was. Southern California certainly has a culture of parents supporting their kids at these events and different styles, with all the regalia of E-Z UPs (a pop-up canopy), drinks, and food. I had not known what an E-Z UP was until the coach sent an email, reminding us to bring the tent umbrellas as protection from the sun and wind.

About thirty miles into the valley, off 101 North, was the site of the soccer match. Courtney's team won, 6–0. She was goalie for the last section and defended the goal perfectly. I picked up cousin Shelby after soccer. Construction on the 101 contributed to my missing the 405 North and sent me two exits beyond and thirty minutes of bumper-to-bumper traffic. I thought we'd be late for Chris's football game, but we were early.

Chris had spent the night at the coach's, looking at film and was coming to the game with the coach and his son. We would pick up Chris after the game. We stopped for In-N-Out burgers and headed to the stadium. The game was at Valencia High School, and another game was in process. When we arrived, Chris was in full uniform. He was a Jaguar, in maroon and yellow, number 34. He yelled, "Hi, Grandma!" It was good to see him.

We headed up to the stands, with more sun and wind. Other parents seemed to take it all in stride. I had the comfy stadium seat with a back that Patsy had provided for me. I had never seen one. I had an umbrella that kept turning inside out with the force of the wind. We could not find refuge from the sun. Paula mercifully called and invited us to dinner at her home after the game. It was after five o'clock, and by then, they wanted to go to a party at the coach's home in a haunted house being given for charity.

Courtney wanted me to get her a costume, all at the spur of the moment and with my blood sugar on empty. I said, "Let's go home, get showered, go by Aunt Paula's for dinner, and see where we are."

Patsy called from the Bahamas to see how the day had gone. They were in the midst of a terrible storm; the hotel was in shut-down mode. The beaches were closed, and it had been raining there for three days. My goodness …

After showers and fresh clothes, we went to Paula's. I looked like the last daffodil of summer, and she suggested I lie down. I was pooped. The sun and wind had done their jobs.

The dinner was magnificent. So good. Chris then said he would like to skip the party. It took a while to convince Courtney, but she said okay. Hooray! We played poker after a couple hours and went home at ten o'clock.

Pat and Rob were due back Sunday evening at seven o'clock.

I now had Sunday with nothing scheduled—heaven—except morning talk shows, coffee in bed, and peace and quiet.

At 8:23, an earthquake rattled the house like nothing but an earthquake can. Courtney ran screaming into my bedroom, saying, "Grandma, what was that?"

Chris slept through the moment. It was centered in Newhall, near us, and was rated at 4.4. I thought, *My God, tropical storms in the Bahamas, an earthquake here. Do we have enough excitement?*

The rest of the day was quiet, except for politics on the TV. Pat's plane was delayed out of Nassau. A text said they'd missed their plane in Miami; another text said they'd got on another plane, arriving at 8:40. That turned into arrival at 9:30 and home after midnight. We were nonetheless grateful for their safe return. Patricia had read three novels, Robert enjoyed the water sports, and they both got plenty of rest, good food, and lots of rain.

And it was an unforgettable week for all.

*Loveable grands, Chris and Courtney*

*Original Work of Patricia Dash, Gift to Me*
*from Dr. Suzanne Turpin-Mair*

*Friendship is essential to the soul.*

*—Omega Psi Phi fraternity*

# CHAPTER 36

## Eight of the Great Women That I Am Blessed to Call Friend

Each of these women, except one, I have known for over fifty years. This chapter is about friendships in my life and what they have meant to me. In my songbook of experience, between each page of pain and glory, they were there. My earliest recollection of any meaning of the term *friendship* was from my father, who said, "Friendship is essential to the soul; the sweetness of life is found in companionship. A man is judged by the company he keeps. The only way to have a friend is to be one."

*Marilyn*

335

## Marilyn

As girls, we were great friends and dreamed about our future. As women, we have remained great friends. Marilyn aspired to be an opera singer. She has a beautiful voice and still sings in Los Angeles today. Marilyn has a beautiful smile and beautiful hair. Her hair turned gray at age eighteen. She is stopped on the street by people who admire her beautiful white hair. Ever since I have known her, she never goes to sleep without setting her hair. I tell her "your hair is your crowning glory"

We have nicknames that go back many years; she is Birdie, and I am Ducky. Marilyn has two sons; she has been widowed twice and is currently married to a high school classmate, Reginal Fields. He has a beautiful tenor voice. "Vibrant and happy" will be her epitaph. Together, we can laugh in the twinkle of an eye. If there is humor to be found, we can find it. She is just the funniest person I have ever known. We attended Manual Arts High School and would sometimes get into trouble for laughing. Our algebra teacher, Mrs. Nash, asked me to tutor Marilyn; that is how we met. I can proudly say she later became a bank manager. I teased her that it was due to my good tutoring.

Marilyn sees the best side of people and things. We have cried and laughed over the years, with the travails of our children and families. We have had good times too numerous to recount—cruises with our families and European trips, Greek isles, Egypt, so many places. Marilyn is like a family member, as we have shared so much—debutante balls, graduations, weddings, funerals, picnics, parties, dances, good food, and our families. We all love each other. Marilyn is in my heart and in my soul; she is my bud as we grow old. We have been so blessed, and we both love the Lord. Today, minor health challenges invade our conversations but not for long, as we soon find a way to insert something humorous to make us laugh.

The one thing that makes Marilyn stand as my oldest and very best friend is that she has always believed in me. Marilyn thinks I can do anything and has encouraged me at every step of my life until I felt I could do it too. I can count on her and have, and she can count on me, and we both know it. Birdie is truly one of God's sweet gifts that has made my life so blessed. I love Reggie too because I believe Marilyn is truly happy being his wife, and he is a great man of God.

*Freddie*

## Freddie

Freddie is a Fisk classmate, my college roommate, and a bridesmaid at my wedding. We have visited and traveled together over these last fifty-plus years and never lost touch.

A beautiful woman by campus consensus, she was voted Miss Junior. We are sorority sisters in Delta Sigma Theta, and she was my big sister and carried me across the burning sands.(Sorority lore not to be shared smiles) Freddie became a high school principal, married, and now has a daughter and grandson. She has a distinct Southern accent, denoting her Texas origins, that I just love. Freddie is admired for her quiet dignity and her purposeful life; her appearance always is impeccable. In school, Freddie did everything with perfection. She loves fun and good times. Freddie has visited me many times in Las Vegas. We both enjoy gaming and shows and the city.

We have enjoyed cruises and talking on the phone or fund-raising for Fisk, when we worked together for the fiftieth reunion.

Freddie has always been there as a great friend, encouraging me but cautioning me at the same time. We shared rooms again at our fiftieth college reunion, and that was special. We visit when we can, email, and call and travel. When I need a friend, she is there. We both got into real estate as a retirement activity and loved talking about that profession. Freddie was a psychology major and became an educator and school principal until she retired.

Freddie is like the stars in the sky—you may not see them, but you know they are there. She is in Houston, Texas, and once gave me a beautiful silver plaque in the form of the state of Texas that I adore. I am blessed to have had her love and friendship all these years.

*Ethel*

## Ethel

Ethel and I met when we were classmates at Fisk University. We were science majors with pre-med aspirations. We have enjoyed a lasting friendship over sixty years and have lived together. We went to Washington, DC, together after graduation from college on a grant from NIH at Howard University. We were going to be doctors.

We lived in an efficiency apartment at 920 T Street in Washington. Life was not a walk in the park. Even though we had grant stipends in pharmacology, neither of us had much money.

After a year, Ethel fell in love with a brilliant twenty-seven-year-old NASA PhD, William Jackson, and decided to get married. This was a shocker to me and to Scottie, her long-time boyfriend. Ethel, our dreams! But life went on. Ethel was in love and life wasn't easy. I moved from our apartment after landing a savior job at Hillcrest with a free room and board. It would have been difficult for me to pay the rent alone. It turned out to be one of the best experiences possible. Love was in bloom.

I got married after my freshman year in dental school, and Ethel and I and our husbands spent time together as married couples. We played cards and invited each other to dinner. After a few years and two babies, Cheryl and Eric, Ethel wanted to again pursue her medical dream. Ethel's husband was not keen on the idea of dental school or med school. Neither was Dan, but I was already in dental school before we married. Ethel did become a dentist. Ethel and Billy divorced and Ethel had second marriage, years later.

Ethel was also a loving caregiver to her mother, who was ninety-four years and has grandchildren: Christian, Kenyon, and Gabrielle. Ethel found a fulfilling career with NIH until her retirement in North Carolina. Even though far apart we were still friends.

We have kept in touch and recently traveled to China with friends and enjoyed a luxurious time in Beijing, Xion, Tibet, a river cruise down the Yangtze River, and Shanghai, staying on the Bund. That trip brought us close together again, and now we talk almost daily. 2020 Update, With the Covid Virus this is a really good thing.

We started a journey of life together. We traveled different paths. I remember how much I enjoyed Ethel's sausage-apple-and-cranberry dressing for one Thanksgiving dinner. The sweetest full circle of our mission as friends is that we both have daughters (Cheryl, Paula, and Pamela) who are physicians and granddaughters (Gabrielle and Shelby) who are freshmen at Spelman College in Atlanta. We met recently in Atlanta, introduced them, and enjoyed the campus activities and time together.

Ethel is a joy to still have as a treasured friend. We now share talk about our mutual back ailments and what's a good movie on Netflix or Prime almost daily. We live near our children and share a great love of family. Ethel is another blessing!

*Frances*

## Frances

We met at Howard University. Frances, a Howard graduate, worked in the Department of Anatomy at the medical school for the renowned Dr. Montague Cobb, anatomist and Anthropologist. I needed to get home to California. One of my professors told me about this lady in the Department of Anatomy who was driving out there with some others who were going to Stanford, and maybe I could ride with them. Money was tight in 1958. This was the beginning of a lifelong friendship that made Frances as close as a sister. She is seven years older, and I have learned many things from her. We have had a ball together. She married a dentist, and she and I are sorority sisters in Delta and Links. Frances is the most fabulous cook of any of my friends. She can lay a spread of food extraordinaire, and she loves to do so. Frances is one of seven children from Charlottesville, Virginia, a large, loving family. Going home with her in those days got me adopted by her family. We have supported one another through triumphs and losses. Frances went with me to take my youngest daughter, Patricia, to Yale. She lived in Teaneck, New Jersey, and now in South Hampton. We drove up the beautiful drive to New Haven, and I cried all the way back.

Frances and her husband had a fixed tradition that endured until he died. They did not just eat meals; they dined. They entertained friends and guests from over the East Coast.

Breakfast was never shorted; it was eggs, sausage, toast or biscuits, grits, and fruit juice. Coffee was never instant; it was brewed the old-fashioned way in a percolator pot. They never ate lunch. They left for the office and worked together all day. Frances was her husband, Colden's, office manager and receptionist.

Dinner was an event every night with a formal table setting. Colden retreated into his study for a scotch "pinch" before dinner and to read his mail. When dinner was ready, the family gathered—two sons and a daughter: Colden Jr, Romney, and Tijuana. On Fridays, there were always three types of fish: scallops, a fleshy fish they loved to do whole, and shrimp. After dinner, Colden had his pipe, and the family sat and talked, or they walked in the garden. Phone calls were not allowed during dinner.

Colden lived a long, storied life until age ninety-two. The Raineses entertained dignitaries, from college presidents to their children's friends. Friends visiting New York or New Jersey stopped by their home, as they knew something good was in the pot. I cannot recount the many feasts with them or friends and family they have welcomed. Frances calls me "Shirley Anne," and we speak every week or so. When she refers to me as her best friend, her friend Jackie, in New Jersey, gets upset and says,

"I thought I was your best friend." To keep the peace, she says, "I told her Shirley Anne is my best friend on the West Coast." Frances loves sports, like I do, and she and her beautiful family have been more than friends; we are all family and all blessed with the richest of friendships and love. God has made me glad indeed. Frances is a blessing!

*Shirley*

## Shirley

Shirley has gone to live with the Lord. We met in church in 1952, and my days at her home and with her family are great memories. Shirley grew up in a family that had the sickle cell trait and the disease. I saw her lose her sister Janet, her brother Leroy, and her mother, in later years. Shirley was a confidant who told it like it was. She was a great musician; she could play Chopin's Polonaise in C-Sharp Minor like Chopin. She could sing, and her song was "Since I Met Jesus." Shirley was fun and adventurous and a risk-taker. Looking back, I understand why winning at cards, bowling, or whatever she did had to be her best. She and I were best buddies and running buddies. I loved to spend time with her. She was honest and real.

Shirley loved Bob Campbell, who was quite a character. We used to have so much fun. I should feel guilty. We bowled, camped, went fishing, listened to Aretha and Al Green, danced, and partied. Of course, we had good food. Music was always a focus, standing around the piano singing and sharing time in the church choir with Eddie Kendrix and Paul Persley, Calvin Norton, and Lonnie Farrell. Oh, the days and nights at the beach. Such beautiful memories of teen years and beyond. After marriage, we shared times at each other's homes; we lived only five minutes apart. Our kids swam together and lived the California dream. We took motorhome trips fishing up to Butterfield lake and lake pyramid with all the children.

Shirley worked for the school board in Los Angeles for over thirty years. Her daughters, Charise and Lesa, are wonderful young women. One is a lawyer with Bank of America, and the other is in corporate business with State Farm since graduating from Spelman College.

Shirley's motto was, "I lived the life I loved, and I loved the life I lived." I learned what a competitive spirit is from her. I loved to be around her when we were girls. I went away to college, but we never lost touch. We were both Shirleys. My first cruise was with Shirley for her family reunion. She is missed. She was a true friend to me.

*Suzanne*

## Suzanne

Oh, what a girl—a Jamaican, adventurous, risk-taking, giving, generous, workaholic, family-loving, food-loving, people-loving woman. Suzanne is a dentist and an educator. She taught at LSU dental school for twenty-five years. She is a researcher and writer and Fulbright scholar. We are colleagues and friends. We have worked together in the trenches, performing dentistry for the underserved in the summers, even during the AIDS epidemic. We have supported one another as our children have grown up, through many a crisis of life and loss. Suzanne is an optimist and very confident when she gets an idea. "Those convinced against their will are of the same opinion still" (Dale Carnegie)—this quote may apply to Sue, with an idea.

She is like a family. We have talked into the night about problems, issues, and challenges, and after all that, she feels better but still may do it her way. Sue makes me laugh. She gets sick and plows back with more resolve than ever. She is devoted to her family, Chantale and Lawrence. Sue loves to Tuk,(Jamaican dance)Reggae,and and listen to good music (oh the steel drums are her passion). She loves Jazz and wine and good food, like crab boils and crayfish. And those New Orleans Mardi Gras celebrations and jazz brunches are legendary.

We share our love of sports—basketball and football. We will talk for hours about our teams, stars, and about politics. She gave me my nickname, Shirleywhirl. It stuck; the whole family calls me Shirleywhirl. Nowadays, Sue calls me Shirls. She gives nicknames to those she loves— Muff, Lars, Glubbs, Pete, Jacks, Rups, Dandi, Pones; you get the idea.

Sue loves steel drums. We took a recent trip to Trinidad Carnival to hear them. Oh, what an adventure. From Chaguaramas by day to a stadium far away into the night, the drums were humming, and Sue was over the moon. Sue and I shared a life-changing trip to Israel in 2018, walking the Via Dolorosa, carrying a six-foot cross—it's the path Jesus walked to jeering crowds—to Calvary and then to the Church of the Holy Sepulchre. From Bethlehem to Jerusalem, it was transformative.

Suzanne lost everything in Hurricane Katrina. She now resides in Fort Lauderdale, Florida, and has two grandbabies, Madeline and

Emma. They have reenergized her, and she loves them mightily. These children are a whole new world for her, Lawrence and Rachel's little ladies. Chantale and I share the same birthday, September 25, making us natural soul sisters.

She's an unforgettable friend to say the least, a loyal, loving friend to say the most. Suzanne's entire family is my family as well, and that extends to Tortola, with David and Alicia. Pete's in Montego Bay, as are Lawrence and Rachel and little Madeline and Emma. Paula and I were their guests at Montego Bay's Half Moon for an unforgettable wedding and holiday of memories that warmed the tummy, the soul, and the spirit. Another blessing in my life is the friendship of this great woman.

*Beatrice*

## Beatrice

Beatrice is a college classmate at Fisk University; we also share Louisiana roots, as Beatrice was born in Shreveport, not many miles from where I was born in Monroe. I was born in September, and she was born in November 1937. Beatrice was a bridesmaid at my wedding, a real treasure; even today, we see a lot of each other in Los Angeles. A Sagittarian, she tells it like it is. No matter—for her, the truth is her reality. That honesty and seeing things as they are and facing them is the gift she has given to me. If she is happy, she says so; if she is not, she describes her issues. She will say *damn* like I do, maybe more often, if the issue requires it. Must be a Louisiana thing. Maybe a Fisk University thing.

Beatrice has a master's degree in social work, and she married a psychiatrist, Amos. She and Amos were a great couple. Amos passed away over twenty years ago; he was adored by everyone. Beatrice has led her family since this loss.

They had a dream life, it seemed. They adopted two children, Amy and Anthony, and then moved to Pacific Palisades. They were blessed with a good life and lovely family. Amos and Bea are what I called social A-listers. They were out and about everywhere; being away from Pill Hill at the Palisades made no difference. They still made every social event in Los Angeles. If they didn't, then it wasn't one you would want to attend.

Beatrice lost Amos, but she is still a social A-listener and loyal to all her friends. We talk about our mothers and our children. Beatrice was a caregiver to her mom during her years of confinement. She went daily to see her. We have traveled together on jazz and Fisk cruises and roomed together. We are in different sororities but are in Links together and have an ongoing dialogue. We lunch at the beach, usually, or El Cholo, with excellent margaritas and green corn tamales. She has a beautiful daughter, Amy, and a very loving son, Anthony, as well as many grandchildren and a great-grandchild. Beatrice is a wonderful matriarch of her family.

We help each other by supporting each other. She is there for me and me for her. We celebrated our fiftieth reunion from college in Nashville and speak almost daily, now that I am back in California. Beatrice has always enjoyed a good party. Beatrice is a connoisseur of excellent wines and gourmet food. She collects art and enjoys theater. We made our second New York theater jaunt this year. We saw four or five shows, Lincoln Center, an exceptional dining experience at the Waldorf Astoria, The new World Trade Center museum tour, and we got the "New York fix" absorbing the spiritual energy that seems unique to any other place in the world.(2016)

This year, 2019 we invited our daughters to New York. All my daughters, my son, and two grandchildren came with us.as well. We too are like family; we are so blessed. Beatrice loved my mom and my dad and said she loved them more than me. She will say, "I miss the Limuary," and we will laugh, as he made us do so many times, especially at Links' affairs. Beatrice is my Louisiana home girl, We share bridge playing, luncheons, theater going and texting each other on something good on TV to see right now, or something coming down the pike. We both take the New York times Sunday editions and enjoy pointing out good stuff to keep or comments by weekly columnists. Beatrice is one of my richest blessings and my joy to call *friend*.

*Margo*

## Margo

My Las Vegas friend, I have known Margo for many years. Our fathers were friends and wanted us to get to know each other. We have both lost our fathers, and we both looked after our mothers until we lost our mothers. Margo has the jewels in her crown. I always tell her that, as she had been a full-time caregiver to her mother for some years. Margo gave up her career in Detroit to care for her mother after she suffered a stroke. This was a labor of love and devotion. Margo lifted her in and out of her wheelchair and into and out of the car. She did it with affection. Impaired or not, her mother loved people too and loved to go. Another fantastic thing about Margo is that she is caring and loving to many of her parents' friends as well. She really has a caring heart.

Margo is also a lot of fun. We went to movies. I'm sure she was exhausted, as Margo would doze off. After I gave her a nudge, she would say, "I'm not asleep, just resting my eyes." We ate at our favorite restaurants, went to parties and plays and casinos, and took our mothers wheelchairs and oxygen until they could no longer go. But the good times are good memories.

Margo was a news reporter and started out with Oprah in Baltimore. She went on to be a television reporter and then developed her own public relations firm in Detroit, Michigan. Margo is a social dynamo. She loves parties and socializing. She and I are Carrousel sisters. (Carrouse is a national Black Social organization) Part of the motto that describes it well is "No work to be done, we just meet for fun"

Margo is also an animal lover. For Frisky (her terrier dog) and Bobo (her cat), I am listed as next of kin, and their vets have called me. We have been on jazz cruises and went on an eighteen-day journey as roomies with friends to Hawaii, where we boarded *Radiance of the Seas* and on to the French Polynesian islands, New Zealand, and Sydney, Australia. We then went to Cairns to fly over the Great Barrier Reef.

Margo can stay up all night, sleep very little, and keep going. She is a survivor and makes every effort to help people, visit, and give care.

A motivated woman, a Christian, and a friend, she calls me *Captain* as a nickname, as we have cruised so much. Margo has a great personality. I encouraged her to go into real estate, and she has. She is doing great with it, and now we talk about her listings and sales. I love mentoring her. I say to her, "Tell your client, 'This is how I work.'" We have consults on her clients; she is having fun and making money.

I am blessed to call her my friend. Our parents were friends, and it's all thanks to her dad, as he wished Margo and me to become friends. Margo lives in Las Vegas, and I in California, but we talk almost daily. Yes, Margo is family too. and yes a blessing indeed.

## Postlude on Friendship

I am blessed to have the friendships in my life that I do. In addition to the family, friends add sweetness to life and sometimes spice.

I think the most significant benefit for me is what I have learned from my friends and in sharing so many good times together. Thank you all, and thanks for the memories.

I've met other memorable friends in my eighty-two years, but the women mentioned have stuck it out. That is something that, really, you cannot put into words. The Bible says, "But there is a friend that sticketh closer than a brother" (Proverbs 18:24).

## Just for Laughs

Lord, Thou knowest better than I know myself that I am Growing Older and will someday be Old. Keep me from getting Talkative, and particularly from the Fatal habit of Thinking I must Say something on every Subject on every Occasion. Release me from Craving to try and Straighten out Everybody's Affairs. Keep my mind free from the Recital of endless Details, Give me Wings to get to the Point. I ask for Grace enough to Listen to the tale's of others Pains. Help me to endure them with Patience. But Seal my lips on my Aches and Pains. They are Increasing, and my Love of Rehearsing them is becoming Sweeter as the Years go by. Keep me reasonably Sweet. I do not want to be a Saint Some of them are so hard to live with—but a Sour Old Person is a crowning work of the Devil. Make me Thoughtful, but not Moody, Helpful, but not Bossy. With my vast store of Wisdom, it seems a pity not to use it all. But Thou knowest, Lord, that I want to have a few Friends at the end. (author unknown)

The biggest communication problem is that we do not listen to understand; we listen to reply.

—unknown

# CHAPTER 37

## *Down Under*

It was September 2014. I was preparing myself for a much-anticipated journey to Australia by ship. I had been pleasantly surprised by an informative bon voyage party. All the highlights to see and not-to-be-missed points of interest were shared over a colorful and delightful luncheon by a lake in Desert Shores. I was traveling with Ten people. four I had not met. Three of the ten were lifelong friends. We all met in Hawaii a few days before sailing and toured around the island, shopping and eating during a three-day street festival of music, wares, and food in front of our hotel, fronting the beach. It was scorching-hot but beautiful.

The cruise was eighteen days, to Sydney from Hawaii, with stops after six days at sea in the French Polynesian islands of Tahiti, Moorea, and Bora Bora.

After many more days at sea and lots of dancing and parties on board, we arrived in New Zealand for a few days, visited three cities there, and then went onward to Sydney, our last point of the cruise destination. We checked into a fantastic suite on the fifty-second floor in our Sydney hotel and had daily adventures that were awesome and nightly entertainment and dinners to never forget.

As a seasoned traveler but a first-timer in this part of the world, I knew I could not see everything. I had read several books and knew what I wanted to see. This meant carefully planning shore excursions to include these desired points of interest, as well as determining how I wished to see some things—via boat, private plane, or motor transport.

For all our shore excursions, this plan worked out very well. We really saw the islands, New Zealand, and Sydney in a variety of venues.

One of the greatest adventures of this trip was not connected to the cruise or shore excursions at all. It occurred after touring Sydney and a flight to Cairns to the north of Sydney to view the Great Barrier Reef—truly a wonder of the world, as the most massive living thing.

Margo was my roommate, and friends Marilyn and Reggie traveled together, sharing almost everything. Before we left, ideas were ruminating as to how we were going to visit the Great Barrier Reef. If there was fog, we would see nothing from a boat, but by air, one could view the reef and many other islands in its entirety, weather permitting. So we booked a tour by air.

We became more familiar with the existence of crocodiles and wildlife endemic to Australia, as well as other creatures of the sea. There was no state of bliss. We became keenly aware of the grave dangers, fears, and risks, as well as the incredible natural beauty. The Great Barrier Reef was a fantastic sight from our small aircraft—five of us were sandwiched in with a very young pilot. I was mortified with fear and realized before takeoff that this was probably a huge mistake. I was crying yet curious. I had traveled an extremely long way to see this wonder of the world. I worked hard to overcome my anxiety. I am pretty sure my fellow travelers would disagree that I succeeded.

Meeting my fears head-on while forced to take unexpected risks began my adventure of the Great Barrier Reef, with too many surprises and overwhelming dangers. One great thing was that the weather was perfect.

It was the break of dawn; the sky was dark gray-blue with a faint streak of orange. I was on the deck of my stateroom balcony. Our ship, the beautiful *Radiance of the Seas*, was inching into the harbor ever so smoothly and slowly. There was little movement or sound from passengers. There was almost a reverent worshipping of the spectacle before us. I could hear the minute clicking sound of cameras, but no one spoke. All the balconies were filled with passengers, getting that first look at Watson Harbor, getting a first look at the wonder of the Sydney Opera House.

Emotionally, it was an unforgettable moment. It was the ending of eighteen days on the ship and the nostalgic reality that it all was over. Our bags were packed the night before for the early rise and early breakfast. We said farewell to people we had met. In those moments on the deck, there was the excitement and anticipation of finally reaching Sydney and all the adventures that awaited us. In that dim light of morning, as the sails of the opera house drew closer, the magnificence of the structure did not disappoint. If ever there was a *wow* moment in my life, this counts as one.

The quiet splendor of this architectural wonder just mesmerized me entirely, with charm and allure that is overwhelming. My eyes were fixed; they focused and refocused to try to see and absorb the whole scene—the buildings in the background, the opera house in its splendor, the break of day. My jaw was loose and opened as I moved my head and my camera to click the changing light upon it. I had been standing, stretched over the rail, for the last half hour, and finally, I sat down on the deck chair. I stopped taking pictures and just began to look. I saw the crease of orange in the sky grow more substantial as the sun parted the dark blue sky, which was becoming lighter. We were very close to docking in a port, and after eighteen days, daybreak and Sydney were here.

It was sheer serendipity. Feelings I knew so well were here again, so many emotions flooded my mind—all the tremendous onboard experiences, hugs, and take-care kisses, and the "Don't forget to email me" from people I had met. I had shared life experiences with people I knew I would never see again.

It was now time to get off the ship, identify our luggage, get to our hotel, and begin our adventures on land—begin our visit to Sydney, Australia.

Our fifteen-passenger van was at shipside, awaiting our party of ten who had been traveling together for three weeks, beginning in Hawaii. There was a trailer attached to the rear end of the van to manage our luggage. Each person had about four bags, grips, carry-ons, and suitcases or about forty pieces to manage. I had four. It took about two hours or so to collect all of our things, disembark, and forage through nearly three thousand people onshore. Everyone wanted the same thing—ground transportation to home or hotel. Our ship had 1,600-plus Australians on board, so many were now home. Those reunions were special to witness. Children and grandmas and grandpas embracing and being welcomed home, smiles and tears and hugs.

Our hotel was another *wow* moment—the Meriton Suites Kent Street. Four of us shared a suite on the fifty-second floor. This was a gorgeous space, great large room, kitchen, washer and dryer, sunroom for games, free Wi-Fi (something I had divorced myself from for the last three weeks), two bedrooms, and two baths. We dropped off the luggage and began the tour, as we were too early for check-in. "Sydney, here we come!"

The city was impressive—clean, beautiful, busy—with a European and Asian kind of feeling. There was the elegance of simplicity in the design of architecture, our hotel, the stores, and in the fashions, parks, art galleries, churches, layout of the city, and the Hopi buses, double-deckers, that narrate the thirty-two stops and relate historical meaning.

We saw the museums, the Queen Victoria House, and the restaurant in the sky in Gucci Plaza, where we had kangaroo rump and crocodile and a hundred other fancy dishes on our first night there. No American dollars were acceptable there, credit cards only, or we would go to money exchanges, which were in every block or so. The familiar Starbucks and McDonald's and frozen yogurt franchises were comforting to see. We could detect the differences in lifestyles there versus America instantly; no tipping, for example.

The omission of the unnecessary. Meaning things were simplified for living and moving about the city. We toured the residential areas. The homes were beautiful; there were many elevations, hills, and lovely houses. The trees were beautiful, green and blossoming. It was the beginning of summer there in our October arrival. The Australian people have such a great sense of humor. They see life in lightheartedness. In a graveyard, there was a race car driver among the deceased, so his tombstone was a race car steering wheel. Their greeting of, "Hello there, mate" was warm and welcoming.

Our journey to the beaches—Bondi, Coogi, and Manly, where the Olympics were held—found us watching thousands of beach dwellers enjoying the waters and the morning sun. It was amazing! We prepared to join them, as it was all too inviting. The beach areas had an energy of rhythmic, musical beats; walking through the streets, there was laughter and chatter. The people seemed very happy, very relaxed, very helpful to tourists, not rushed, and many were barefooted. Australians were not a particularly good-looking people but possessed a rugged look, with great features and natural smiles. The many Asian people there were into high fashion, entrepreneurship, business, and commerce. They worked to live, rather than living to work. That was very apparent. I want to go back again.

*Watson's Harbor at dawn*

*Sydney Opera House*

*Best friends on the Bund*

*Our lives are a series of defining moments strung together by the passing of time. Surrender fully to this moment, because it is not the moment itself that sets us but how we choose to live it.*

*—Jill Pendley*

# CHAPTER 38

## *Something Good*

Arriving in New Orleans at the Louis Armstrong International Airport was as much of a circus as any airport in the world and more! Throngs of people, heat and humidity, baggage everywhere, and I had worked in the office up to the day I was leaving. I was exhausted when I got on the airplane in Los Angeles. Once there, quite shortly, I spotted Suzanne, who shouted, "Shirleywhirl, over here!" It was a welcome relief to see her. I knew I was going to settle in for some excellent rest and relaxation, if only for a few hours. I anticipated the great food and conversation we would enjoy before our journey began. Suzanne and her beautiful family are Jamaicans who fled the island when Michael Manley took over as prime minister in the 1970s, and Jamaica declared its independence from England.

Her family was upper-middle class and erudite; they were well versed in the culture of the arts, international travel, music, higher education, and the good life. Suzanne is a dentist, a graduate of Leeds College in England, with postgraduate work at Marquette University in Canada, and at the time (in the 1980s), she'd been on the faculty of LSU Dental School operative dentistry for the last twenty years.

She married David Mair and became the mother of two beautiful children, Chantal and Lawrence. Her mother and father were wonderful and were friends with my parents as well. Sue's father was a certified public accountant for the Opera Society in New Orleans, and her brother was a CPA for the Marriott Corporation. I make a note of this because Peter, Sue's brother, arranged for my family to be his guests at a jazz brunch at the Marriott. That event remains unsurpassed in total entertainment and magnificent food that was as tasty as it was beautiful—New Orleans at its finest.

Suzanne and Peter, as well as their children, took after the mother's side of the family and have Chinese blood; their skin color and features are not typical features of Jamaicans. I took off a few weeks from the rigors of my dental practice to assist Sue on an expedition to Jamaica. We would deliver care as well as mentor fifteen students traveling with us. I had done this type of volunteer dentistry many times before, only now, the AIDS epidemic had hit the United States and many other cities and countries, on its way to becoming a pandemic. This introduced some fear and a lot of caution and a need for protection. In addition to soliciting medicine, antibiotics, disinfectants, anesthetics, syringes, and needles, we needed paper gowns, hats, masks, gloves, goggles, and general protective gear for ourselves and the students, at a minimum. Upon arrival, Dr. Suzanne Turpin-Mair's home was our destination. Beautiful home with crepe myrtle trees in the backyard. The fish pond, beautiful green grass, and comfortable patio chairs caught me quickly easing onto a chaise lounge. I could smell the aroma of food boiling in a big pot. Sue had a crab boil going on. The container was huge, at least twenty gallons or more, and three feet high. Everything was put in with the crab—corn on the cob, potatoes, onions, carrots. The smell is delightful.

Newspaper was spread out on boards in the garage, and we pounded open the crab and made our plates or ate with our hands. We then drank excellent wine, put on good music, and talked into the night. Many people had come over by this time to say welcome and hello and to have dinner and wine. Whiskey pudding is dessert her mother always made for me when I visited. It is the Jamaican version of English trifle—a layer of sponge cake, fruit, and whiskey, and another layer and so on. We had a couple of days of this good life, and then took off for Jamaica.

The students were eager to go; this was a once-in-a-lifetime trip for them.

The students were all white males, as Suzanne was one of two black faculty teaching all white students. This was Louisiana. David Duke lived only a few miles away in Metairie, and segregation was alive and well. Poverty was widespread. Louisiana is one of the poorest states. The students loved Suzanne and had great respect for her skills and for her dedication to the underserved.

The day came to depart. We had twenty-six huge boxes of medicine, more than twenty boxes of supplies, and our bags. It's still a miracle to me how we got those things on the plane, Air Jamaica, without paying a fortune. I only remember hearing Suzanne, in her heavy Jamaican accent, saying, "Get the manager, please." I am sure they had never seen a similar scene and did not know how to handle us. But somehow, each of us checked two boxes or more, and by the grace of God for the people of God, we got through. We got on the plane with all of our boxes.

Suzanne, a Fulbright scholar, had secured some grant money for necessities, but we all paid our way, and she took care of accommodations, food, and transportation. Arriving at night was a blessing and a curse. It was scorching hot but more relaxed at night. Customs was a nightmare. The New Orleans airport seemed like paradise compared to the chaos of Kingston. We had to check in with the Ministry of Health to get our transports and hotel for the night. It was hours before we were all cleared, as there is no hurry in Jamaica. "Soon come" are bywords. We were to journey to the north coast the next morning. The atmosphere was busy. We could hear the steel drums playing in the hills and saw Jamaican Rastafarians with their braids. We smelled ganja in the air, a type of grass that is smoked. Goats strolled freely on the roads.

We were off the next morning after breakfast. Finally, we reached Duncans, the village we were going to set up in. We had a house set up with cots, living room, dining room, kitchen, great room, bathrooms, and a swimming pool. The house came with a cook, a maid who cleaned and washed our clothes, and four jeep-like vehicles. After a beautiful Jamaican dinner—curried goat, rice and peas, salad, tea, and prune whip for dessert—we had a meeting and shared the plan for our work the next day. With a diet full of nondetergent foods and mostly sugary fruits—mangos, papaya—dentures were commonplace for Jamaicans by age twenty. A public health dentist came through the main cities once every five years. Only extractions were done.

We were set up to deliver comprehensive care, emergency care, and preventive care. At every setup, there were as many unknowns as knowns. The only constant was hundreds of people lined up, hoping to get treatment. There is no Social Security, welfare, or other programs to help the needy. A persons only support are family and friends. So people suffered; we saw tumors and growths, broken legs and arms, amputees without a prosthesis, and compromised diets due to poor dentitions. Antibiotics were like gold—very scarce.

Independence from England had not meant much more than that; certainly not prosperity. The bauxite ore that is mined there has made great wealth for Reynolds, maker of aluminum foil. There was general low-pay labor and few benefits for workers, as well as corporations praying on minerals and riches of the land and leaving the people behind. Our mission was to make a difference, if only a small one, and we did.

The days were long; the work was rewarding; our bodies and minds were exhausted. At night, we all plunged into the pool and cooled off, had a good meal, and slept. We followed this routine day after day, moving north to predetermined centers, and we saw the throngs of people standing in line in peaceful patience. The gratitude and smiles were more pay than we deserved.

Our favorite drinks were lime squashes. One of the significant sports activities was cockfighting, and the music was reggae. I could almost hear a beat all the time. We slept with the windows open and sheets only; it was so hot. The fatigue in our bodies and the drinks made us sleep pretty soundly.

There was excellent fellowship—academic, professional, and humorous—as we reviewed our days, and the experience for the students was terrific. They diagnosed and provided treatment under supervision and were enhanced personally. I represented California as a member of the state board of dental examiners of a state larger than fifteen northeast states, and I was a commissioner of the American Dental Association. Nevertheless, two women led fifteen men daily into treatment for people in need. They were grateful beyond expectations. We did good things for many people, and it was suitable for each of us.

Dr. Mair published some of the preventive therapy results in *Dental Abstracts* the next year. As a precautionary measure, sealants were placed into the fissures of teeth of young people to prevent dental caries. We returned a year later to check on these patients, and a five-year study was done after that.

Dental disease is entirely preventable by fluoridation of the water supply, topical applications of fluoride, controlled sugars in the diet, and the placement of sealants into teeth (a resin material cured via ultraviolet light).

In the United States, 70 percent of children were caries-free. Amalgam, used for the last 150 years, primarily has been replaced with tooth-colored resins. Our service to these patients was something good.

*An empty wagon makes the most noise.*

*—Southern proverb*

# CHAPTER 39

## *Electronic Devices*

Young people are very adept at multitasking, a term that describes the performance of many activities at the same time. Electronics has provided enhanced opportunities. For example, young people can watch television, while texting someone on a smartphone, while talking to someone next to them and playing with the family pet with their feet. The text message next evolves to a video game and on and on. Rarely do people sit down to watch a big screen on the wall and do nothing more. Even many senior-age people are reading and watching at the same time. We are not fully engaged.

This is not a judgment of bad or good, unless people are endangering themselves or another, like operating a car while doing these things. It is just an everyday occurrence and a way of life for millions all over the world. It's almost like everything is so slow that we have to occupy the time in between. Electronics are delights and dilemmas. They can help us do, see, and experience amazing things—YouTube video piano lessons, gardens in Dubai, documents, newsletters, reports, puzzles, games, pictures, graphics, art, surgery, all kinds of medical applications, engineering applications, weather, space, ships, automobiles, refrigeration, supermarkets, pharmacies. Everything in our way of life has found a way, through computer programs, to look at our businesses and to measure our lives differently. Medical records, x-rays, and all kinds of reports can be transmitted electronically in seconds, anywhere in the world. There are many amazing applications, and I have only named a few. Emailing a document requires several steps: finding the material, saving it, copying it, sending it as an attachment, formatting it, and so forth; it's simple for someone who is adept in computer skills.

For a graduate of "Computers for Dummies" or a graduate of the hunt-and-peck typewriter skills, still using DOS and Windows XP, life is a bit different. This industry is moving so fast that if you do not keep up, you are left behind.

That brings me to my frustration—the necessity of constant updates, the need to upgrade devices. I have all Apple devices, making the bold change about four years ago. From the iPhone 8, there is now a 10 and X and XR, I believe, or it's sure to be on the way; the iPad, the iPad Mini, the large iMac, which sits as big as any television. Engineers have a self-driving car, robots, and enough creative energy to continue to create exciting new things daily. The Apple company works to get things tremendous, and then they begin from that point to see how to make the same thing super-great. They will work all night on a problem until solved. That work ethic is excellent and exhausting at the same time. The stamina to keep up and stay in the race is quite significant. New apps occur every day.

How people use these devices is the next frustration. The etiquette for social use of these devices has not been written, so common sense must prevail, and for many, that does not exist. For example, try speaking to someone with earbuds or headphones—those who bring devices such as a phone to the dinner table.

There is something excellent, however, about texting and tweets and following someone on Twitter. A text can be sent to someone in a meeting, who can get a confirmation without a conversation—home safe, received the document, see you at 7:00, meeting at 2:00. Tweets shout out how you feel; expressions. On Twitter, you can follow your heroes or exciting persons. Love it or lose out; it touches every realm of life from religion to banking. It has been around in the consumer reach for about thirty-six years. The good outweighs the bad. It keeps getting better, and there's an app for everything. If only I could remember my passwords and user IDs, life would be better. Oh, they have an app for that too. Finally got one.

Imagine life without electronics today—no internet, no emails, no texting, no Twitter, no Snapchat, Facebook or FaceTime. No Skype, Zoom, or web posts—all the things we do. At my age, I can imagine it because my life, growing up, had none of them. But I have tried to stay relevant and learn every new thing. I let go of a flip phone and got a smartphone. I left my DOS tower computer and moved everything to Apple. Yes, I shop online; no more traipsing around the mall until I drop, looking for pajamas for eight grandchildren. I go online. So life is different and changed, and it may be good, until it's not. One thing is for sure, you must keep up with technology or risk being left behind. New apps every day, and there is the word that China is developing a whole new communication system better than our current internet. So, to all my senior friends I say keep up so you can stay connected.

Heap see, but few know.

—Big Mama

# CHAPTER 40

## The Appointment

The telephone rang about three o'clock on a Friday afternoon, and a gentleman with an unsteady voice said he was referred to me by a relative.

I instantly recalled to whom he was referring and answered, "Why, yes. Thank you for calling. I was hoping to hear from you. How can I help you?"

The gentleman stuttered but said he wanted to sell his mother's home. I took his name and address and asked him if Tuesday at ten o'clock in the morning would be all right for me to come over and meet him and see the home. He agreed that it was a good time.

In real estate, a lot of research and preparation is done before you view the home. I allowed myself a few days to do computer searches. I did a title search, a search on the sale price of comparable homes in the area and subdivision, which homes had sold in the area, and how many days they took to sell. After using the market-data approach to value and doing some additional research, I was prepared for the appointment. I packed my briefcase with my measuring tape to check the size of the rooms, placed my Ipad in the case with some business cards, and I was ready for the appointment.

On Tuesday morning, I arrived earlier than the appointed time and drove around the neighborhood, studying the neighboring houses, observing the curb appeal, and also the number of for-sale signs; there were not many. I did not know if the client was staying at the home or a hotel, but I was meeting me there, so at ten o'clock, I walked up to the house, which had gorgeous roses bordering the sidewalk, a huge palm tree, and a partial desert landscape. For a first impression, it was very charming and welcoming.

I rang the doorbell, which was to the right of a wrought-iron enclosure around the front door. A friendly man of about sixty welcomed me in. He wore shorts, spectacles, and a loose-fitting shirt. He said, "Come on in." He said it was from Boston and would only be there a few days. He'd be taking his mother, who had been the resident there, back with him to reside in a home there, nearer to him.

I said, "I see, and that would be Gladys." Her name, along with his, was on the title.

"Yes," he said. "She currently is in a home here but won't be able to live alone any longer, which is the reason for selling her home. She's ninety-three years old. She bought the home new in 1988, along with a new car." The car was in the garage and in pristine condition, just like the home. It had only twenty-two thousand miles on it at twenty-four years old.

Instantly, I could see this home was warm and colorful and beautifully furnished, and Gladys had enjoyed her life here. Everything was as she'd left it when she was taken to the hospital. Her favorite books were in the den, her bed was turned back, china cup and saucer were on the kitchen counter, tea towels were neatly hung in the kitchen. There were charming window treatments, a crystal chandelier in the dining room, and warm tuxedo-backed chairs beside the fireplace. The living room had a vaulted ceiling, tastefully placed sofa end tables and a coffee table. It was a charming home.

Soon, we sat down at the dining table and discussed the items in my file. He indicated he was leaving next Thursday and wanted me to take care of everything.

I was momentarily stunned because I expected he would have packed some of his mother's favorite things to ship them back to Maryland.

He said, "No, she has lost so much weight. Just donate her clothes and items and sell the furniture."

I was still taken aback but did not show it and calmly offered a consignment store as a method of liquidation of the furniture and Safe Nest as a charity source to pick up the clothing.

"Great," he said.

My heart thought of his mother, whom I had not met. I took out the listing agreement and disclosures, which were forty to fifty pages of initials and signatures. I told him to obtain a specific and general power of attorney for his mother, so he could sign for her but that I would like to meet her.

Again, he thanked me and got a power of attorney. I got to meet his mother in a brief visit, and he presented me with the notarized power of attorney. She watched him sign her name and initial each page. She was once a much larger woman, I was told, but she appeared entirely gentile, with snow-white hair neatly groomed, weighing about 135 pounds, with beautiful, smooth skin and a powerful voice and feisty spirit.

Her brother and son were there at the signing, and she said, in a combination of helplessness and hopelessness, "What can I do? I have to go along with this. I wish I could punch them both right in the nose."

She did not want to leave her home. She loved it; she loved her life. She loved her evening beer. She looked great to me, recovering from a mild stroke. She was just old and needed assistance. There was not a close relationship between the son and his mother. They had not lived near one another or kept close contact. The son seemed dutiful but perfunctorily so. He was doing a job, and that was it. There was no abuse or discussion. It was just that the time had come. The brother was not especially close either, as this woman had lived a happy life as a recluse and avid reader.

*It's over*—that thought kept circling in my head. All her clothes in the closet, bedding in the linen closet, dishes, china crystal. The son seemed oblivious to it all. "Just get rid of it and send me the bill."

I called my handyman to come out and repair some minor things— check the filters and smoke alarms. We summoned the gardener to trim some things that were a bit overgrown since Gladys had been in the hospital and I received all the keys. We went to the consignment store; it took an authorization for me to act on behalf of the owners.

He sold the car in the garage. They were to leave at 9:00 p.m., flying back to Maryland. Just like that, twenty-four years after Gladys came to Las Vegas after her husband died and moved to Shady Grove Avenue, it was over. Her son selected a few family pictures, which he put in an envelope, and left the cup and saucer as it was, the kitchen counters as they were, and he said he would wait for me to call when we had an offer.

The pictures my photographer took were lovely, and in a few days, the home was listed. We showed it half a dozen times. Everything would go forward in due process—trucks would come, and people would clean up, and a new family would move in.

The love and care Gladys put into her home were evident. I can't help but remember she was not ready to leave. Are we ever prepared to leave, I do not know.

Thinking carefully about it all and trying very hard not to be judgemental, I know what seemed to be missing. Love, caring, kindness. The son Stevie, took her to a nursing home upon arrival. Her new home. He would visit often and do what was needed as a duty. No emotion was visible other than business and responsibility. But that was the life Gladys had built so I must respect that this is how many people live their lives and close their lives. The home sold quickly. Gladys is alive and well.

*Don't take life too seriously; you will never get out of it alive.*

—Elbert Hubbard

# CHAPTER 41

## *Clocks and Calendars*

Looking at the medium of time, just living to retirement age is, in itself, a milestone, a benchmark, a blessing. Like anything else, the passage of time can present formidable challenges, as well as magnificent opportunities. This might mean your life's important work is behind you. Accomplishments, achievements, changes implemented, awards, plaques, recognitions. Somewhere to some people, you mattered. You made a difference in the lives of others and in your life. You touched something on the earth and made it different, maybe better or not, but you were there, and you did what you did. Whether you were a teacher, worked as a clerk or as a salesman, were a stay-at-home parent, volunteer, analyst, doctor, lawyer, or athlete, whether you raised children or raised crops, you are done with that phase of life. You gradually realize you now possess a kind of freedom you never before enjoyed. You are retired. Done, finished.

For the first time in your life, you may be able to make decisions as to what you wish to do with your time. At first, it is exhilarating to not have to be at the office or wherever. You play golf, bowl, travel, call people on the phone who are still working and some who have retired also. You read, play bridge, and finally indulge those passions you had been waiting until you had the time to do them, that hobby—scrapbooking, knitting, woodcarving, sewing, gardening, mountain climbing, photography, collecting things, grandchildren, children, family time.

You soon realize that you are still very busy. Even with this freedom, you have many things to do. Exercise, watering the plants, email, phone calls, doctor visits, medicines, vitamins, eating well, hair appointments, manicure and pedicures, shopping.

What is it? Do we not know how to slow down, stop, and smell the proverbial roses? When you have not had control of your time for over fifty years, probably not.

Is there guilt associated with doing something different?

My dad used to say, "I am retired. I don't do anything, and I don't start that until noon."

My mother used to say, "I am still so busy. I wonder how I ever found the time to go to work."

We all look at time differently.

My goals for 2012 were written down, and I read them frequently. The mechanism for measuring my progress was also written down, as was my reward system upon accomplishing each one of them. January, the first month of the year, always represents a fresh start, a new beginning. Having failed so many times in making these resolves, evolving wisdom has taught me to make smaller, realistic goals so that they can be accomplished, even incrementally, rather than be abandoned—for example, getting my workout clothes ready and laid out the night before and athletic shoes by the door. That's the first step to doing my walking.

My first week, as always, has been very successful—focus, execution, progress, motivation. A month later is the real test. I have so many distractions, or should I say *passions* because I have so many interests that I enjoy with vigorous enthusiasm and fervor that compete with new goals. In thinking it through, I have to learn to combine my goals with my current passions so that I will not give up. For instance, spectator sports, football, basketball, tennis, golf, and baseball. I love to watch these events and record them all the time. That barely scratches the surface of time expended. Moving on to my favorite TV programs: *American Idol, The Good Wife, Real Time with Bill Maher, Murder She Wrote, Matlock, The View, The Chew, The Talk, Let's Make a Deal*, as well as films such as *Warhorse* and *The Iron Lady*, and we have not discussed politics. These are all distractions from daily goals if I spend too much time watching the television and the variety of shows that take my time.

I am somewhat of a news junkie extraordinaire, a political pundit. I watch liberal and conservative commentators, the polls, the debates, the candidates, the prognosticators, the president and his detractors, and all the hype, truths, half-truths, and partisanship.

President Bill Clinton recently said to an audience of Georgetown students that the last bastion of triumph that Americans face after the economy, racism, same-sex marriage, gun control, and immigration issues are let's agree to disagree. That statement came into our language to replace duels, which used to be the way to settle disputes. Cardinals and popes have used it; world leaders, especially in the Middle East settlements and agreements, live by it, and now the Congress of the United States of America.

What it really means is that if we do not agree, I do not want to be around you. It really says that if our ideas are not congruent, there is no place in our American way for your dissent in my circle of thought. This juxtaposition of ideas is what makes for twenty-four hours a day of political talk shows. We have to ask ourselves, "Am I better off for just knowing what each side thinks?" Maybe not, but it sure is entertaining. Whoever thought of news as entertainment? Sadly, because networks have made news bureaus into profit centers, they no longer report the news; they create the story.

I remember all the time spent with social clubs with women and groups. These were luncheons, bridge, Carrousels, Links, Urban League, and so forth. After years of service, these clubs have run their course. It is difficult to measure what was the value of the club meeting, other than the apparent benefit of acceptance, belonging, and the current project at hand.

That need also waned as time passed. The substance of this time is seen as far less important or needed. Hence, I have been getting out of clubs. I am learning to be a non-joiner; learning to say, "No, thank you." The time has come.

Children, grandchildren, Mother, doctors' appointments, mail, investments, taxes, memoir writing, picture archiving, music concerts, opening of the Smith Center—what fun that has been. We have tickets to Broadway shows, and the Jazz Roots series for Reynolds Hall. We saw shows at the Cabaret Theater.

Let's just casually throw in right here that I can do this activity in my pajamas, and I do, but I am still licensed as a broker in California and Nevada, so I am not correctly doing nothing. It keeps me active and is something for my brain to do besides go to physical therapy for my back and pains. Technology is grand. The telephone and computer is 99 percent of the administrative aspect of real estate today.

Hence, it's suitable for an at-home retirement activity.

New York City, the city that never sleeps, or Las Vegas, a twenty-four-hours-a-day, seven-days-a-week city. On any given day or night, you can enjoy a casino, a show, a quality restaurant experience. You can go shopping at any number of exceptional venues. The Fashion Show mall, premium outlets, Town Square Las Vegas, The District—to name only a few. There are no clocks in casinos, as they do not want you to think of time. They want you to lose all thoughts of time and spend and spend.

So back to a time when I lived in a city that is fascinating, arguably one of the most exciting in the world. If we had a river or an ocean, we would be right there. Having none, the Venetian, for example, recreates Venice and St. Mark's Square. We do have Lake Mead.

To accomplish a solitary goal, it is necessary to say no to some things so you can say yes to others. I never dreamed—never came close—that I would be this busy as a senior citizen and would enjoy it this much. The year 2011 was quite a challenge, as I was in California for January, February, and March; it was a blur, and April was not any better as to activity.

I was not back in Las Vegas until October, and I was able to get back into my routine. I was just as grateful as my kids were for the experience I had of helping out with family needs when a hand was needed.

For example, one of my daughters moved from Los Angeles to Valencia, settled and cleared the old house, and found a new home and the best schools. It was a monster job for a physician single mom of three girls, ages ten, twelve, and fourteen, who summoned Mom to assist. Her live-in housekeeper of twelve years had returned home to Mexico to start a business. I felt blessed to be able to say, "Yes, I can help with that," and we got it done. I loved the time with the grandchildren, dogs, school activities, and settling in. I appreciated the thought all the while that I was so happy that I was done with all of that. The homework was really a challenge. Believe me—the math was out there, and I am speaking of middle school. Of course, we found the highest-ranked school in the state, Westridge at Stevenson Ranch, which was new and had a high school, middle school, and elementary, all on the same hill. We placed one child in each school.

Then it was back home for the last quarter of the year. The year 2012 was an exceptional time for me, as I had a milestone birthday, as did a number of my closest friends. I also had a life-changing loss, in that the father of my four children and former husband passed away in July 2012. I admired the care, concern, devotion, and gratitude each of our children demonstrated throughout the prolonged illness of their father.

As a total family, many events of significant proportion met us head-on, and everyone worked together to create the success and peace we have found. We have a great family, and we have evolved from a great and giving family.

I am poised, mentally and physically, to continue to pursue my personal goals this year, and I believe I will be successful. I have this big push, internally, to put the past into perspective in the form of packaging, organizing, and ensuring a meaningful frame of reference, and it is happening. I cleared out one storage locker and located most picture albums. The next project is to try to match pictures with writing. Life-extended learning begins this month, and more new adventures in learning are before me. I live in a retirement community that is four-tiered—independent, assisted living, skilled nursing, and memory care. I feel incredibly blessed to appreciate all the rich experiences of the array of events in my life.

To be able to see due to cataract surgery recently, to hear, walk, talk, and breath are not gifts that are not recognized daily as a blessing of health. Also, still in my right mind, I wake up with a memory of yesterday and beyond. Time seems to be a conscious presence, more so than in the past. Calendars clocks alarms—I see the clock ticking another hour, another afternoon, another day. I write in the calendar, another week, month, year. I hear the alarm; it always means now.

One day or day one; it's your decision.

—unknown

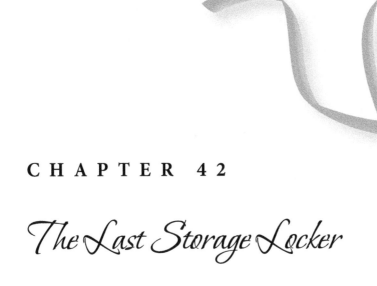

# CHAPTER 42

## The Last Storage Locker

Using storage lockers began for me in Las Vegas in my first significant downsizing in 2009.

This saga will describe ten years of hanging on to "stuff." Having sent two huge trucks to California to my children, one might wonder what was stored. Furniture, lamps, sofas, tables, china, dishes, linen, towels, bedding, art, collectibles, plants, books, crystal, silver sculptures, and rugs went to the kids.

I was left with the storage of file cabinets of film, pictures, DVDs, VHS tapes, albums, LPs, plaques of recognition, awards, certificates, black women dentists' history, dental patient files, x-rays, and real estate transactions from 1974 onward of complete data.

Three of my four children lived in Los Angeles at the time and had come to Turnberry in Las Vegas and picked out what they wanted and what was to go to each home.

My son, Danny, managed the move and transfer of items to Los Angeles while nursing, of all things, a toothache, which had him kind of cranky during the move. Independent and stoic as he could be, not much solace could be received. But that was Danny.

Storage Depot out on Rainbow in Las Vegas was charming, first-floor air-conditioned, and near the door and car. Completely inside and no worry of goods becoming damaged or altered. The move to Las Ventanas in 2010 and all my investment ventures with the Orphalese ship project were safely tucked into the storage, as well as over fifty years of marriage, divorce, children, club activity, hobbies, travels, collectibles, records of dentistry and of real estate, of dental school, continuing education, and awards.

In 2016, I moved to California, leaving one storage locker in Nevada. I secured two additional lockers in California near Paula's home, as I lived with her for the next two years.

Now that you have the history of this stuff, here are the details of the March 1, 2019, pilgrimage to Las Vegas to do the cleanout and bring to California what I wanted to keep out of this storage.

This well-planned and well-executed mission began at 5:00 a.m. My granddaughter Sofia and Scott, my trainer, accompanied me. It took five people—three women (Sofia, Elaine, and me) and Scott and Lonnie, Elaine's nephew. The locker was twelve-by-fifteen feet, and boxes were packed to the ceiling. In other words, it was full. We arrived in Las Vegas at 10:30 a.m. and went directly to Enterprise Car and Truck Rental to pick up the truck. My team was poised to work, and Elaine and Lonnie met us at the storage facility at noon, and work began immediately.

And worked until 4:30 p.m., closing down to check into the West Gate Hotel, formerly the Las Vegas Hilton, to freshen up and have dinner.

We had a lovely evening and even did a little gaming and a lot of winning. The next morning, we were on the job early, leaving in a misty rain, which prompted a stop by an auto parts store for a tarp and tie-downs to cover the truck. My job was to review what to keep and what to discard. That meant a cursory review of thousands of files and papers. The men moved items to the truck for dumping. Elaine pulled the boxes to me, as did Sofia, and sorted things I identified to keep or let go.

Observing my life in pictures, papers, and collectibles pass by for two straight days was to experience emotions I had not imagined. It was exhaustive and exhilarating. Baby pictures to million-dollar real estate transactions were the story of my life in boxes, in file folders, in actual print. It was, "Wow, wow, wow!" I looked at the people who had crossed paths in my life, many for a minute, some for a season, some for life.

Business associates, clients, patients, teachers, friends, family, coworkers, doctors, lawyers, homes, church, school, clubs, professionals, recognitions. The flow was overwhelming, some moments brought tears, some laughter. The people who passed through my life and those who stuck amazingly. Believe me, this was way more than moving stuff; it was a walk down memory lane, and it was being in touch with raw emotions.

On Monday, we had a lovely lunch at Vintner Grill in Summerlin with my brother, Limuary, and his wife, Marilyn; my sister, Carolyn Booker; and dear friend Margo Williams. My favorite free-range broiled chicken was still on the menu, and it was yummy. The event ended with sorbet and goodbyes. Sofia and I returned to the hotel for packing up and an early 7:30 a.m. appointment with Dr. Taylor at Shepherd Eye Center for my check-up. After a proper exam and report, we headed for the 15 South to Los Angeles and to home, safely. Sofia put on an audiotape of an Agatha Christie Poirot murder mystery. After a lunch stop and a couple of minor events, we were back home, and the locker cleanout was concluded.

We purchased a key lime pie from Marie Calendar but were too tired to have a gathering that evening. Instead, it was quickly a shower, cozy pajamas, and bed.

*I don't need you to remind me of my age;*
*I have my bladder to do that.*

*—Stephen Fry*

# CHAPTER 43

## Detroit Memory

I recall the time when I was nearly ten years old and loved playing outdoors with my friends. We lived in Detroit, Michigan, at the time at 574 Horton Street. I remember the trees on our street like it was yesterday—the bark was dark and rough and was a favorite for those white cocoon-like creatures that produced caterpillars. It was amazing to watch them work their way out of the envelope, and many fell to the ground. Kids would step on them. I can still remember the awful squish sound and the look of triumph on their faces, as if something had been achieved. They had squashed a caterpillar, partly out of fear and partly out of curiosity. I had probably crushed some too, but the gelatinous, gooey slime of the colorful creature did not attract me nearly as much as my desire to admire the changes taking place.

I recall how much time I had to just sit in the grass or on the tree branches and observe the sights of nature. I would reflect on the smells of the bushes and flowers and trees. It was hot and humid there. I had a bike with a basket and loved to ride. I would raise myself off the seat and stand on the pedals with my arms out in the wind and would whiz down West Grand Boulevard as if I owned the block. I also could skate really well and had my skate key around my neck. We made scooters out of skates and painted them.

Getting to go out and play was a great joy. The punishment was not getting to go out and play. I loved softball too and could really hit. We kept bats and balls in the hallway near the door. There was one rule: I had to be in before the street lights came on. So near dark, get in the house. If friends were still over or around the home, we would plead to play games on the steps, such as Simon Says and Mother, May I until all kids were gone home to dinner and family. I remember a wonderful dinner always with our family, conversation of the day, and a homemade dessert, such as tapioca or Jell-O or cake. After dinner, I did the dishes and hated doing the pots and pans.

Sometimes, I hid them to soak under the sink. It was then the routine of getting ready for the next day, taking a bath in the tub, and getting down on my knees to pray before climbing into bed. Life was good. I also remember VJ Day and riding proudly with flags on my bike in 1945. America had won.

*The greatest thing in this world is not where we are but the direction in which we are moving.*

## CHAPTER 44

# *What I Will Miss; What I Will Not Miss*

1. The telephone, great conversations
2. My children, grandkids, family, extended family, friends
3. Quiet time with myself (meditation, prayer, praise time alone)
4. Television, big-screen movie mysteries, inspiring shows, news
5. Toasted English muffins with butter and strawberry jam, orange marmalade, fig or blackberry jam.
6. Christmas tree lights (All holidays are great; Christmas is the best.)
7. Hugs and grunts (human contact of touch)
8. Smiles and eyes that tell a story
9. Sound of onions and celery sizzling in the skillet
10. The waves at the beach, roaring with energy and power
11. Football, basketball, tennis, golf, baseball, horse racing
12. Sunrise and sunsets
13. All mornings; the quiet serenity of a new day
14. Corn (all things corn—syrup, cornmeal, cornbread, corn tortillas, corn on the cob, white or yellow corn)
15. Pajamas—my favorite piece of clothing next to socks

16. Music, mainly piano, ballads, singers, easy listening, horns, violins, drums, harps, and guitars
17. Fresh sheets on my beautiful bed
18. Comfortable shoes that are pretty
19. Hot coffee (Starbucks, my favorite)
20. A crackling fireplace, standing in front of it or sitting and watching the fire
21. Laughter with good friends (nothing compares)
22. Gel writing pens—smooth
23. Vacations anywhere on a luxury cruise ship
24. Rain, cloudy days
25. The smell of fresh-cut grass
26. Pasta
27. A great movie, a compelling story
28. A warm coat or sweater or blanket
29. Church (the refuge and place of shelter for the soul)
30. My computer, iPads, cell phone
31. Broadway shows in New York City
32. Chinese food
33. Winning, every aspect of winning
34. My car, the magnificent machine that it is
35. Josie (our Maltese poodle)
36. Indian food
37. C'est La Mour—nail salon
38. My office sanctuary
39. Paula's morning calls
40. Alexa
41. My beautiful home
42. The blue skies of Santa Clarita
43. Fun at Bella Vida
44. Reading
45. Puzzles on my iPad
46. Magazines that I love
47. Stuffing
48. New ideas

49. Making plans
50. Talks with my grandchildren
51. Playing bridge

## What I Will Not Miss

1. Hospitals
2. Lines at the post office
3. Cold soup
4. Rock music
5. Nighttime driving
6. Heights of all kinds
7. Surprises
8. Phonies of any kind
9. Great white sharks
10. Heavy traffic
11. Dry eyes
12. Guns
13. Storms at sea
14. Turbulence in flight
15. Escalators
16. Deadlines
17. Fifty pounds of fat
18. Double chin
19. High heels
20. Unpacking after a trip
21. Aches and pains—leg cramps; ouch!
22. Picking up dog poop while walking the dog
23. People who do not know what they are doing (patience and tolerance in short supply)
24. Overly opinionated announcers on worldwide media, sports, news
25. Freezing temperatures (Some like it hot; that is me.)
26. Losing (mostly my sports teams; hate the whole feeling of losing)

27. Steep stairs
28. Smoky rooms, casinos, bars
29. Visits to the doctors
30. Political pundits
31. Wrestling or boxing
32. Fox News
33. Funerals, loss, tears, and sadness
34. Loud, noisy places and people
35. Liars
36. Fake people
37. Unauthentic souls
38. Whiners, complainers
39. People who talk too much
40. Mediocrity
41. Unpatriotic elected officials
42. Cowards
43. Unbelievers
44. Smug people
45. Selfish souls who can't realize it
46. Narcissistic leaders
47. High winds
48. Backaches
49. Deadlines
50. Ignorance
51. An unimaginable Covid virus Pandemic
52. Poor Leadership at the National level of the US

*It is better to light one candle than to curse the darkness.*

—Chinese proverb

# CHAPTER 45

*Leaving*

This title could have been one of many—"The Long Goodbye," "Time to Go," "Final Surrender." It began four years ago, before, during, and after Dan Jr.'s marriage and wedding celebration to Marcela in 2008. Dr. Dan appeared heavier and bloated and had haltingly slow mobility at the sequence of events. I was told his diagnosis was grim, with a description of two cardiac aneurysms, cardiomyopathy, high blood pressure, and the sequela of organ failures associated with this condition. Surgery was not an option.

Dan was depressed but masked it as best he could. He was insistent on directing his own treatment in refusing hospital care until there were no choices about it. Three of our four children live in Southern California, and Pam, the East Coast daughter, flew out monthly at a minimum. Dr. Dan's current wife, Shirley "Marty" Martinez, a Filipino nurse for more than ten years and one who has been warmly received by all of the family, was a constant companion, and she was at his side, directing his care. Paula, our oldest daughter, was to call me repeatedly and give me the prognosis and share her feelings of concern and the prospective loss of her father.

Dr. Dan was more than irrational in wanting to make his small condo into "medical central," with his disdain for hospitals, especially in July, when new interns and residents arrive, and the death rate is the highest in all hospitals. Paula resisted going along with her dad in converting his home into a mini-hospital. She consulted with his physicians and got him as much home health care as possible.

Over the next year, he lost over one hundred pounds and began to get better. His high blood pressure subsided and became low blood pressure. We began to see the therapeutic benefit of weight loss alone, and he seemed to be much improved, only thin and frail, loss of muscle mass, weak, but less depressed. The family was encouraged; he was encouraged. Emotions were fragile; his recuperation toyed with ups and downs of hope and optimism to exhaustion, despair, and depression.

Year three became acute periods of sudden crisis, telephone calls ("Dad's back in the hospital"), making him accept dialysis three times a week or die, and the negotiations of that. A crisis began to occur almost monthly—a respiratory event, unable to breathe, screams for help, 911, and admission, several days to weeks, in the hospital, into rehab. And back home with hospice care.

Year four brought longer crisis events, oxygen, CPAP and biPAP, dialysis daily, drugs to elevate his blood pressure, tubes out of every orifice—nose, stomach, etc.—and forced air through the biPAP. Our kids were nearly out of their minds; our family was in wait mode. Waiting for the phone to ring with news, needs, some news.

Dan's battle to live was not an easy thing to watch. I am not sure there is a difference in the battle not to die and the battle to live. No one knew exactly how to cope. The children were all impacted, as were the grandchildren and our friends, as everyone's life was affected. Everyone dumped emotions on friends and other family members.

Year four, 2012, was the most difficult, as we moved through our lives with a sense of normalcy but our emotional lives were quite the opposite, anything but normal. Pam flew out to California even more often, talking to her dad and Marty and helping where she could. Paula, Patricia, and Dan were there at Glendale Adventist Hospital all the time and contributed generously of themselves over the entire period.

Dan's wife was literally keeping him going, as the physicians responsible for his care had given up on him four years earlier. They continued to say there was no possibility of life for him. He kept dispelling the prognosis, no matter how impossible his diagnosis was.

I spoke to him on his seventy-fifth birthday on June 22. He labored to speak, and we shared a moment of conventional humor about age. There was no getting around the fact that we had spent thirty-five years together, meeting fifty-one years ago. I did not like seeing him suffer so. I watched my four children react and wither over the years of devotion and loyal attention. I looked at the long faces and sad eyes of our eight grandchildren, seeing Oompah so helpless and vulnerable—this huge figure in our family, so bent and broken beyond repair. After a four-year virtual vigil, in the final analysis, there seemed, for me, to be a relief.

Each of our children managed in observable sadness and grief, kind of an empty space, a void, a loss. The call came at 5:45 a.m. on a Saturday. They simply said, "We cannot get a pulse."

I was all packed and ready to leave anyway, as I was driving there to see him that morning. I told my daughter I was on my way and would see her in four and a half hours. I was of course living in Las Vegas, Nevada in 2012.

I was glad it was morning and not that great dark night I think Dan feared. It was morning. I knew Dan was safe at home, at last, with God. I know the children and Marty will see him there too, in time.

The final rites gave the closure we all needed. Dan was a special doctor. Many wonderful tributes were made regarding his care of patients and his life with the medical staff. A top student, an esteemed surgeon, a good man, a good father, a good husband who tried very hard to be his best, left a legacy of excellence in his life. He was a fighter who never gave up.

*Every job is a self-portrait of the person who did it. Autograph your work with excellence.*

—unknown

# CHAPTER 46

## My Favorite Passions and Why I Like Them

After years of raising children, a rewarding and successful career, years of volunteer work, philanthropy and charitable giving, historic preservation, and community service, I am at last entertaining my time. Hopefully, it does not sound woefully selfish, but I think the time has come. I am the captain of my ship, the master of my fate, and I have a bad back.

Well, it's September, my favorite month of the year, endings and beginnings. Triple-digit temperatures end, and football begins. New seasons of television programming begins. Summer lazy days have ended. Briskly, the days start to whiz by, as the holidays are only days away. Halloween is not yet here, but Christmas trees and decor are up in Costco, Hallmark, and many stores around our city and nation. The rush is on; soon they will begin the countdown as to the days left for last-minute shopping before Christmas, when I have not even started. This season is the beginning of getting-ready time.

To quote a famous line from *Ragtime*: "Looking back to this time last year, we were in a frenzy of national elections, debates polls, posturing, and urgency."

The last quarter of the year is upon us. Time to get your flu shot, eye exam, medical physical, dental exam. For me, it is a birthday month, and oh, what a year this was—a surprise party, so much fun, so many well wishes, so many good moments, so many smiles and hugs.

My dad had a September birthday, as did Uncle David and Auntie Allene. I love this month. My favorite day of the week is Sunday, hands down. I love the serenity of this day that no matter where I am, I know and feel Sundays are different. If I go to church, it is a good day and a good week; if not, I will hear some words of the Bible from a television ministry or just read the text myself. It's a sobering day of the week, when you can usually find some quiet time to readjust yourself, spiritually and emotionally. I subscribe to the Sunday edition of the *New York Times* newspaper. This an indulgence for me, in the guilty-pleasures category.

Additional delightful perks are coffee and a sweet accompaniment, such as coffee cake. As I read the editorials of journalists, sometimes reading it is not accomplished in one day. The *New York Times* magazine, book reviews, art and culture, what's on Broadway, the buzz of the Big Apple, and sports are my favorites. This Sunday morning bundle on my driveway is one of my favorite things.

So to what now, in these years, do I commit my precious time? My latest passion is back to the piano. My core training helps me to sit up for about twenty minutes.

I love music; it is life, breath, joy, peace, energy, harmony, balance, rhythm, and beat. I have never mastered much of it, but that has not quelled my passion for continuing the chase. I am further than I ever thought I might be, equated to the commitment I devote to it. Amy, my new teacher, recently told me that you can struggle in music for a long time, and then, one day, a light comes on, and you get it. You really get it. So here is hoping. I saw the sign that read PIANO LESSONS last year, while attending UNLV lifelong learning classes in Sun City.

I made a mental note and stopped in one day and bought a music book, and the people seemed friendly enough, so I kept going back. While I had taken pretty much all the OLLI (Osher Lifelong Learning

Institute) classes, and there was nothing I was interested in, I said, "This is my time to get back to music."

I am in a music class in Sun City that is quite exciting. The first month, I sat in on several different types until I found the right two categories. I even went over there twice a week. Now, everything is on a Tuesday, and I have probably the most gifted teacher I have ever known. She is not only a sensational performing artist on the piano, but she has the gift of being able to show others. She has taught children and can simplify things to that level, which is probably why she is so successful and why I am getting it. She played in a band for years. She just knows how and why and even has a class called Tricks of the Trade. I am in a class called Fake Book and another called Music Theory. Although so much is over my head, I come away from there feeling lucky to be able to be there. I only wish I had met her fifty years ago. There is no telling how different my life might have been.

Our class has about eight people, all seniors with lots of life history. One of the best decisions made this year was to make music.

My second passion is sports, in the order of football, basketball, tennis, golf, baseball (New York Yankees—though not this year; too many injuries), track and field, and horse racing. I do not care for hockey, soccer, swimming, diving, or auto racing, which they say is a sport. I used to play the French horn in the band, and we marched during halftime at football games. I began to learn the game, and by the time I was married, we were tailgating in a motorhome outside of the Los Angeles Coliseum for the Raiders.

Football is a game played with a leather egg-shaped ball, fourteen to fifteen ounces in weight, and about twenty-two inches in center diameter. It's made of three-ply rubber panels sewed together with white laces and dates back to the eighteenth century. Players fight to gain yards, inches, downs, and field position, leading to goals and touchdowns. The running and passing of this elusive elliptical pigskin are intercepted, passed, fumbled, kicked, and tipped, but the excitement is like nothing else. The players are padded and helmeted and wear colors, numbers, names, team logos, and shoes with cleats and pads. Still, it is like the gladiator days of primitive times, almost a fight to the death, as players are injured as frequently as not. It seems to be putting everything on the line, a factor that is so attractive to fans.

The game is played in all kinds of weather—rain, snow, ice, heat, day, night, cold. There are domed stadiums now, but this is for fan convenience—luxury boxes, food courts, bars, and so forth. The season is only a few months long, but the sports talk and drafts and millions of dollars to be made are legendary, from college to professional ball.

Winning has an exhilaration like nothing else! Learning how to win is enormous. No one likes to lose. Someone has to lose, but victory is better. So when we lose, we mourn and work harder and fix it and come back next week, determined to win.

Peyton Manning was my favorite football player. I watched his dad play, Archie Manning, his brother Eli, and their whole family is right for the sport. They have discipline, humility, excellent work habits, persistence, patience, determination, and the know-how to win. Now, my favorite is Kansas City Chiefs quarterback Patrick Mahomes. Phenomenal! Best I have ever seen for the game, I believe. He was in the Super Bowl 2020.

My favorite baseball players are Alex Rodriguez, Derek Jeter, and Mariano Rivera. Baseball is as uncomplicated as it was when we played it in school. Three strikes—you are out. Of course, they have high-tech pitching now and schools to learn every position. But pitching and hitting are the basics of baseball, along with running and catching the hit balls.

Pitchers are very important; there are all kinds of pitches to use to try and fool the batter. There are cut fastballs, sliders, fastballs, curveballs, sinkers, knuckleballs. The pitch must be in the strike zone. Too high or too low, and it's a ball and not a strike.

If you understand pitching, you will love baseball. It is a war between a batter and a pitcher, trying to guess inside, outside, low, high, fastball, or curve, coming at ninety-five miles an hour, straight at you, and, ultimately, three strikes and you are out—over, finished until next at bat for nine innings.

The planet earth is round, and all these balls are a form of round, except the size of the series is different—football, baseball, tennis ball, golf ball, basketball. Dimples were added to golf balls. Most of these sports began in England in the eighteenth century. All have specific weights and have evolved, over time, from available materials to more high-tech equipment that is amazing. In school, we learn to play these sports. Some perform well enough to have careers in sports or related fields as trainers, coaches, and so forth. If not, we become fans; we develop loyalties and favorites.

Basketball—I loved Kobe Bryant. What a work ethic; what a professional. Kobe was a sensation, from high school to retirement. Great father, magnetic talent, one of the best ever.

In tennis, I love Serena Williams today, as well as Steffi Graf and Chris Evert.

In golf, Tiger Woods is a sensation. Even now, he is number one again—five wins in 2013. He is amazing to watch. His stroke and form are what thousands work to achieve. Tiger is one of the greatest ever in golf.

That takes a little of those favorite fall Sundays, watching my favorites on the television. Breakfast at Wimbledon, the Masters, the World Series, the basketball NBA finals, the Super Bowl. Oh yes, there are the parties, the food, the beer, the shouting and screaming, and the pain and agony of defeat. Still, there is also the thrill of victory— nothing else like it. When my teams or favorite players win, I walk around all week, just as if I had won. Isn't that some transference? And when they lose, I mourn the loss as well.

Music, sports—the family is right there in the middle, and sometimes, when necessary, they move to the top. Whatever, whenever, the family is primary as a passion. Mother, grandchildren, children, sister, brother, nieces, nephews, and now, Josie, my little dog, who is so smart it is almost scary. Those eyes look at me with such a knowing look. She speaks to me in a language that is so clear as to what she needs or wants, and I know what she is saying. I am understanding more now why pets are so adored and valued. They are exciting. Josie helps me get my exercise, like it or not.

I still work. I am not sure why, but I always find enjoyment in it— real estate. I am sure, when this license period is up, I will not renew my license in 2016. I may finally retire before that, but I find I need the time to commit to my passions, my projects.

The final passion that I feel is so important is writing. The very act of putting thoughts on paper makes what I am thinking a *thing*. It has moved from the thought process, the idea, the flash of the moment, to the written word. It can stay around for centuries—what a vain thought. The writers' group has accomplished the feat of keeping the passion alive. We have listened to tapes from a Princeton English professor on descriptions of writing, making sentences more interesting, long-winded sentences, and short, syntactic sentences that have an impact, descriptive adjectives, and power.

We have worked around holidays, members' travel, illness, family trips, busy schedules, looking for and finding that elusive time to come together to share what we have been working on. The times together are always right. There is a dynamic synergy that is pervasive and ever present that weaves surreptitiously from writer to writer until we have all shared, and then the best part is always like dessert, after the main course. After we have encouraged and critiqued each other and learned a great deal about Wisconsin, Nebraska, civil rights, Saudi Arabia, China, family members, and ourselves, we wistfully and factually call ourselves writers, and we always will be. It has been said in many forms that the complete person is the written life.

If I used food metaphorically, life, for me, seems to be the buffet. Las Vegas knows how to put on a meal. The Wynn is outstanding. The Mandalay Bay is excellent, and the Golden Nugget knows a few unique things. The Paris Hotel and the Red Rock hold their own—the beauty, variety, the international cuisine, the salad bars, the continental foods, the fruits, the meats, and seafood. The Wynn has a total room of desserts, from lemon bars to homemade gelato.

These are some of the passions in my life. I am so grateful for the gift of life and the buffet before me.

In closing this chapter, my passion for the Word of God is very real and very present. The Bible is the procedure manual for life. Daily, I read, without fail, Jesus calling. It really makes me pause, center myself, and begin my day, hopefully with steps ordered by Jesus. There are those I pray for in my family, people who ask me to pray for them, my friends, and our world. We need leaders who will work on global and national problems of clean water and food for everyone, accessible health care, immigration, climate change, crumbling infrastructure, housing, education, diplomacy, and so many things and ways of coming together. The young and the old need many things.

*Cowards never start, the weak never finish, and winners never quit.*

*—unknown*

# CHAPTER 47

## Recalling a Day I Overslept

The sun was shining brightly into my Marina del Rey condo when I opened my eyes and slowly lowered my head toward the clock on the nightstand. I squinted to see the hands on the clock—9:10. I shrieked! My plane to my twenty-fifth class reunion was to leave at 9:30. I knew immediately that I was going to miss my flight.

Several of my classmates were on the flight and knew me to be punctual or early, so never in anyone's mind did a thought appear that I would be late. Beatrice said to Angie, "She'll be here; don't worry."

When the boarding of the aircraft was nearly complete, Angie stated, "She had better hurry."

Then the stewardess walked through the cabin and began to close the overhead bins. Beatrice said, "She'll be here any minute now."

When they closed the door and locked the hatch and asked passengers to turn off all electronic devices for takeoff, they both realized Shirley was not on board. Oh, my God. What has happened?

Back at the marina, I quickly dressed, grabbed my bag, hopped into my car, and drove less than ten minutes to LAX. In my mind, I was reviewing what had happened to cause this once-in-a-lifetime misadventure. I wildly drove to the airport.

It was going to be a short trip of three days, so I had not ordered transportation. I was going to do airport parking, I had not requested a wake-up call, as I'd had company the night before, was up late, and had only planned to catch two hours of sleep. I arrived at the airport to see two hundred people in line at the American Airlines ticket counter. I went back outside to the curb and spoke to a Red Cap, telling him of my dilemma. I embellished my story considerably by telling him I had to get to Nashville, as I was a keynote speaker at the reunion events. I pressed fifty dollars in his hand. I was well dressed, carrying a briefcase, and looked panic-stricken.

He said, "Give me your ticket and bag and wait here."

After fifteen minutes, which seemed like thirty, I thought, *This is the worst day of my life. I overslept. I missed my plane. I have given a stranger fifty dollars, my ticket, and my suitcase. I exaggerated the truth a bit. Have I lost my mind? And I am now going to miss everything?*

Then I saw the Red Cap pushing a wheelchair. He said, "Doctor, please sit down. Your plane will leave in about twenty minutes, and I will take you to the gate. This is the fastest way to get you through security. Here is your boarding pass, your ticket, and your baggage check. You do not have to pay a change fee, and the only seat available was in first class, so they put you there."

I had a great time. I arrived three hours after my classmates, feeling great after having drinks and fun in first class, and the party was on. I thanked the Lord that this story has a happy ending.

*In the game of bridge, a peek is better than a finesse any day.*

—Limuary Alja Jordan

# CHAPTER 48

# Looking Back and Looking Ahead

When I contemplated a look ahead at 2014, a reflection over the past year was inevitable.

It was undoubtedly a year of significant events. Mother's ninety-fifth birthday party with every member of all immediate families coming to Las Vegas began the year on January 19, 2013. The Camp Shirleywhirl cruise was in June 2013. Planning for this had started. Seventeen family members were going. A stop in Washington, DC, was included so I could bid farewell to my oldest granddaughter, Natalie—the first off to college at West Point.

Then it was off to Fort Lauderdale for a pre-cruise jaunt gathering before setting sail. Oh, what a time that was—a Hilton Resorts suite with a spiral staircase to the second floor, right on the ocean. We had a party there and dinner in the restaurant, with friends from Florida joining us. Josie, a fourteen-pound white Maltese poodle, came to live with me in August, a life-changer for sure but such a joy!

Sister Carolyn and Cary Booker moved here in May. I helped her furnish her Las Ventanas apartment. She returned to Atlanta to clear their family home and returned to Las Vegas in August. Within hours, Cary was felled by a stroke that ultimately, after a few months, claimed his life. On October 10, six days later, their son and my nephew Cory won election to the US Senate from New Jersey. We all attended his swearing-in, with all the grandchildren and children in Washington, DC. Mother was too fragile to travel and remained in Las Vegas.

This extraordinary event was a blessing for all of the grandchildren to experience. It was quite a proud moment for all of our family and for my sister, Carolyn, especially. Ultimately, we attended a memorial service in Atlanta for brother-in-law Cary on December 14, 2013.

What a year! As a sidebar, sometime during the cruise, I tore the medial meniscus on my right knee. It was not much of a problem and healed entirely after physical therapy. Still, a month later, feeling energetic and spry, I was trekking across the soccer field across from Las Ventanas with Josie. I heard something go pop on the left knee. It responded to the same intense physical therapy but is not back to normal yet.

I had a dental implant squeezed in all of this, and Mother faced renewed medical challenges that continued, but she had positive responses. The hours in doctors' offices in 2013 seemed countless but very beneficial.

Before beginning 2014 from my perspective, I wanted to share a story that I found so compelling in the *New York Times* magazine. I found the lesson simple, evident, and vital. It became the thesis of my outlook for 2014. Paul Tough was the writer of the article titled "Man Overboard."

It was about John Aldridge, a commercial fisherman who fell into the ocean in the middle of the night, forty miles off Montauk, Long Island. He had no life vest and no way to signal where he was. He was a speck in the ocean, and his partner was fast asleep. It was 3:30 a.m., and he was pumping water into holding tanks for the lobster and crab to chill so that when they reached their first string of traps, the water would be cold enough to keep the lobster alive for the return trip. To do this, he needed to open a metal hatch on the deck and pull over two hundred pounds of ice to the cooling tanks. It was when he was hooking the side of these ice chests and leaning back and pulling that the accident occurred. The handle snapped, and he found himself flying backward across the deck, toward the back of the boat, where the hatch was open. There was just a ramp leading into the black ocean.

The water hit him like a slap. He swallowed a mouthful of water and then tried to yell as the boat, on autopilot, moved due south at six and a half knots and was already out of reach. He was alone in the darkness, and a single thought gripped his mind: *This is how I am going to die.* At forty-five years old, he had been a fisherman for two decades. What despair! What aloneness and utter fear and astonishment he felt in those moments. Then, he quickly determined to have no more negative thoughts. Instead of kicking off his tall rubber boots, as survivalists tell you to do immediately because of their weight, John gently took off the left boot and pushed it upside down into the water. This captured an air pocket, and he slid it under his left arm. Then he took off the right boot, pushed it upside down, and pushed it under his right arm—and like pontoons, he could stay afloat. Trying to tread water was already exhausting him.

John's goal was to hold on to these boots and strive to stay awake until daylight. He would then look for floating debris to hold on to. It was very hard. He knew that in the cold Atlantic, his hours were numbered before hypothermia set in.

In the meantime, his partner and best friend awakened and realized John was not there. Emergency rescue procedures began, as well as volunteer boats, and air and sea patrols.

John was but a speck in the water. There were no coordinates to track him, and his partner had no idea if he'd gone into the sea shortly after he fell asleep or moments earlier. The Coast Guard, air-sea rescue helicopters, and volunteer fisherman all joined the search, as every moment was precious.

I won't detail all the drama of the search, but it took twelve hours, with constant thinking, using buoys and trap flags, before John, who nearly drowned, ultimately was rescued. After hospitalization and after offering his profuse thanks, John said—and here is the lesson— "You guys did a hell of a job in finding me, but let me tell you—I did my part."

John Aldridge kept positive thoughts. He used his knowledge of trap flags and buoys, and he stayed awake. How easy it would have been for him to give up. The ocean was claiming him. Sea lice and

415

shrimp were attaching themselves to his clothing, and he was shivering uncontrollably. He knew the odds of someone finding him were slim to none. As long as he could stay awake, though, he thought positive thoughts. Indeed, how sturdy his resolve was for the small window of time he had before there would be no hope.

Is this something from which I can gather strength? I think so. Can I do a fraction of the positive thinking that John did when I think about my goals for 2014? Thank you, John Aldridge, Paul Tough, and the *New York Times* magazine. Is this something I can gather strength from? I think so. Can I do a fraction of the positive thinking that he did about my goals for 2014. Thank you, John Aldridge, journalist Paul Tough, and the *New York Times* magazine.

The year 2014, for me, is, first and foremost, a decision to take better care of myself, safeguarding the health I have. I have learned that an injury is a real inconvenience. I appreciate my knees more than I ever have. There was a time when it was a given that I could walk anywhere I wanted to go with total freedom. Now I walk Josie as far as the knees will allow.

Weight loss will help a lot of things, my knees at least. That said, yes, I have a plan. Weigh myself, record the number, and move to lose five pounds. I cannot lose twenty-five pounds if I cannot lose five pounds. Invest time and effort, and work at keeping positive and record my results. Come on in, 2014.

I plan to go to my fiftieth dental school reunion in May at Howard University. There is also the high school graduation of Sofia's second-oldest grandchild. More travel in 2014.

I was invited to join friends on a South Pacific adventure, beginning in Hawaii and ending in Australia, including Tahiti, Bora Bora, and New Zealand in September. This trip would occur during the period of my birthday. Australia was on my bucket list, so I planned to go on that trip. Knees, please get stronger, and back, please hold up.

The decision to join a piano music class in 2013 was a great one, and it's something I want to continue and even add some private instruction. I love the course. Spending quality time with family and strengthening relationships is always essential. Family togetherness has been very enriching. All are agreed we should have more in the future. With my children and grandchildren, we have such a great time.

Three of my granddaughters—ages thirteen, fifteen, and seventeen—were recently here. We had such a memorable visit, talking and listening and answering questions. The usual activities of going to shows and looking for entertainment were scraped, and we just spent quality time together. I believe we did things in the right way.

One of my goals is to encourage them to have big dreams and be global thinkers without limits. We laughed and talked about subjects they generally discuss with their peers—sex, dating, dancing, college. They love boy bands; currently, One Direction is hot. They adore Adele, the singer. They are pragmatic but also want glamour and chic things when shopping. A favorite store is Forever 21. We set out to go there while they were here in Las Vegas. I took them to Town Square; it had a Forever store but not Forever 21. I was directed to try the Fashion Show mall. There, in a dynamic splendor, it appeared. It had just turned dark; there sat this mega-store with bright lights about one hundred yards from valet parking, from Maggiano's across from the Wynn Hotel.

The girls saw the store and were in heaven. They stood in front, let out a shriek, and began running toward the store. After parking, I went inside. It was bright and colorful. Ubiquitous blaring musical beats steadily added energy to the experience. It had escalators streaming to the second floor, sizes from petite to plus, glamour, accessories, everything a kid could want and more.

This was far more than a department store; it felt like a rock music experience—with merchandise. Forever 21 had everything—designer clothing, shoes, boots, accessories, and jeans. as knockoffs at minimal prices. You can look great if you know how to put things together. Los Angeles did not have a store this large.

All I could hear was, "Grandma, this is awesome," and "Look at this, Grandma." Their mom was helping and smiling, accustomed to their glee. They bought boots and clothing accessories and still did not spend all of their money. They were in heaven, and I was one of their heroines— for that day, anyway. In 2014, I could use a lot more of that.

The knees held up well.

I don't need you to remind me of my age;
I have my bladder to do that.

Don't you love judging other people? It makes all
my fears disappear and all the things I don't like
about myself seem so much less important.

When it rains, look for rainbows; when it's dark, look for stars.

—Unknown

# CHAPTER 49

*A Profile in Trust*

I moved to Las Ventanas in 2010. This is a retirement community, located in Summerlin, on seventeen acres of prime real estate. It is branded as a continuing-care product.

The life-care plan offered three tiers of care and ideas for a fourth tier—independent, assisted, skilled care, and, in the future, memory care. Lifestyle selection is made according to the level of care you require; I selected an independent-living model in building D.

Being in my eighties now, with grown children, single, mostly retired, with a ninety-four-year-old mother also here in assisted living and a brother living nearby in Nevada—these are the "golden years." Mainly being of sound mind and body, I did considerable research before making the decision to move here. The research on the internet provided many visual tours of facilities and accreditation standards and designations, the highest being CCRC—Continuing Care Retirement Communities. Site visits to Carlsbad, California, and Thousand Oaks, California, with overnight stays gave more insight on the residents and lifestyles, food and dining, activities, amenities, staffing, estate planning, returns on investment, and—last but not least—medical care, hospitals, and procedures for getting attention.

It took a few years to make a decision. After attending promotional lunches and even a preconstruction promotional invitation. I was being sensitized to a different style of living. The residents seemed happy wherever we visited.

The concept of community living, I believe, is the first consideration for anyone considering a move to a senior residential facility. As I'd personally lived in high-rises for the last twenty-five years, this was not an issue for me but could be for some.

I liken life here to cruising on a large ocean liner. There is one world inside your quarters and another outside your quarters. With my medical background and real estate background, I have learned that people move in two stages. The first is the emotional move, with visualization and mental images, and then there's the physical move. Visualize, actualize, let go, and learn that less is more. There are necessary emotional adjustments that have to be made as to space, size, square-footage differences, private pool or community pool, private dining or community dining, and the mental examination of values and priorities for one entering independent living as a choice. For others, their state of health or limitations may be such that just obtaining the care needed or the assistance with cooking, housekeeping, less bill-paying stress, etc. is reason enough. Many people are just tired. Change is welcome in any form.

It is the prime option. The biggest positive for me was the ability to live in a setting that meets the challenges of aging, allowing me to manage and thrive on site. The initial investment added to my estate is positive. What are the immediate differences? Lots of people with white hair, bald heads, walking devices, riding devices, hearing aids, visual issues, mobility limitations, and other identifiable medical challenges. It is a visible reality; fortunately, there are also smiles and waves and winks and hugs.

Human nature makes us think, *Oh, that's the other people; that's not me.* We console our psyches that we are unique, and maybe some distant day in the future, I may develop some limitations. What are some typical profiles of entering residents who enter these doors to live at "The Windows" (*Las Ventanas* means *the windows* in Spanish)? First, and vital to any decision, a trust must be developed in the business part of operations—the marketing staff is efficiently trained with these answers and processes—and then trust in the contract presented. Second, the message and mantra of the lifestyle also must be trusted, as the deliverables must meet the expectations or exceed them. My experience has been that Las Ventanas has met and exceeded my expectations of life here, even though many opportunities exist for more deliverables to the quality of life here for residents. The area of greatest strength, from a resident's perspective, is staffing. Compassionate, caring staff, from housekeeping to security, is a huge positive.

The following shows what the resident population here may have experienced or considered before coming here:

- Stay in the family home, and make adjustments—stairlifts, alarms, ramps (no care in this scenario, except home-health care, private care).
- Downsize to a smaller house; move from a two-story to a one-story; sell the house, and lease an apartment or condo.
- Move near the children; move in with the children.
- Make a physical move to a popular retirement area—Florida, California, etc.—or out of the country, like Italy or the islands of the Caribbean.
- Move to a senior (over age fifty-five) community, like Del Webb Sun City (still have your home, just live with seniors; activities).
- Move to a senior residential rental community (group activities; no health care).
- Move to a life-care facility, such as Las Ventanas—the only one in the state of Nevada.

The following are basic profiles of the resident population at Las Ventanas:

1. A couple, getting on in years and tired of the upkeep of a home (children or grown children and grandchildren may factor in). No big health limitations. Forward-thinking decision. Downsize, minimize, reduce stress, travel or hobby interest, read, volunteer.
2. Loss of a spouse; alone; children worry. Not taking care of oneself. Children want a safer, predictable setting for Dad or Mom. An aging parent alone.

3. Single or divorced men and women, eager for the companionship of other seniors. Do not wish to be alone. Need some of the amenities offered.

4. Medical needs dominate decision. Chronic or degenerating medical condition for one or both in a couple.

That is the *why* of moving to Las Ventanas—age, health status, financial status, social status, married or single, group activities.

Now to the *how*.

Disposal of current residence—sell, lease, gift

- Furniture, collectibles—liquidate, sorting process
- Must keep—family pictures, records, keepsakes to bring with you
- Maybe keep—books, clothing, art; storage, children, give away to charity
- Donate—let go of it (kids say no; let it go)
- Sell to consignment stores—little value; half of the agreed price and less

Move date

- Packing, wrapping, relooking, rethinking, moving
- Unpacking

Adjustment

- Joining, visibility, reaching out, finding activities, learning new crafts
- Learning what is available and utilizing what you wish.
- Continuing to learn and grow; age is only a number.
- OLLI, activities, trips, programs, events, celebrations, holidays, games, family events (Olli is extra mural learning associated with UNLV)

I think residents have a responsibility to stand up, dress up, show up, if only for a short while, for the sake of program continuity and integrity of programming.

In summary, unless an unexpected event takes our decision powers away, seniors who have designed productive, happy lives for themselves and their families in their middle years will continue to do so in the golden years, when the legs no longer work, or the eyes are dimmer, or the spoken word is inaudible.

With good attitudes and medical aids available, these changes can be accepted. Many residents have pain every day. Some suffer considerably. Some have chemotherapy or dialysis while we are still sleeping. Others take a lot of meds. A thriving population is supportive of others and encouraging. That spirit seems to be very contagious here, from the staff to the residents. You develop an extended family—those who check on you, miss you, are eager to see you.

As of this writing, memory care, the fourth level of care, has been completed at Las Ventanas. It is a beautiful, functionally designed, state-of-the-art wing of the total physical plant. This division of Las Ventanas has been actively treating residents for five years. We have a choice: either curse the darkness or light a candle. Fortunately, at Las Ventanas, we live at the windows. A lot of light and enlightenment can enter.

Senator Edward Ted Kennedy on the occasion of the 1980 Democratic convention at Madision Square Garden, New York City shared these words with the world that has been deemed one of the great orations of the 1980's. I am so inspired by these few but powerful words.

The Dream shall never die Speech exerpts :

> "The work goes on, the cause endures, the hope still lives and the dream shall never die."

# EPILOGUE

These final days of editing my life story in this book are occurring during the Covid 19 Pandemic. To be living in these times is to be described as an at risk person due to my age and all accompanying health history that abides with me. It is now almost August 2020 as I complete this labor of love and send it off to the publishers.

I have been confined to my home as have most Americans and the world since March of this year. Watching the news showing the loss of more than one hundred fifty thousand lives, and 4.5 million people infected in the U. S. alone are staggering statistics that are not static but changing daily. I cannot know the numbers by the time this book is in your hands.

Life has changed, many work from home, schools are closed, businesses are closed, churches,restaurants, and travel is restricted, Doctors treat you remotely from the office via zoom or skype. We are all wearing masks and social distancing six feet from each other. We have physicians in our family on the front lines of fighting this virus and caring for their patients. We are washing our hands and disinfecting surfaces and being very wary of infection control. The beautiful summer weather and long term confinement sent our young people and old to the beaches and to establishements who attempted reopening as cases decreased, only to have to reinstitute health advisories when numbers began to climb again in a resurgence. While my grandchildren have been here studying on line summer courses we cannot cuddle, hug or kiss each other. I miss that terribly. I play bridge on Bridge base on line with other senior friends and that is just a blessing. I look at movies on

Netflix, Prime and elsewhere and have really enjoyed that. I do a little gardening, lots of reading and telephone talking but so many friends are having trouble hearing. They say the phones are just not as good? Keeping busy has been a life saver as well as a schedule and exercise. I discovered Youtube seated exercises for seniors and there are some wonderful ones to choose from. You can do fifteen minute sessions listing calories burned up to an hour. People have been so inventive in these times of trying to stay safe and have fun. My neighbors have organized block parties. We all sit in a lawn or folding chair and mask up and catch up. People have planned drive by parties for family to get a glimpse of a loved one or friend. Whatever it takes to be wise and safe. We do not see an end in sight as of this writing. My profound sympathies to all the families who have lost members. I know how devasting that can be especially when one is otherwise healthy.

We lost Dan's brother James R.Bailey in April of this year to the virus and currently two family members have tested positve. Life has changed in so many ways but not all for the worst. The freeways are less crowded, you have no place to go so home really is where the heart is and everyone else. Adaptation to working at home has been something more than fifty percent love doing and never want to stop doing.

Social contact has been the biggest loss other than lives. As humans we really crave the touch, the being,the presence of our loved ones, work associates, school mates, church congregations and sports events. Base ball, basketball, football are really our passions as are all the sports for men and women that entertain us. The teams we root for, we cannot gather people in large crowds.

The virus can stay in a room three hours, from a sneeze, droplets can travel 35 feet. Coming together for events really can mean loss of life, severe illness, or infecting others who may have that fate.

Our nation is lamenting the challenge of fighting this virus and it's toll on America and the world. Our streets are filled with peaceful demonstrators such groups as Black Lives Matter. The United States is bracing for a national election in less than one hundred days, Police reform is on the lips of everyone due to massive excessive force and the need to address many calls as a social service team response instead of police. Climate change is still a huge concern, a clear path to citizenship for immigrants is needed and more humanity for childen of immigrants and refugees. Our homeless people populations are subject to multiple threats,povery homelessness and disease. The unemployed population due to business closures is in the millions. These are the most unusual times of my entire life. People are doing their best to cope. We clearly understand the things we miss and why. We can only hope our best and brightest doctors and researchers develop a vaccine that willl allow us to express our humanity again with longed for hugs to the special people in our lives and allow us to embrace our passions of sports and outings that we so love. My thank you, love and forever respect to our medical personnel in hospitals. The janitors who manage all the waste in our hospitals, the parking attendants and ambulance drivers, the administrators who are compiling all the record keeping and interacting with families, the nurses, xray technicians, laboratory technicians, the laundry workers who keep sheets and towels and all needed linens at the ready for our patients, the people and restaurants who have donated lunch and food to hospital workers. Of course our doctors everywhere, America and around the world who have been working every single day caring for their patients sometimes with limited personal protective clothing and masks. Our Governors and Mayors in California, New York and many states have been extraordinary leaders in fighting this Corona Virus. World wide at this time from February of 2020 to the present August 1, 2020, there have been over seventeen million persons infected with the virus. Over six hundred seventy nine thousand deaths. Recovery world wide has been over ten million, however thousands are suffering organ damage including cardiac and kidney as risidual effects. In the United States, We have over four million six hundred seventy thousand diagnosed cases and over one hundred and fifty six thousand deaths. According to CNN, The United States of America has 4 % of the of world's population but 25% of its corona virus cases. So, what's next?